FATHERING THE ADHD CHILD

FATHERING THE ADHD CHILD

❖ ❖ ❖

A BOOK FOR FATHERS,
MOTHERS, AND PROFESSIONALS

Edward H. Jacobs, Ph.D.

𝒜

JASON ARONSON INC.
Northvale, New Jersey
London

This book was set in 11 pt. Berling Roman by Alpha Graphics of Pittsfield, New Hampshire and printed and bound by Book-mart Press, Inc. of North Bergen, New Jersey.

Copyright © 1998 by Jason Aronson Inc.

10 9 8 7 6 5 4 3 2 1

Library of Congress Cataloging-in-Publication Data

Jacobs, Edward H.
   Fathering the ADHD child : a book for fathers, mothers, and
professionals / by Edward H. Jacobs.
     p.   cm.
   Includes bibliographical references and index.
   ISBN 0-7657-0068-9 (alk. paper)
   1. Attention-deficit-disordered children—Family relationships.
2. Father and child. I. Title.
RJ506.H9J33   1997
618.92'8589—dc21   97-2061

Printed in the United States of America on acid-free paper. Jason Aronson Inc. offers books and cassettes. For information and catalog write to Jason Aronson Inc., 230 Livingston Street, Northvale, New Jersey 07647-1731. Or visit our website: http://www.aronson.com

I dedicate this book in loving memory to two people:

my mother

Rita Lillian Finkel Jacobs,

who nurtured my love of books

and

Peter Kolack, M.D.,

physician, humanitarian, teacher, and friend

❖　❖　❖

Contents

❖ ❖ ❖

Preface

This book addresses the needs of fathers who want to do a better job of parenting the child with Attention-Deficit/Hyperactivity Disorder (ADHD), of mothers who want to understand the special needs that fathers have in parenting these children, and of professionals who face the challenging task of involving the fathers of ADHD children in treatment in a productive way and of facilitating cooperative parenting between fathers and mothers. This book includes ideas to help fathers deal with the assessment process; work with their child's behavior and attention problems; understand their child's emotional, learning, and behavioral needs; form a better working alliance with their spouses; and understand their own struggles and uncertainties in dealing with this confusing diagnosis. As a father, I realize that applying psychological theories to real children is not easy. As a psychologist, I have worked for more than 20 years with individuals and families coping with ADHD. I have struggled to understand the sometimes very different worldviews of men and women, and the different ways in which they think, see the world, solve problems, and relate to children.

I grew up in the 1960s when the women's rights movement was flowering. The reality of male superiority in society was under attack, as were the ideas that could justify that superior position. That movement did what was necessary to attack the institutions, behaviors, and ideas that kept one half of our population in an inferior economic, physical, and social relationship to the other half.

Differences between men and women were minimized because being different was often the excuse men used to treat women as inferior. One unfortunate consequence of this was that discussing differences between men and women often became taboo and politically incorrect. When I was in high school, we had a discussion in class about job possibilities for men and women. Some of the students vociferously denied any general differences in physical strength between men and women because these general differences were not true for *all* men and women. I agreed that all opportunities should be open to anyone regardless of sex, but I also perceived a tendency to deny that there were any differences between the sexes.

In recent years, the differences in how men and women parent have become a subject of interest to psychologists. Understanding these differences will help parents of difficult children become more effective in parenting, which is a different experience for men than it is for women. Therefore, helping a mother develop the understanding and skills to parent a challenging child, such as one with ADHD, takes a somewhat different form than the same help offered to a father. Addressing fathers' needs requires an understanding of what makes fathers different from mothers.

In my clinical experience of working with hundreds of families over the years, I have found that mothers seem to readily understand what psychologists say to them, and psychologists tend to feel validated in working with mothers. Working with fathers is a different experience. They are often less accepting of what the psychologist has to offer, and they ask more questions, express more doubts, and anticipate more pitfalls. Fathers are more difficult and less immediately gratifying to work with than mothers are. They either fail to come in for treatment or drop out of treatment prematurely more often than do mothers (Forehand and McMahon 1981). Fathers often rely on their wives to represent the family to the therapist and to relay back to them what the therapist has to say. I have always considered it a failing of mine and of other psychologists that we lose so many fathers in treatment.

The issues outlined in this book are ones that I have struggled with personally in my life and professionally in my career. When I speak of the thoughts and feelings that are common to fathers, I am speaking not just from knowledge of research, theory, and technique, but from my personal struggles as well and from my work with fathers who have been either my patients or the parents of my young patients.

Fathers might recognize themselves in this book, and therapists might recognize many of the fathers and couples. However, I do not expect that everything in this book will ring true for every father who reads it, as everyone is different. Yet the tendency of fathers and mothers to parent differently remains, and even men who pride themselves on not being "traditional" men, or who fancy themselves as "New Age Dads," if they are honest with themselves, will probably recognize some of these differences between themselves and their spouses.

The concerns that therapists have in working with the fathers and families of ADHD children are intertwined with the issues that these fathers have in helping their children. For these fathers to benefit from our knowledge and clinical experience, therapists must consider new ways of thinking about fathers' experiences and must develop new ways to reach them. These fathers can gain some benefit from reading articles and books that are intended for them, but they could gain much more from working with professionals. If they and the professionals better understood each other, they would have even a greater chance of success.

In working with families of ADHD children, I have found that the rigid distinctions between schools of psychological theory can hinder our options and flexibility. Much of the intervention with ADHD children and their families is behavioral in nature. Some research has been done utilizing family systems theory in understanding and treating these families (Cunningham 1990). There is also a strong place for understanding the role of the self and the empathic process in this work, as articulated in writings on narcissism (Kohut 1971, 1977,

1984, Solomon 1980, 1985). Rather than lending itself to simple, cut and dried strategies, working with ADHD children and their families challenges the therapist to integrate many forms of psychological understanding and technique. This should not be done haphazardly. The challenge for the therapist is to be consistent, to be helpful, and to integrate different psychological perspectives in a systematic way.

In writing about a subject that is the basis of much of my professional work, I found it impossible to eliminate my perspective on evaluating and treating ADHD in general, even if these ideas were not exclusively oriented to fathers and fathering. Through hundreds of interviews; test batteries; consultations with schools, courts, physicians, and fellow therapists; and discussions and debates with colleagues, I have developed my own sense of what is useful in clinical practice. This perspective is an integral part of the theme of the book. This book, then, is not just about fathering children with ADHD; it presents a point of view about working with children and families coping with ADHD. I hope this will be useful to fathers, mothers, and professionals in understanding these children and in obtaining for them the services that they deserve.

I am attempting to accomplish several things. One is to discuss, for the enrichment of both professionals and parents, what men bring to parenting that is different from what women bring, and how this difference has an impact on the parenting of children with ADHD. I am attempting to reach out to fathers of children with ADHD to help provide them with an enhanced understanding of the disorder and with the skills to deal with it more effectively. In addition, it is my hope that, in receiving validation for their perspective, fathers will also gain a better appreciation of their spouses' perspective as being different but valuable. It is my hope that fathers will appreciate that empathizing with their spouses' perspectives is important and possible even in the absence of agreement, and that this empathy is critical to the working of an effective co-parenting team. This book also seeks to provide more guidance to mental health professionals in understanding the needs of these fathers, and in incorporating this understanding into their clinical work to increase its effectiveness. Finally, this book is an attempt to help mothers understand their spouses and to appreciate the differences in their perspectives, even if there is disagreement. It is my hope that mothers will read this book and give it to their husbands, and that fathers will discover this book on their own and give it to their wives.

It is also my intent to reach out to fathers who are separated or divorced and therefore deal with their children on their own. These fathers need to understand the unique perspective that they bring to parenting in order to improve their own parenting skills and their interpersonal skills with their children, so that they can more effectively parent a child with ADHD.

❖ ❖ ❖

Acknowledgments

This book has one author, but that authorship has been enabled and nurtured by several. I want to express my gratitude and appreciation to:

Vicki Touster Jacobs, M.S.W., my wife and colleague, who granted me the time to write when there seemed to be no time at all, who kept telling me that I would complete this project, who tolerated my anxiety, and who read my manuscript, discussed my ideas with me, and gave me valuable critical feedback. Her steadfast and boundless love has created the foundation for my ideas, my work, and my life;

My children, Rebecca and Joshua, from whom I stole time, and who kept me entertained when I tried to write at home. They have selflessly given me the privilege and the wonder of parenting them;

My good friend and colleague, Pamela Enders, Ph.D., who generously gave of her time, thoughts, and editorial expertise in reviewing the manuscript;

Robert L. Weber, Ph.D., a friend who is as rock-solid as he is intelligent and kind, who told me to stop obsessing, find my own voice, and put it on paper, and, when I did, showed me how to make it better. He has been the catalyst for my development as a writer and, therefore, for this book;

Anne Constantinople, Ph.D., who helped me, as an undergraduate, to pursue my own path in the study of psychology;

Stephen Rousseas, Ph.D., Michael McCarthy, Ph.D., Michael Murray, Ph.D., and Peter Stillman, Ph.D., who taught me to think and read critically;

Morris Chandler, Ph.D., who taught me the value of rigorous scientific inquiry;

Ellen Berger, Ph.D., who showed me the therapeutic nature of my relationships with my patients;

Phoebe Schnitzer, Ph.D., who taught me to assess the individual rather than the test results;

Anne Alonso, Ph.D., and Richard Geist, Ed.D., two extraordinary supervisors, who taught me about the depth and complexity of the therapeutic relationship;

David Kaplan and Judy Cohen, who, through painstaking editorial attention to language and detail, and commitment to making this work readable, crafted this book into its final form;

Michael Moskowitz, Ph.D., of Jason Aronson Inc., for his encouragement and support of the concept of this book;

Holly Eddy, M.L.S., Librarian at Columbia Parkland Medical Center, for her professional, prompt, thorough, and thoughtful help in procuring research materials;

My patients, past and present, and their families, who taught me most of what I know, who shared with me their ideas for the book, who trusted me with their hopes, dreams, fears, and confusions in their efforts to make their lives and the lives of their children better, and who struggle every day to make the rest of the world understand the phenomenon called ADHD.

❖ C H A P T E R 1 ❖

Why a Book on Fathering the ADHD Child

THE CHALLENGES OF PARENTING AND FATHERING

The challenges of parenting a child with Attention-Deficit/Hyper-activity Disorder (ADHD) has been the focus of many books and articles. Although books on parenting written for the general population might be useful, it is clear that special skills are needed in parenting a child with ADHD. A parent needs abundant love and wisdom, a parent must be knowledgeable about education, a parent must acquire the skills and sophistication in managing behavior that psychologists have acquired after years of study, and a parent must develop the patience of a model clergyman or -woman. Although it can take a lifetime to acquire any one of these skills, the demands of parenting an ADHD child necessitate that all of them be acquired in an instant.

The normal challenges of parenting are demanding enough. But they are exaggerated when dealing with a child who has an attention deficit. Parenting an ADHD child often leaves parents outside the mainstream, unable to be guided by conventional wisdom or advice from friends and family. The normal stresses of parenting are worse for parents of ADHD children, because the problems that these children have are more frequent and intense. For example, school children frequently need reminders to get out of bed in the morning and get ready for school. But the ADHD child might need more frequent reminders, and might not respond to gentle prodding or pleading. If told to do two or three things in order, he might do the first one and neglect the others, or he might be overloaded by this multiple-step demand and wander around the house or be found playing on his bed. The parents' reminders might become less gentle over time. Their demands might become more urgent and intense. Their voices might be raised more quickly and more loudly. Being more overwhelmed by his parents' increasingly intense demands, feeling more inadequate in meeting the demands that the world is placing on him, and experiencing a lot of attention and control by avoiding responsibility, the child might intensify his resistance to cooperating.

Parents normally have to guide their children through the process of making friends, including the ordeal of being teased and rejected, and have to help their children learn to resolve disputes with peers, deal with aggression in themselves and others, and assert their needs. But friendships are often more difficult for children with ADHD. The problems are more frequent; the rejection is often more severe; and the learning of effective ways to resolve disputes, be assertive, play cooperatively, and control aggression comes a lot more slowly and with a lot more of a struggle.

The solutions to children's behavior problems that make sense, that work with most children, and that seem to be intuitively "right," often do not work with children with ADHD, and when they do work, they might take longer to work, might require great effort and persistence to make them work, or might result in unanticipated and undesirable complications and problems.

Some examples might clarify the above points. You might tell your child that if he cooperates with you that day, he will earn a special privilege that night, such as a later bedtime or the right to watch a movie. Your child might get very excited about this prospect, think about it all day, talk about it, and use it as a means to guide his behavior. You might even use some reward closer in time to the desired behavior, such as a trip to get ice cream in the middle of the day. The child with ADHD might get similarly excited when the reward is mentioned; however, after five minutes his behavior will return to its usual uncooperative state. The promise of rewards does not seem to have a hold on his behavior for longer than a few minutes, and sometimes not even for that. The repeated experience of missing these rewards, and even getting genuinely upset about these deprivations, does not seem to result in changes in the child's behavior.

Barkley (1993, 1995b) believes that these children lack a well-developed sense of the future, and have difficulty using language to help them delay gratification and anticipate the future. They are ruled by the present. If rewards are to work, they must be administered immediately. Even then, it might take repeated rewards and consequences, over a long period of time, for the child's behavior to be affected.

Another intuitive notion is that talking through problems with your child, and helping him to understand what you are doing and why, is productive. Since children with ADHD are more driven by the moment, since they are unable to delay gratification the way other children are, and since they have a deficit in anticipating future rewards and consequences, there is limited value in using language to affect their behavior. It is not that a parent should not try to talk to the child about why things are happening, and verbally tie the consequences of the behavior to the behavior itself, and to the choices that the child makes. It is that the ADHD child's behavior is much more controlled by real-world consequences and actions than by words. It is often more effective to deliver consequences without emotion, without extensive explanations, without negotiations or justifications, and without verbalized compassion for the child's expressions of distress at being punished and deprived of toys or activities. Much of this approach runs counter to what many of us intuitively think of as good parenting. Most of us value the idea of emotionally relating to our children, strengthening the bond between us, and helping our children understand motives, consequences, and feelings in greater depth. But with an ADHD child, remaining in control and structuring the environment, which includes our actions as parents, might be more important much of the time.

Much has been written about parenting in general and parenting the ADHD child in particular. However, parenting is treated as a generic activity, and there seems to have developed a bias that mothers are the more important parents and fathers are important but secondary. Most parenting books seem to be written for women with the implication that fathers have to learn how to tune in to their children in the way that mothers do.

As Bell and colleagues (1961) indicated, fathers also have historically been underrepresented in clinical child and adolescent research. This bias toward studying mothers has resulted, until recently, in a lack of knowledge about how fathers respond to teaching, guidance, and clinical intervention in parenting. These trends have left fathers' needs incompletely addressed (Phares 1992).

Therefore, there has been a lack of appreciation of the unique perspective and insight that fathers bring to parenting children. This has also been reflected in the clinical experience of many family and child therapists, who have difficulty engaging fathers in the treatment process. Fathers often do not come in for therapy and often drop out of therapy, at times very angrily. Comments from fathers often reflect the fact that they do not find therapy to be productive. They often do not see the point of talking about the problem and do not see change as happening quickly enough. Many fathers leave therapy without feeling that their needs are addressed. Even if these issues are not expressed, fathers often "vote with their feet" by becoming too busy at work or elsewhere to come into the office. Meeting with the child or family therapist just does not become compelling enough to make it the most important thing.

This is not said to fault fathers for their behavior. Rather, it behooves those of us who are therapists to find ways to reach our clients and to make our work relevant to them. It is our failing, not our clients', if we are not deemed relevant to their lives. The same responsibility holds true for writers of parenting books. The reason these books seem to be read by mothers more often, or that mothers read them first and then have to convince their husbands to read them, might also be because fathers do not feel spoken to by these books.

Fathers often start off feeling out of place in dealing with domestic and child-rearing matters. Although times have changed, the home is still largely considered to be the province of the woman. Osherson (1995) describes men as associating "home" with their mother's house, which creates a feeling of being an outsider in their own homes and families. There is a fear that many men have that they are fundamentally nonessential, that the family would continue just fine even if they left the picture. In addition, men are often ambivalent about how present they want to be in the life of the home. Due to their own feelings of strangeness and their resulting ambivalence about belonging to and connecting to their home, it is a struggle for many men to find their places as insiders in a home in which they must take on the roles of adult and parent.

When a father attempts to become more of an insider, he can find himself struggling to break into the tight circle of dependency and allegiance that has formed between his children and their mother. This mother–child coalition can become quite comfortable and comforting for the mother over time, and there might be some unspoken resistance or feeling of threat when the mother is faced with the expectation that this must change. This unspoken resistance can lead to greater feelings of frustration and anger in the father and can intensify his feelings of alienation (Bell et al. 1961).

Mothers often assume that because their husbands are negative or turned off to their way of dealing with the child, they would not be interested in coming for counseling and exploring options. I have often had mothers tell me that their husbands would not come in, and insist that nothing could get them to come for an appointment. Usually, if I could prevail on the mother to allow me to call her husband and invite him in, he readily responded to the invitation.

It is not that the mothers purposely excluded their husbands or wanted them to stay away. I believe that they correctly perceived that their husbands were out of touch with how they, the mothers, felt and saw things, that they were worlds apart, and that they were unable to understand the way their husbands felt and saw things. They probably correctly perceived that their husbands were resistant to coming in. Wouldn't you hesitate to go to a place where you could predict being attacked, ridiculed, and told you were wrong? Wouldn't this be especially true if you were uncomfortable communicating your point of view in the language of feelings and relationships? Going to a therapist with your wife would be like going to a foreign country where your wife and the therapist spoke the language and you did not! None of us seek out experiences where we expect to be misunderstood or invalidated.

The fact that most of the men I have contacted readily responded to my invitation tells me that they were yearning for a chance to tell their side of the story, be heard, feel understood, and get the help that they felt they needed. They were at an impasse, too, with their wives not understanding them. Before these fathers received a call from the therapist, they might have felt that they were being asked to engage in a world in which their wives were already the acknowledged experts—the home and the family. Both parents knowing this communicates an inferior position to the father and leaves him vulnerable to being judged as inadequate and in need of correction and change (Bell et al. 1961).

Many fathers are also puzzled by the need for them to participate in psychotherapy. After all, they work full time and do not spend a great deal of time with their children. They believe that the mother has much more accurate and detailed information about the child than they do. If the mother has difficulty handling the child's behavior, they reason, it is she who needs help, as the father is not home often enough to really have this problem (Bell et al. 1961). I have even observed this belief in fathers who were married to women who themselves worked full time.

Mothers are usually genuinely surprised, even shocked, that their husbands so readily agree to come in. I used to wonder at the ease with which so many of these men agreed to an appointment, following the repeated insistence from their wives that it would be impossible. I wondered if the wives had covert reasons for wanting to exclude their husbands. This may have been true to some extent, but I believe that the stark contrast between the mothers' insistence that the fathers would be unavailable and the fathers' unquestioning willingness to come in reflected how far apart the two were in their minds and how unbridgeable the gap seemed to be. Although part of the mothers' insistence that the fathers were unavailable might have been self-protective against feeling misunderstood and invalidated, and to prevent another plunge into unproductive disagreements, I believe that most couples truly want to work out child rearing with mutual understanding, respect, and cooperation.

Some fathers might also hesitate to come in for psychotherapy because of their own feelings of inadequacy at having a child whose deficiencies are so obvious to the outside world. The impact of having an ADHD child can be more severe on the father's self-esteem than on the mother's, as fathers have traditionally based much of their sense of adequacy on how they are perceived by the outside world (Bell et al. 1961).

PARENTING STYLES OF MEN AND WOMEN

There is increasing evidence that men and women often parent differently, and find different methods of parenting effective or ineffective. The varied parenting styles of men and women can arise from different ways of perceiving reality, different assumptions about right and wrong, different bases of experiences, and the different roles that each adult adopts within the family. Mothers and fathers differ in the ways that they communicate with their children and with each other, in the ways in which they play with their children, in the ways in which they solve problems, and in the beliefs they hold about their children's difficulties.

These are not stereotypes. Just because we happen to be a man or a woman does not mean that we have only one way of seeing or doing things, or that seeing the world in one way excludes other ways of perceiving reality or problem solving. Differences that apply to men and women in general do not apply to all men and women, and do not apply to any man or woman all the time. Each of us is complex. Any personality trait can exist in a man or a woman. Any personality trait can also exist along with a multitude of others, even with contradictory traits. Nothing in the human personality exclusively belongs to men or women. However, certain characteristics are generally more common in one sex than in the other in this society. These differences have been supported by research and clinical experience, and understanding these patterns of differences is important in helping parents acquire skills that will improve their parenting. When a mother and father are in the home, these differences exist because there are two people sharing responsibility, and because one of these people is a man and one is a woman. No matter how open or flexible a person thinks he or she is, most of us are, to a good extent, stuck in our maleness or femaleness. This fundamental fact of our existence frames our perceptions about ourselves and others. Furthermore, children benefit when they experience their mothers and fathers as being different, respect those differences, and work out a way to use those differences productively.

That fathers and mothers deal with their ADHD children differently is no secret to the many mothers who feel that their husbands do not understand what they deal with every day, who get the message that their concerns are exaggerated, who feel belittled for believing that their children's problems are quite serious, and who, in spite of their superior effort, care, and time with their children, find that their children behave better with their fathers than with them.

That men and women parent differently is also painfully obvious to many fathers. Although their wives often find psychologists helpful, fathers can feel turned off by the psychologists' involvement. When they do accept input from psychologists, they often become frustrated with their wives for not implementing the advice literally and consistently. They also feel that decisions about punishment, rewards, limits, and expectations are revised and modified without consulting them. Many a father has conscientiously followed through on a punishment in the way that was planned only to find that the rule was changed (perhaps with good reason) without his knowledge.

It is important not only to understand how to parent a child with ADHD more effectively, but how to do this as a mother or as a father, and to appreciate what men and women can learn from each other. These differences between mothers and fathers not only result in differences in how they understand their children, but can also lead to a breakdown of understanding and empathy in couples' relationships. One unfortunate outcome of having different points of view is arguing against the other's point and not responding to the feelings out of which the investment in that point of view arises.

Mr. and Mrs. Paulo argued incessantly over how their fifth-grade son Dan should deal with a bully who was picking on him when he was dismissed from school. The bully would ridicule Dan for having ADHD and receiving special help. Their encounters would often lead to physical fights. Mrs. Paulo felt that Dan should walk away and report these incidents to the nearest teacher. She believed that Dan needed to learn how to avoid this bully, as other students were able to do. Mr. Paulo was incensed that this bully would pick on his son, and felt that if his son would only fight back forcefully and decisively, the bully would learn not to pick on him. The Paulos' discussions deteriorated into arguments over the right way for Dan to handle this situation, which intensified with their frustration over each new incident. Mr. Paulo was afraid that his son would turn out to be a wimp, become a target for bullies, and develop into an anxious and fearful person much like his learning-disabled brother had. Mrs. Paulo was afraid that her son would get into trouble with the authorities, who would not be pleased with their son, and by extension, with the family. Both parents lost sight of exploring with Dan what he wanted to do, and became preoccupied with imposing their way of dealing with the situation on Dan and on each other. They found it difficult to try to understand the fears and concerns that were fueling their opinions and their strong emotional investment in them.

Once Mr. and Mrs. Paulo were able to suspend their control struggle and listen to each other's fears, they were open to listening to Dan's feelings and opinions. Dan did not want to be picked on, but he did not want to fight either. We then helped Dan to respond verbally to the bully in an assertive manner, and then to walk away. Dan agreed that if the bully pursued him he would tell a teacher. He would fight back only if the other options had been exhausted.

The breakdown of an empathic connection between the parents has dire implications not only for the marriage, but for the effectiveness of their parenting and for the well-being of the child. The disruption and dysfunction this can create in the family system can be very destructive to the child emotionally. Once two parents become polarized and are unable to respond to each other's feelings, they stop functioning effectively as a parenting team. Instead, they become invested in their stands or positions and enter into a competition for control of the family. One parent might cede control to the other, but this outward compliance can mask underlying feelings of depression and rage (Jacobs 1991), which can lead to subtle attempts to undermine the other parent's authority.

Once two parents stop functioning as a parenting team, the child no longer has a firm basis of authority and guidance. He receives confusing messages about what is right and wrong. His parents might lean on him to bolster their own self-esteem in ways that would be appropriate to do with a spouse, not with a child. The parents might subtly or not so subtly undermine each other and develop an alliance with the child that makes the other parent an outsider. The hierarchical relationship with the child that is essential for effective parenting (Hoffman 1981) becomes eroded.

Children are comforted by the stability of the parenting subsystem. They need both parents to be in positions of authority, to be working together, and not to invite the child to side with one of them to undermine the other's authority.

The challenges posed by a child with ADHD, on the one hand, and the discrepancies between a mother's and a father's thinking, perceiving, and problem solving, on the other, often has a synergistic effect, where each problem escalates and fuels the intensity of the other. We often see a spiraling effect, with disorganization, disagreement, anger, failure, hopelessness, and helplessness getting more out of control. The stances of the mother and father can become so polarized that the parenting subsystem is rendered ineffective and the child is left without consistent discipline, authority, or protection against his impulses and his own disorganization.

In contrast, when mothers and fathers complement each other, both they and the child derive enormous benefit. One of the potential advantages of a two-parent household, which also creates many of the potential pitfalls, is that each parent presents different assumptions about behavior, expectations of the children, ways of negotiating problems, and personality styles.

This variety of points of view and expectations can provide great benefit to both the child and the parents. Having two parents who fulfill similar functions for the child, such as nurturance, protection, and limit-setting, forces a child to learn to discriminate among the different expectations and ways of communication from different people. The child learns at an early age to be more sensitive to social cues and the subtle differences between people. The child learns to tolerate the frustration inherent in having two people have slightly different expectations of his behavior. The child is compelled to understand that these two people have differences of opinion, and therefore he must learn to consider more than one side of an issue. This can help increase the child's analytic problem-solving skills. Furthermore, ADHD children are exposed to many negative messages about their behavior, such as the message that they are the source of much frustration for their parents. Exposing the child to two points of view increases the likelihood that if positive messages about the child are not coming from one parent, they will be available from the other (Lewis et al. 1981).

For parents who are able to work together, having someone who sees things differently enables one to learn flexibility and to see alternative solutions to problems. It therefore can improve the parents' analytic problem-solving skills as well. Seeing one's spouse handling certain situations and issues more productively or easily than oneself forces one to confront one's own weaknesses and limitations. Having a partner also enables the parent to focus his frustrations on the partner, rather than leaning on the child for support and validation, or blaming the child when things go wrong.

The broader understanding of their children that men and women can gain from each other, and the greater effectiveness they can develop in responding to their children's behavior allow both parents to form richer relationships with their children. Fathers and mothers share a need to be understanding of their children, to guide them into becoming successful in their relationships with others and in their occupational endeavors, and to have their children develop into good, moral citizens. Although their needs and goals might be the same, fathers and mothers tend to have different assumptions about how to meet these needs and reach these goals. They will inevitably clash with and challenge each other about their different ways of seeing the world, and they will struggle with each other to resolve these differences. Out of this struggle can develop a child who has more options and a fuller perspective on life. Out of this can develop parents who can communicate despite their differences, and who are not merely able to tolerate their differences, but who can understand them and make use of them. Throughout this book, I will attempt to add to our understanding about effective parenting of children with ADHD. The inevitable conflicts between parents can result in their fuller appreciation of each other and of their children.

Most of these observations apply also to single-parent households and households where the parenting responsibility is shared by people of the same sex. The main point is to understand how men and women approach parenting differently, and to understand what assumptions or biases one brings to parenting because of one's sex.

FATHER'S ABSENCE

One particularly negative result of the inability of parents to communicate with each other is the removal of the father from active involvement in the child's problems. Fathers can be physically absent, as a result of separation or divorce, or they can be present but emotionally removed, or they can be there to run errands or play with the children, but be unavailable to participate in child care.

In their frustration and helplessness, men often turn to silent, angry withdrawal to cope with conflict. This withdrawal is a last-ditch attempt to exert some control and maintain some dignity in a situation that feels out of control, in which the man feels misunderstood. John Gray (1992) refers to "the Cave" to illustrate the tendency of men to retreat into noncommunicative silence. When this withdrawal, emotional or physical, becomes chronic, it has important implications for the emotional and cognitive development and the behavioral control of the child. Men often do not appreciate the effect that their silent withdrawal has on their children.

Uninvolved or absent fathers can have profound implications for their children's intellectual development. A father's involvement has been found to facilitate boys' cognitive development from infancy. For boys, a father's absence has been correlated with a deterioration in academic achievement and intellectual abilities, and the lack of development of analytic reasoning (Blanchard and Biller 1971, Bronfenbrenner 1967, Deutsch 1960, Deutsch and Brown 1964, Landy et al. 1969, Lessing et al. 1970, Maxwell 1961, Santrock 1972, Sciara 1975, Sutton-Smith et al. 1968). In reviews of the literature (Lamb 1981, Radin 1981) a father's encouragement of intellectual performance in girls has been found to be positively related to achievement, while a father's rejection has been found to be detrimental to achievement.

The father's absence can have substantial effects on a child's social development as well. Delinquents have been found to be more likely to come from homes where the father is absent or in which there is a poor father–child relationship, such as one marked by hostility and a lack of empathy on the part of the father. This was found to be true even when the relationship between the child and the mother was normal.

For sons, a father's nurturance and participation in child rearing has been correlated with the development of masculine traits, self-esteem, and personal adjustment. Nurturant fathers have also been found to promote the healthy psychological adjustment of their daughters and their happiness in heterosexual relationships (Baumrind and Black 1967, Fish and Biller 1973, Fisher 1973, Lamb 1981, Lozoff 1974).

Being involved with one's children on an emotional level counters the strong socialization to which many men are exposed and which

shapes their identities. Men have been socialized to be good provid-
ers, which is the role with which men have most strongly identified
(Brooks and Gilbert 1995). This is an easy role to fall back on, and
the danger is in convincing oneself that being a good provider is a
sufficient way to be loving and nurturing to one's children. Such a
strong identification with this role allows fathers to rationalize and
justify opting out of other fathering roles and leaving those aspects
of parenting to the mother.

In extreme cases in which the father is absent, there has been observed what psychoanalyst James Herzog (1982) refers to as *father
hunger*. Herzog described several patients who experienced in a very
forceful way throughout their lives that they were lacking something
that they vitally needed, which was related to the absence of their
fathers in their lives. This hunger had profound effects on how these
patients related to others, how they felt about themselves, and the
values and goals that they established for themselves.

The more antagonistic and hurtful a divorce is, the more it seems to
exacerbate this feeling. A mother's interventions can soften the effects
of father hunger, but the need for a father does not go away, and his
absence leaves a void in the child's life that a mother cannot fill.

One family with which I worked consisted of a mother and her two
adopted teenagers. Connie had married Frank with the expectation that
they would have children. However, through the course of infertility
and the adoption process, Frank became less emotionally available,
perhaps reflecting his own unacknowledged ambivalence about having
children. The adoptions of Carla and Stephen left Connie feeling fulfilled as never before, but also left her with a greater sense of loneliness and abandonment as her husband drifted further away. Frank and
Connie eventually divorced. Over time, Stephen became an intensely
angry, belligerent young man, who defied everything Connie asked him
to do, and harassed her by following her around the house screaming
at her. Carla adopted a passive, compliant stance toward both parents.
Her ability seemingly to get along with both parents elicited the ire of
her older brother, which fueled his resentment toward the mother for
favoring his sister.

All three members of the family were intelligent and verbal and were able to describe their disputes in rich detail. Attempting to negotiate some agreement involving specific behavioral changes resulted in escalating arguments about who would have to change first, or who should have to change more, or how fair the division of responsibility was. The changes that we were working on were, on the surface, simple, and within their ability to carry out. However, there were obstacles every step of the way.

In one session, I discovered that helping the children talk about the absence of their father changed the tone of the entire meeting. All of a sudden, the conflict, the animosity, and the blaming were gone, and there were two children and a mother united in their sadness, grief, and helplessness. The children discussed their different adaptations toward their father—Stephen adapting through angry rejection and hurt, and Carla through passive compliance in the hope of gaining some small measure of love either through time with her father or through gifts that were often promised and delayed. Each understood the needs out of which their adaptations arose. Stephen, who was older and angrier, was able to give compassionate advice to Carla about dealing more productively with her frustration while maintaining the relationship she chose to have with her father, without trying to convert his sister to his own solution to the problem. Each time Stephen and Carla became stuck, discussing their unresolved grief about the father united them.

Stephen was also able to decrease the struggle with Connie and to encourage his mother to discuss her feelings rather than continuing to try to control him. Stephen became more responsible in following through with his efforts to de-escalate the conflicts at home.

This example is presented to show that the father's absence from the family often has a profound effect on the children, even if there is a competent parent left to care for them. Men often feel that they are nonessential to the family, or of secondary importance to the mother. This feeling often leaves men on the periphery, or results in their gravitating there when there are conflicts with their wives. Furthermore, there is a tendency in many men to be attracted to the periphery more than women. As Osherson (1995) describes, there is a conflict inherent in men in being enveloped in the family, in feeling swallowed up and losing their individuality.

Men yearn for their families, just as their families yearn for them. Yet men also tend to feel threatened by their immersion in family life. It saps them of their individuality and independence. It brings out more of their dependency needs. Many men opt for the loneliness and emotional isolation of the periphery of family life, which is made easier by societal messages that it is all right and even masculine to spend most of one's time on work, and not to be dominated by one's wife and children.

The father's absence is painful to the children, and robs them not only of an emotional connection that is important to their self-esteem, but also of the unique contributions that fathers make to parenting. In ways that are unique to males, fathers contribute to their children's ability to deal skillfully with the real world, to accept realities that are different from their wishes and expectations, to follow through on tasks and goals, and to relate to authority.

FATHERS AND INTERVENTION

Fathers are also in a position to make a valuable and irreplaceable contribution to the process of assessment of and intervention for their ADHD child. Dealing with the school system can be a challenge for some parents and a nightmare for others. Often, an adversarial relationship develops between the parents, who see their child and his needs in one way, and the school, which views the child in another way. The parents are at a disadvantage in dealing with professional educators who are more familiar with the resources and options that the system has to offer, with the legalities of the assessment process, and with the procedures used. The language of special education is one that is familiar to the school personnel, but often not to the parents. It is difficult to sit in a room with experts who seem to know more about your child than you do, and who are entrusted to make important decisions about your child while you are not armed with all of the specialized knowledge that they have.

Also, if the parents are facing a team of professionals, they may feel outnumbered. Therefore, parents need their partners to be actively involved as advocates for their child. One parent simply cannot do what two parents can. Although many men believe in simplifying and economizing ("If my wife attends the meeting, why is there a need for both of us to attend? I can be involved by listening to my wife's report of the meeting"), two parents attending a meeting is better than one. Not only is the emotional support important, but two people thinking through ideas that are presented can be critical.

A father attending a school meeting might have his own feelings of authority challenged, which might contribute to some fathers' reluctance to attend these meetings. For fathers who have never attended such a meeting, it is important that they understand that these meetings can be quite intimidating. The parents are often put into the uncomfortable position of wanting to please the professionals in order to maintain a friendly relationship because the professionals will be teaching their child for many years. Thus, parents may not be assertive enough about feeling dissatisfied with the educational services being provided to their child. On the other hand, the parents might want to assert themselves and "do battle" for their child, which risks alienating the school personnel and jeopardizing the relationship, to the possible detriment of the child. Do parents go along with the school and make compromises with which they are uncomfortable, or do they go into battle for their child and pay the price of being disliked and opposed by the very people the child needs? Two parents can play different roles and therefore have greater flexibility in dealing with the school system. One parent might be disliked, or have an adversarial relationship with the school, while the other can preserve a friendlier negotiating position. Men also bring the unique perspectives on authority and negotiation to dealing with the school system that they bring to parenting.

In a meeting with Ted's parents, the school presented evidence of progress in Ted, a sixth-grade boy who was highly intelligent but very immature and unfocused. The child had some learning problems over the years that had not been definitively diagnosed and categorized. Ted's stepmother was trying to cooperate with the school, because she knew that Ted was getting help, and she felt bad that he was such a difficult management problem. She also had quite a temper and was easily upset emotionally, so she felt a need to keep her irritation under wraps so as not to risk alienating the school personnel. For Ted's benefit, she wanted them to feel that they could talk to her.

On testing that had been completed recently, all of Ted's abilities ranged from low average to superior, with one exception. Ted's spelling achievement score was in the fifth percentile, indicating a severe deficit that involved the encoding of language-based information. The school personnel dismissed this as unimportant, but when questioned further about it, the school spokesperson maintained that sixth graders were all poor spellers, and the boy's abilities were therefore typical. Because the stepmother did not want to rock the boat, and because she was not sure of what significance this score had, she did not challenge the school personnel. The father, who was much more easygoing than the stepmother, looked the school spokesperson in the eye and asked, "If his spelling is typical of a boy his age, his score would be in the fiftieth percentile, not the fifth."

During the ensuing negotiation over Ted's school program, Ted's stepmother was able to support the positive things that the school had done and wanted to do, while his father challenged them to do more.

Likewise, there is value in having both parents involved in dealing with health professionals, such as pediatricians, neurologists, psychologists, and social workers. Parents can come away confused from a medical appointment where they discussed medication options with the physician, even with a physician who seems to be sensitive, thorough, and a good communicator, because the issue of medication for ADHD children is very complicated. There is no clear, universally agreed upon treatment regimen for ADHD. It is a disorder that has been intensely studied and extensively treated, about which a great deal is still unknown. This can be intimidating and frustrating. In addition, the parent is often asked to share in the medication decision making, about which the parent knows nothing or very little, and what the parent has heard might be based on rumors or sensationalism. There are so many choices, that the decision comes down to a judgment call. The doctor in effect is a consultant to the family.

It is particularly important for fathers to be involved in meetings with psychologists and other mental health professionals or behavioral specialists. Behavior management plans and techniques have to be applied and tailored to the specific needs of the child and the parents. It is impossible simply to prescribe a technique for any situation and expect it to work. Fathers must be part of the team working with their child. Since each parent sees his child somewhat differently, a technique or program that seems fitting to one parent might have flaws that are only seen by the other parent. But it is the parents who have to carry out the plan together. What may fit one parent's personality, style, and philosophy might prove to be difficult for the other. Furthermore, much of what is asked of a parent with an ADHD child is counterintuitive; that is, it differs from what the parent might intuitively consider to be good parenting. For example, a parent who values understanding the child's feelings and verbally explaining the reasons for things to the child might find it difficult to accept the need for no-nonsense, authoritative limit-setting. A parent who is concerned about how he will be seen in public might find it difficult to administer a time-out in a supermarket. Once the rationale for these methods has been discussed with the parent and the parent can see how new techniques are consistent with an effective behavioral plan, the parent is often open to trying new things.

If the father does not attend the meeting with the psychologist, it is up to the mother alone to express her thoughts about a procedure, and work through her assumptions, fears, and misunderstandings with the psychologist. Then she must convey the information to the father. If he has reservations that the mother is unable to clarify, his ability or willingness to follow through on the plan and function as half of a parenting team may be compromised.

Fathers should not expect their wives to learn about ADHD by themselves. Fathers need to be equally involved. While educating themselves might seem like an arduous, time-consuming task, it is not necessary for them to have a professional's understanding of ADHD in order to help their child. They should strive to understand the child's disorder well enough to communicate effectively with the child, help the child with his schoolwork, and assist the child in planning how to meet his academic, social, recreational, and vocational needs and responsibilities. Parents must develop an understanding of how the world looks through the child's eyes, and how he sees himself.

Parents also need to understand ADHD enough so they can create an environment for their child that provides structure and consistency. Such an environment is essential to fostering productivity and skill development. Another area in which a parent needs sufficient knowledge of ADHD is in providing guidance and assistance to the child in dealing with the outside world, such as the school, recreational organizations, or peers. This might take the form of guiding the child through difficult decisions or social situations, or dealing directly with schools and other institutions on behalf of the child.

Another problem that parents of ADHD children have is the amount of aggression the children exhibit toward their siblings. Many parents are very concerned about the safety of a younger sibling when that sibling is playing with the ADHD brother or sister. Even if safety is not a pressing concern, the amount of time and energy these parents use up in refereeing fights and disputes between the ADHD child and his sibling is draining. Paternal involvement can have a softening effect in this area, too. Fathering that is affectionate to and helpfully interactive with the children has been associated with positive social interactions between siblings (Volling and Belsky 1992).

FAMILIES UNDER STRESS

Families raising ADHD children are often family systems under chronic stress. The key word here is *systems*, since a family is a web of interlocking relationships in which whatever goes on in one part affects every other part, every other person, and every other relationship. Stress increases if the father is not home much, spends little time with the children, and participates little in the direct discipline and management of the children's behavior.

The day-to-day stress of raising an ADHD child usually is encountered in the mother–child relationship. For this reason, fathers and mothers often feel that it is not necessary to include the father in the interviews with professionals if it is inconvenient for him or his work schedule. But even if the mother of an ADHD child is primarily responsible for disciplining the child, the quality of that discipline, and her self-esteem while disciplining, is inseparable from her relationship with her husband. The stronger the husband–wife relationship, the more supportive it is, and the more the parents agree with each other on issues of child rearing and discipline, the more capable the mother will feel in disciplining the child. If the mother feels ineffective in disciplining the child, if she feels inadequate as a parent, if her attempts at child management do not work, there is a good chance that there is trouble in the relationship between her and her husband. Furthermore, the more distance that develops between them the more likely it is that an emotional alliance will develop between the mother and child that excludes the father. If there is a breakdown in communication between mother and father to the point that the parents are no longer working as a team in child management, with shared understanding and goals and a mutual feeling of emotional support, then the mother may, by default, lean on the child for emotional support, thereby excluding the father. The father therefore becomes the "odd man out" emotionally, making it harder for him to parent and to feel effective.

All people need emotional support. If the parents support one another, each is reinforced in the parental role, making each more effective and self-assured in disciplining, setting limits, and providing healthy role models for the children. If the mother does not feel supported by her husband, she might try to have her emotional needs met through her relationship with her child. This might manifest itself by the mother feeling that only she is capable of understanding her child's needs, and that only her child understands how difficult it is for her to meet those needs. The mother might see in the child an ally on whom she depends for her feeling of adequacy as a parent. The increasing emotional dependency between mother and child might serve to further exclude the father, which results in the primary alliance in the family developing between mother and child rather than between mother and father. The mother then might see her husband as the source of the difficulty in the family. This type of alliance can be very destructive, as the mother then cannot separate herself enough emotionally from the child (since she is getting too many of her emotional needs met in that relationship) to parent effectively, and it becomes more difficult to develop a partnership with her husband because she will have to give up a valuable part of her relationship with her child for something that has not worked for her in the past.

It is impossible for anyone in a family to stand alone. There are always alliances between individuals, some stronger than others. If the parents' alliance is weak, it will be natural for them to develop stronger alliances with the child or children. This undercuts the healthy and effective functioning of the parenting team.

Having the father become more involved can be threatening to the mother's emotional security, even when the mother–child relationship is fraught with conflict. This can be true even when the mother insists that she wants her husband to be more involved. She still might be wary about letting her husband in and allowing him to co-parent if she is used to doing it on her own. It might be hard for the mother to give up control, even when she feels out of control much of the time.

This can be very difficult to understand, and the signals that the father gets can be confusing and contradictory. On the one hand, he might be criticized for not doing enough of the practical, day-to-day caregiving and disciplining of the child. On the other hand, whenever he does become more involved, he might be criticized for not doing things the same way that the mother does them.

> Cora James, the mother of Billy, a 5-year-old, hyperactive child, criticized her husband, William, for not taking a more active part in controlling Billy's behavior during dinner time. They all had dinner together fairly regularly. One rule this couple developed for Billy was that he must eat what was on his plate. Cora interpreted this rule to mean that Billy would eat everything that he was served. But when William agreed to take responsibility for enforcing this rule at the dinner table, he used a different criterion, that of "eating enough dinner," of trying at

least *some* of each type of food, which was the practice in his family of origin. Thus, a new control struggle ensued between Cora and William over the fact that William's way of handling the rules at dinner time was different from Cora's. William became more alienated and frustrated because his increased involvement, although effective with Billy, resulted in greater criticism from Cora. He felt that he could not win. Cora used her frustration with William for failing to do things her way to focus on him as the cause of the family's strife, thereby further disempowering the parental team.

Cora then formed a stronger bond with Billy, an "us against him" mentality, in which her struggles with Billy became attributed to William's failure to support her and to be involved with Billy. Because Cora felt that William's involvement with Billy was peripheral, she did not see a need for him to attend the sessions with the psychologist. However, her attempts to manage Billy's behavior remained ineffective, despite her ability to grasp the principles of behavior management and to put them into practice, until she finally participated with her husband and they began to resolve their differences regarding control, mutual understanding, and mutual support. Only then were they able to understand the different ways in which each needed to parent, to accept each other's different styles, and to support each other as individuals. This was necessary even though Cora did most of the parenting work.

CHILDREN AT RISK

When fathers are uninvolved or absent emotionally or physically, it increases the risk of maladjustment in ADHD children, who are already at very high risk for problems throughout life. Children with hyperactivity have been found to have lower self-esteem, poorer adjustment in adolescence, lower educational achievement, and lower occupational rank when they reach adulthood. Low self-esteem in adolescence has been associated with lower psychosocial adjustment in both adolescence and adulthood (Slomkowski et al. 1995).

Peer rejection results in poor self-esteem, which leads to social avoidance, and thus to a further decline in social skills. In adulthood, many individuals with ADHD feel like underachievers, and they exhibit a greater number of symptoms of psychiatric disturbance (Weiss and Hechtman 1993).

SUMMARY

- Special skills are needed to parent an ADHD child.
  - The normal stresses of parenting are increased.
  - Conventional wisdom and commonsense solutions often do not apply.
  - The ADHD child has more difficulty maintaining friendships.
  - The ADHD child is more driven by the moment than by rules or future consequences.

- Fathers and mothers parent differently.
  - Most parenting books seem to be written with mothers in mind.
  - Fathers often do not feel that their needs are addressed by therapists.
  - Many fathers still feel like outsiders in the home.
  - Fathers differ from mothers in the way they communicate, play, and solve problems, and in the beliefs they hold about their children's problems.

- It is important to maintain an empathic connection between fathers and mothers.
  - This is essential to the parents' functioning as a team, which is essential to providing the child with authority, security, consistency, and organization.
  - Strongly held beliefs are often based on unexpressed assumptions and emotions that need to be communicated.

- Having two parents who can work together provides the child with alternative ways of seeing the world and himself, solving problems, and relating to others, and the ability to respect differences and to compromise.

- The emotional withdrawal or physical absence of the father from the child's life can be seriously detrimental to the child's development.

- Fathers can make a valuable contribution by attending school meetings and meetings with health professionals.
  - These meetings are less intimidating with two parents in attendance.
  - Two parents can adopt different roles in the meeting.
  - The father's attendance increases the consistency of follow-through with behavior management procedures.
  - Fathers need to have an understanding of the nature of ADHD as well as do mothers.

- Even when fathers are not home much of the time, they are affected by the stress on the family of having an ADHD child.
  - The stress profoundly affects the mother, if she is home more with the child, which in turn affects the father's relationship with her and with the child.
  - The father might get confusing messages from the mother about how involved she wants him to be.

- Children with ADHD face a higher risk of low self-esteem, poorer adjustment in adolescence and adulthood, and lower educational and occupational achievement. The risks are increased if fathers are not involved.

❖ C H A P T E R   2 ❖

The Deficits of ADHD

Although each child who has ADHD is unique, there are symptoms, problems, and characteristics that are commonly associated with it. Some of these are formally included in the diagnostic criteria of the disorder. These symptoms are commonly considered by professionals as the defining characteristics. Other symptoms are not part of the formal diagnostic schema, but have been frequently associated with the disorder clinically. Few children have all of the formal, diagnostically significant symptoms and the associated characteristics. Each ADHD child has a unique combination of symptoms and characteristics that differ in their severity and frequency, and in how they interact with the child's own personality traits, learning style, and interests. Any two ADHD children can be confusingly different from one another.

A detailed discussion of the process of diagnosing ADHD can be found elsewhere (Barkley 1990, 1995b, Garber et al. 1995). Here is a brief review of the major deficits or problems that characterize the ADHD child, to give fathers a sense of where their children might encounter problems in their lives. This review will be helpful in applying some of the ideas in this book to the father–child relationship.

ADHD has been found to occur more frequently in males than in females. Depending on the study, the male-to-female ratio ranges from 4:1 to 9:1 (American Psychiatric Association 1994). The higher ratio occurred among clinic-referred children, indicating that boys with ADHD come to the attention of professionals more than do girls with ADHD. Because of the higher prevalence of the disorder in boys, the male pronoun will be used when referring to ADHD children in general.

THREE MAJOR SYMPTOMS OF ADHD

There are three major symptoms associated with ADHD that are considered to be diagnostic of the condition: (1) inattention, (2) impulsivity, and (3) hyperactivity. Since almost all children exhibit these characteristics some of the time, they have to exist to a degree that is developmentally inappropriate in order to be considered diagnostic. The ADHD child exhibits these characteristics to a much greater degree than his peers and to the point at which they interfere with his functioning in major areas of life, such as home, school, recreation, and peer interaction. These characteristics are diagnostic if they appear before the age of 7 and last at least six months.

The American Psychiatric Association (Table 2–1) has developed examples of these three symptoms that describe how they interfere with a person's functioning, and has formalized them into the criteria used to diagnose ADHD.

Inattention

The descriptions offered in the formal diagnostic criteria provide examples of ways in which the child's functioning is impaired by ADHD. The nine criteria of inattention provide examples of different ways in which inattention can be manifested. Requiring the presence of six out of nine symptoms in order to make a diagnosis is an acknowledgment that the average child may demonstrate a few of these symptoms. These criteria, however, do not demonstrate how

Table 2–1. Diagnostic Criteria for ADHD

A. Either (1) or (2):

  (1) six (or more) of the following symptoms of *inattention* have persisted for at least 6 months to a degree that is maladaptive and inconsistent with developmental level:

Inattention

    (a) often fails to give close attention to details or makes careless mistakes in schoolwork, work, or other activities

    (b) often has difficulty sustaining attention in tasks or play activities

    (c) often does not seem to listen when spoken to directly

    (d) often does not follow through on instructions and fails to finish schoolwork, chores, or duties in the workplace (not due to oppositional behavior or failure to understand instructions)

    (e) often has difficulty organizing tasks and activities

    (f) often avoids, dislikes, or is reluctant to engage in tasks that require sustained mental effort (such as schoolwork or homework)

    (g) often loses things necessary for tasks or activities (e.g., toys, school assignments, pencils, books, or tools)

    (h) is often easily distracted by extraneous stimuli

    (i) is often forgetful in daily activities

  (2) six (or more) of the following symptoms of *hyperactivity-impulsivity* have persisted for at least 6 months to a degree that is maladaptive and inconsistent with developmental level:

Hyperactivity

    (a) often fidgets with hands or feet or squirms in seat

    (b) often leaves seat in classroom or in other situations in which remaining seated is expected

    (c) often runs about or climbs excessively in situations in which it is inappropriate (in adolescents or adults, may be limited to subjective feelings of restlessness)

(continued)

Table 2–1. (*continued*)

    (d) often has difficulty playing or engaging in leisure activities quietly

    (e) is often "on the go" or often acts as if "driven by a motor"

    (f) often talks excessively

Impulsivity

    (g) often blurts out answers before questions have been completed

    (h) often has difficulty awaiting turn

    (i) often interrupts or intrudes on others (e.g., butts into conversations or games)

B. Some hyperactive-impulsive or inattentive symptoms that caused impairment were present before age 7 years.

C. Some impairment from the symptoms is present in two or more settings (e.g., at school [or work] and at home).

D. There must be clear evidence of clinically significant impairment in social academic, or occupational functioning.

E. The symptoms do not occur exclusively during the course of a pervasive developmental disorder, schizophrenia, or other psychotic disorder and are not better accounted for by another mental disorder (e.g., mood disorder, anxiety disorder, dissociative disorder, or a personality disorder).

Reprinted with permission from the *Diagnostic and Statistical Manual of Mental Disorders, Fourth Edition.* Copyright © 1994 American Psychiatric Association.

multifaceted the concept of attention is, and how much variability exists in individuals who have attention deficits. A child's ability to pay attention to some things in some situations is often cited as evidence that the child could not possibly have ADHD. Indeed, children with ADHD might have some types of attention that are relatively intact; however, there might be other areas in which their attention is significantly impaired.

Inattention can refer to several different problems. Some ADHD children may be characterized as being distractible, for when these children are engaged in a task, their attention is easily diverted by another stimulus in the environment. If the child is doing a writing assignment, he might look out the window at every passing car. If he is engaged in a conversation with another student, he might look away every time he hears another student speak across the room. His attention will be diverted by even small, insignificant things that other children would barely notice. A stimulus that for other children is part of the background and therefore gets screened out becomes for the ADHD child an intrusion on his consciousness and a demand on his attention.

Distractibility, therefore, refers to the difficulty these children have focusing their attention on one thing and screening out other stimuli that are less important or unimportant. These children have difficulty with *focused attention*, which is the ability to attend to one stimulus or piece of information at a time, to simultaneously resist interference from competing stimuli, and to attend with an intensity that locks onto the stimulus.

Not all ADHD children are distractible. Many focus their attention very well on one thing at a time. However, the length of time for which they are able to focus is very short. These children might appear distractible to some because they frequently go from one activity to another, but their problem might be persistence of mental effort and performance rather than focus. These children have difficulty with *sustained attention*. Their focus might be good and strong, but it is not long-lasting.

There are many ADHD children who do focus on one activity intensely for long periods of time. The ability to do this is often cited as evidence that these children do not have ADHD. ADHD children can often focus very well on something that they find highly interesting, rewarding, or stimulating. However, these children have difficulty with *attentional shift*: it can be difficult to get them to shift their focus to something else when the rules or procedures of home or school require them to do so. Many ADHD children can play video games for hours on end, much to the consternation of their parents, as it is very difficult to get them to stop when it is time to do homework or come to dinner. Other children can spend hours building with construction toys. However, when these children are required to sustain their attention on something that they do not find intrinsically rewarding, such as schoolwork or chores, they have difficulty mustering the effort.

Thus, ADHD children have a highly selective ability to focus and sustain attention, often accompanied by difficulty shifting attention when they are engaged in something that they find rewarding.

Another component of attention is an orienting response, which informs us that there is something in the environment to which we should be paying attention. It is often difficult for ADHD children to tune in to what they are supposed to do. The teacher calls the class to attention, and the ADHD child keeps on talking. The parent tells the children to get their shoes and coats on to leave the house, and the ADHD child keeps playing with his toys.

Many ADHD children are weak in the reflex that tells them automatically what is important in the environment as opposed to what can be ignored. They have difficulty with *selective attention*: they pay equal attention to relevant and irrelevant stimulation and information. They have difficulty engaging relevant stimuli. They fail to be alert to environmental cues that inform them of what is important and what will be rewarded and punished. They might be the children who get caught and punished in class when everyone is fooling around because they do not know to stop when the teacher turns around. They have difficulty scanning the environment and automatically becoming alert when important information enters their perceptual field.

Learning is dependent not only on attentional abilities but also on different sensory modalities. The two major areas of sensation involved in higher order learning are visual and auditory. In school, and also outside of school, we interact with the world through what we see and what we hear.

Many children's attention deficits are modality specific. Some children have difficulty processing auditory information (Halperin and Sharma 1994). They have difficulty listening and doing what they are told to do. They are better able to process visual information. Therefore, when they must process auditory information, the simultaneous presentation of accompanying visual information is helpful. Other children have just the opposite set of strengths and weaknesses. They get distracted or have difficulty sustaining their effort on visual tasks, but do better on auditory tasks.

Whatever the specific attentional deficits that the child experiences, children with ADHD can and do exhibit good attention skills much of the time and in many situations. They are more likely to show very good attention when tasks are highly stimulating and when there is a high degree of novelty. This is why they can play video games for hours on end and be the best at them. If life were more like a video game, with intense, constantly changing stimulation, these children would do quite well. This is also why children with ADHD often behave and attend very well when they are in a psychologist's office. The unfamiliarity of the situation, along with the high adult-to-child ratio, helps to keep their behavior under control. ADHD children generally behave so well in the psychologist's office that parents initially think the psychologist will question their concerns about the child. However, it is the child's problem attending under ordinary conditions, on tasks that are not that interesting to him, or in situations to which he has grown accustomed, that gives him problems in life.

Impulsivity

Impulsivity refers to the tendency to act before you think. It is not that the thoughts of the ADHD child are abnormal; it is his tendency to act on them, or his failure to inhibit his actions, that distinguishes him from others. Many children might notice something potentially embarrassing that the teacher says or does. It is the ADHD child who will blurt it out. Many children might be tempted to pull the chair out from under a classmate; it is the ADHD child who will do so.

Their impulsivity makes many ADHD children accident prone. They injure themselves as they jump off things, dive for things, and run into things without looking. Their impulsivity makes them say and do things that get them rejected by their peers and punished by adults. Their impulsivity makes them put down the first answer that comes into their minds to a question on a test, without carefully reading the question or checking the accuracy of their answer.

Hyperactivity

Hyperactivity refers to a developmentally abnormal degree of motor activity. The activity level of ADHD children is often tiring to watch; they have been described as acting like they have motors running inside them that will not turn off. Many are so overly active that it is readily apparent that the activity is involuntary. Some engage in excessive gross motor activities, such as moving their arms and legs, walking or running around the room, constantly humming, singing, or talking, or taking out toys and games until there is a pile of them on the floor. Others engage in more subtle actions, like tapping their feet or fingers, and seem fidgety or squirmy. Older children and adults with ADHD might not exhibit readily observable, excessive motor activity, but might be bothered by a persistent feeling of restlessness. This can take the form of feeling like they have to leave the room or get up out of their seat, or feeling impatient with someone with whom they are speaking.

Recently, impulsivity and hyperactivity have come to be regarded as different aspects of the same symptom. When children are impulsive they also tend to be hyperactive and vice versa.

The diagnostic criteria distinguish between children who are primarily inattentive but do not show signs of developmentally inappropriate impulsivity and hyperactivity, and children who are primarily impulsive or hyperactive but do not show signs of developmentally inappropriate inattention. It is also possible to exhibit both types of symptoms to a clinically significant degree.

Children who are predominantly impulsive and hyperactive get noticed more easily and tend to get more negative feedback, but they are also the children who are most likely to get help. They are the squeaky wheels that get greased. They are active and disruptive, break-ing rules in ways that interfere with the smooth flow of events around them, and with the goals and needs of others.

The predominantly inattentive children are often quiet, withdrawn, and daydreamy. They might sit unnoticed in a classroom, and tune in and out of the lesson. They might experience symptoms of anxi-ety or depression. Since they do not tend to shout out and run around the room, they might not be noticed as having a problem, as the class-room functions smoothly with them there. They might be noticed by teachers as being underachievers whose performance and grades are inconsistent, but this might be attributed to poor motivation or laziness, and it therefore might not be investigated further. They can present so differently from the impulsive-hyperactive children that it can be hard to see the two as sharing the same disorder.

PRIMARY PROBLEMS

Deficits in Rule-Governed Behavior and Reinforcement Sensitivity

ADHD children have great difficulty following rules in many settings. This difficulty is so pervasive that it has often been considered a de-fining characteristic of ADHD. Rules are commonly understood ab-stract concepts that communicate behaviors that are appropriate in different settings. They inform us of what behaviors will be rewarded and what will be punished. They control the behavior of most people in a clear fashion. Rules organize behavior, and promote the consis-tency, fairness, and predictability of people's behavior in different situations. They ensure safety. Without rules, games could not be played, organizations could not exist, and social life, business, and education could not be conducted.

Rules establish the kinds of behaviors that are rewarded in differ-ent settings. For example, the behaviors that are valued in school are attentiveness, punctuality, work completion, and accuracy (answer-ing questions and demonstrating mastery of material on tests). The behaviors that lead to success in these areas are rewarded by good grades, praise from teachers, positive interactions with parents, and possibly greater freedom granted by parents in one's social life. These rewards that follow success in these areas are usually powerful motivators of behaviors.

The three deficits of inattention, impulsivity, and hyperactivity have the common characteristic of making it enormously difficult for an individual to follow rules. Following rules involves organizing one's behavior to conform to the expectations of others, delaying immediate gratification of one's own wants and needs, and understanding that one's behavior must conform to abstract guidelines that might not offer immediate rewards and feedback.

A child who is inattentive and has difficulty sustaining his attention for long periods of time will tend to follow rules inconsistently, especially if he is not constantly reminded of these rules or rewarded for compliance. If he has difficulty selectively focusing on the most important information in the environment, he might not even notice that there are rules, or understand how they apply to his behavior. The ADHD child is less motivated by rewards for his behavior. His behavior is so internally driven that the environment has less of a hold on him.

If the ADHD child is not capable of attending to the environment, if his activity level makes it impossible for him to control his behavior even when he understands he is required to do so, and if, in spite of many reminders of what is expected of him, he blurts things out and behaves inappropriately because he feels like it, it is not hard to see why rewards that reinforce certain behaviors for most people, and consequences that punish other behaviors, will have a weaker hold on his behavior. It is for these reasons that rewards and consequences have to be stronger, more immediate, and more tied to specific behaviors for ADHD children. Rewards and consequences have to be varied more often, as children with ADHD get used to them quickly and they lose their power over the children's behavior.

Inattentive children are also forgetful. They fail to hand in their homework because they forgot to do it, or because they did it and forgot to bring it to school. In class, they fail to follow directions. They do the wrong thing at the wrong time. They take a test and have no idea of the way in which they are supposed to answer the questions.

Impulsive children constantly violate rules and expectations. Following rules involves putting the expectations that others have on one's behavior first, and putting one's own immediate impulses and needs second. Impulsive children tend to do the opposite. They blurt something out when it comes to mind, no matter how inappropriate the comments might be. They also have difficulty waiting their turn and working independently without the benefit of prompts and reminders. They are the class clowns. They run into the street without looking; they get into fights.

Hyperactive children have a hard time sitting still when they are expected to and sticking to a task for the required amount of time. They leave things unfinished as they go from one thing to another. Their behavior lacks order and direction. They talk to the students sitting next to them when they should be working.

Deficits in Executive Functions

Executive functions are those areas of thinking and behaving that are necessary to carry out tasks that require sustained effort. The symptoms of ADHD can be conceptualized as constituting a deficit in executive functions.

Effortful tasks require the interaction and maintenance of several cognitive and behavioral processes at once. They require the individual to sustain attention over the period of time necessary to complete the task (Schachar and Tannock 1993). They also require the ability to formulate plans and problem-solving strategies, and then to carry out these plans or strategies while inhibiting competing responses or impulses (Reardon and Naglieri 1992). These abilities also are dependent on the individual's controlling his level of arousal, or mental alertness, in order to match the demands of the situation.

These requirements are met through an individual's ability to organize his time and his physical surroundings, to regulate his own behavior and cognitive functioning, to rehearse or practice solutions to problems, and to practice flexibility in considering alternative responses for meeting challenges (Reader et al. 1994, Robins 1992). The tasks that demand executive functions often require memorization and computation (Dykman and Ackerman 1993).

Barkley (1993, 1994, 1995a,b) has argued that the diagnosis of ADHD is more accurately described as a deficit in behavioral persistence rather than one of attention. To persist in effort over time is a hallmark of executive functioning, as it is a requirement for task completion, compliance with rules and expectations, and fulfillment of goals. It requires intrinsic motivation in the absence of immediate rewards and consequences and environmental prompts (Koziol and Stout 1993).

Deficits in Anticipating the Future

In a reformulation of the theory of ADHD, Barkley (1993, 1994, 1995a,b) hypothesizes that the various symptoms and characteristics of ADHD children commonly arise from their problem in inhibiting behavior. They have difficulty regulating their behavior with an orientation to the future. What is commonly perceived as inattention in ADHD children is actually a deficit in inhibiting certain behaviors for a period of time in order to complete the task at hand.

The ability to delay responding immediately to events around us, to inhibit our urges, and to suppress our need to respond based on our feelings, is what separates our thought processes from those of lower animals. This enables us to respond to events more objectively rather than solely on the basis of how we feel about them. This ability to insert a delay between an event and our response enables us to keep that event alive in our memory, to analyze and understand what happened, and to plan a response that will affect what happens in the future. It also allows us to talk to ourselves about the event and therefore guide our behavior according to rules, plans, and goals.

Our ability to inhibit behavior and to use language during that delay to understand events and plan for the future enables us to break down information into smaller parts. It allows us to understand information in different ways. We can then take these aspects of reality and put them together in new ways. Thus, we generate new ideas, new ways of understanding and seeing things, and new approaches to solving problems. Keeping ourselves from responding immediately to events based on our urges and emotions, therefore, enables us to be flexible in our approach to problems and to formulate more effective ways to solve problems and succeed in the world.

SECONDARY PROBLEMS

There are other deficits that are not considered to be the major symptoms or primary problems of ADHD, but they are so pervasive and so linked to the major symptoms and primary problems that they are almost as defining of the condition.

Social and Communication Deficits

ADHD children often have problems getting along with other children because the intensity of their reactions is often out of synchrony with the situation. They have difficulty modulating their intensity to fit the expectations of others with whom they are interacting. They often appear to be insensitive to the subtle nuances of social interaction (Whalen and Henker 1985). They therefore respond in ways that seem unusual to their peers. They become too upset or angry, or too intensely happy, or they overreact to minor difficulties, and these emotional reactions last for too long. They become explosive and unpredictable or overly aroused. They have difficulty shifting gears, and require more time than normal to de-escalate their emotions and behaviors.

Some ADHD children might respond with less intensity than others expect. They might ignore the questions or moods of their peers and might therefore appear unresponsive. They often do not adjust their communication to the changing demands of the situation (Guevremont and Dumas 1994, Whalen et al. 1979).

Since their attention wavers, ADHD children overlook important cues that would inform them how others are feeling, what others need, and how others are reacting to them. They therefore have difficulty evaluating the intentions of others and taking the perspectives of others. These difficulties lead to inaccurate judgments and to inappropriate reactions to their peers, which creates the basis for rejection and scapegoating (Dodge 1986, Giddan 1991, Whalen and Henker 1985).

Peers tend to perceive ADHD children as being more aggressive, disruptive, domineering, intrusive, noisy, and socially rejected than other children (Frederick and Olmi 1994, Johnston et al. 1985, Pope et al. 1989). They respond to ADHD children with avoidance, criticism, and often aggression, sometimes after only a few contacts (Barkley 1990, Frederick and Olmi 1994). Peer rejection can have devastating long-term effects. It increases the risk of dropping out of school, delinquency, and psychiatric maladjustment. Social rejection results in even poorer social skills and greater interpersonal problems, and in decreased social interaction over time (Weiss and Hechtman 1993).

Memory Deficits

Inattention limits the amount of information that can be processed and stored at any one time. ADHD children have been found to have difficulty remembering previously stated rules and directions (Maag and Reid 1994). Other tasks that depend on short-term memory can also be affected. For example, children with ADHD might have difficulty copying information from the blackboard onto paper, since this process requires the storage, for a brief period of time, of the information that is on the board. Memory abilities are also required in transferring information that one has studied previously onto paper during a test. This can be especially challenging to the ADHD child as the conditions for taking a test are often more distracting than the situation in which one studied (Umansky and Smalley 1994).

Response-Speed Deficits

Task performance for ADHD children is also hindered by their difficulty performing accurately under timed conditions (Robins 1992).

When their performance is based on speed, they become less planful in their approach and less accurate in their results. They have difficulty maintaining a balance between speed and accuracy, and they often sacrifice accuracy for speed. This is one reason why many educational plans for ADHD children include the modification that they will be able to take tests under untimed conditions.

Self-Esteem Deficits

The peer rejection that many ADHD children experience takes its toll on their self-esteem (Weiss and Hechtman 1993). ADHD children experience many frustrations in life. In addition to failures in getting along with peers, they also experience inadequacies in their school performance and in meeting the expectations of their parents.

Since the manifestations of ADHD are quite variable, and since other people in the child's life often have an inadequate understanding of the disorder and might not even be aware that the child suffers from it, the child constantly experiences that others expect him to do what he knows he cannot. Being able to follow rules, complete work, or perform well in school on one day leads others to expect that the ADHD child will be able to do the same every day. When he does not, others become disappointed in or angry at him, and might attribute his failure to some personal characteristic such as laziness or lack of caring.

Intelligent or verbal children with ADHD are often met with expectations from parents and teachers that are based on their intelligence and their verbal abilities, while their very real attention problems are ignored. This is analogous to expecting a strong, athletic person who then had his arm disabled by a stroke to throw a ball well.

Many intelligent and talented ADHD children believe that they are dumb or stupid. They frequently fail on tasks that society deems important: getting good grades, behaving well in school, and making friends. They fail to meet the expectations of others, and are confronted with anger, disappointment, criticism, correction, and monitoring. All of this diminishes their self-esteem.

SUMMARY

- Inattention is a core deficit that includes the following:
  - Distractibility, or poorly focused attention.
  - Poorly sustained attention or persistence.
  - Difficulty shifting attention.
  - Deficient selective attention.
  - Visual and auditory inattention.

- Impulsivity, another core deficit, entails the tendency to blurt out answers to questions, to act without thinking, to have difficulty waiting one's turn, and to interrupt others.

- Hyperactivity, the third core deficit, entails excessive motor activity, difficulty staying seated, feelings of restlessness, and fidgetiness.

- ADHD children also exhibit deficits in conforming their behavior to rules.

- ADHD children lack sensitivity to rewards and consequences. Rewards and consequences must be strong, immediate, specific, and varied.

- ADHD children experience difficulty with tasks that involve planning, problem solving, sustained effort, and behavioral persistence.

- ADHD entails deficits in behavioral inhibition, delayed responding, and the orientation of behavior toward future goals and consequences.

- Social behavior and communication problems are very common.

- Memory problems often exist.

- Slow response speed in problem solving often coexists with ADHD.

- Self-esteem problems are pervasive for ADHD children.

❖ C H A P T E R 3 ❖

What Makes Fathers Unique

The significant differences between men and women are what make the experience of fathering different from the experience of mothering. These differences provide mothers and fathers with different skills and different areas of vulnerability. Men and women tend to think, communicate, and form relationships differently. Thus, there are differences in how mothers and fathers play with, speak to, understand, and discipline their children. Despite these differences, fathers are just as capable as mothers in their ability to interact with and form attachments to their children. Emotional attachment to children is not the sole province of mothers.

FATHERS SEE BEHAVIOR PROBLEMS AS BEING LESS SERIOUS

Even when fathers experience as much stress in parenting as do mothers, mothers tend to perceive child characteristics as more stressful (Baker 1994). Mothers tend to see their children's problems as being more serious than fathers do. Mothers usually function as the early warning system that something is not right with their child.

Sometimes there are specific things that the child does that indicate to the mother that there is something wrong, like hitting other children, not sitting still in school, or failing to learn. At other times there is nothing more dramatic or specific than a nagging feeling that the mother has. Fathers are apt to dismiss such worries as overreactions by the mother. Fathers often see their son's overly active and zealous behavior as being typical boy behavior.

Fathers might minimize their spouses' concerns partly because the children also behave better around them than around their mothers. Fathers might not see the amount or intensity of the misbehavior that the mothers see. If they do witness the severe temper tantrums and defiance that the mothers report, the fathers might be able to resolve them quickly. This makes the problem seem to be more manageable than it in fact is when the father is absent.

Edwards (1995) found that mothers of ADHD teenagers reported greater conflict with their teens than did fathers. Mothers were more likely than fathers to see that areas of conflict actually existed, that these conflicts occurred with greater frequency, and that they were fraught with greater intensity compared with parents of non-ADHD teens. Mothers tended to engage their teens in more heated discussions, and their conflicts had an adverse effect on the mothers' mental health.

Barkley (1981) cited research indicating that children tend to misbehave more when they are with the parent with whom they spend more time. Since in this society that is more typically the mother, it is no wonder that children's behavior problems are worse when they are with their mothers. Fathers, then, often see a different child than the mothers see.

FATHERS REASON AND COMMUNICATE DIFFERENTLY

Linear Thinking

Men and women often feel completely misunderstood by each other. People feel frustrated when they are misunderstood. Men and women seem to speak different languages, and research on male and female communication patterns and problem solving has shed some light on this apparent language barrier between the sexes (Tannen 1990).

Men tend to think very linearly, relying on logical analysis and facts to interpret events and solve problems. Problems are seen as things to solve as efficiently and quickly as possible. The operating principle seems to be the old geometry axiom that the shortest distance between two points is a straight line. Circuitous routes are not as valuable as direct routes in solving a problem.

Men therefore tend to be instrumental problem solvers. This strategy also applies to problems that involve people. Men seem to be good at seeing solutions in simple terms and at plotting the most direct route to get there. There is a focus on the goal as the primary objective. Whatever contributes to meeting the goal is considered worthwhile.

Fathers make great behaviorists. They often can identify specific behaviors that disrupt family life, what they want their children to stop doing, and what they want them to do instead. Once the goal is defined, fathers often consider meeting the goal to be dependent on an act of will and choice. They believe that their children can simply make choices and can be the agents of their own behaviors. This attitude is also found in male school teachers and administrators, especially with parents who attempt to obtain special services for their children who the school personnel feel should be able to behave and perform well through an act of will.

This perspective can create a sharp focus on the goals of behavior management and promote clear ideas about what behaviors and skills the parents want to develop in their child. It can also lead to a great deal of frustration, helplessness, and giving up when the goals are not met and when the process is not easy. If things do not change as quickly as they "should," the blame can be cast on the child or the mother for not wanting things to be different.

What fathers often overlook is that there is much more than observable behavior and will to consider in helping a child change his behavior. For example, social interaction is a very complex phenomenon that involves organizing a great deal of stimuli simultaneously. We tend to do this automatically, by attending to a person's words, tone of voice, gestures, and body language all in a split second and unconsciously, factoring in our own feelings about the person and our expectations of being treated well or poorly by him or her. Therefore, behavioral strategies are often confounded by the needs and feelings of both the parent and the child.

Early in my career I worked at community mental health clinics where I was referred many children with behavior problems. I designed many logical and goal-directed behavior management plans that I thought would work well, in theory. The only problem was that the clients would not cooperate! It was their inner motivations, feelings, fears, and expectations that complicated the process of simply getting from point A to point B. And it was my own inner need to see my clients as logical and uncomplicated that led me to believe that these plans would work as designed, and that created such disappointment when they did not. If I had thought about it, I would have realized that if a simple and logical behavioral plan could work right away, the client probably would have been doing it already.

Men often make the mistake of ignoring the emotional side of the ledger in an attempt to simplify the world and make things conform to the way they think they should be. Problems exist in order to make them disappear. Emotions are obstacles to solutions, and should be set aside lest they interfere with reaching the goal quickly and efficiently.

Women, on the other hand, are more likely to take into account their own and the other person's subjective feelings and experiences that might complicate the process of solving the problem. Women are more likely to respond automatically to their emotional needs and those of others, and these needs are likely to be more important than progressing to their goal exactly as planned. Admitting emotions and subjectivity into the equation introduces a greater number of variables for which to account. It is like expecting to cook something with only two ingredients and then having to work with five, and balancing their flavors, interactions, responses to heat, and everything else that goes into the recipe. The planning takes longer, the process is more complex and more delicate, and the chance of making a mess, a mistake, or a disappointing dish is greater. But the possibility of a richer, tastier, more satisfying and memorable dish is also greater.

These differences in communication style have been observed in the ways in which mothers and fathers interact with their children. Researchers have found that fathers tend to concentrate on more instrumental factors, and are more action oriented when providing support for their child, while mothers tend to be more supportive and encouraging in an affective sense (Lamb 1981, Starrels 1994). Research with fathers and daughters has found that girls shape their interactions with each parent based on the parents' interactive style. Specifically, girls in one study exhibited more task-specific behaviors with their fathers and more interpersonal interaction with their mothers (Lamb 1981).

This information has important implications for what happens when parents help their children with homework. Fathers might be stronger at structuring the homework, setting clear and concrete goals, and guiding the child through the step-by-step process they have set up together. However, if the child hits a snag and becomes emotionally overwhelmed or unduly frustrated or has a reaction to the work based on fears or personal feelings about the teacher, the father might have difficulty tolerating this diversion from the straight and narrow path. He might find it difficult to deal with the emotional problems of his child in a productive way that facilitates the child getting back to the task. The mother, on the other hand, might be more skilled at dealing with these emotional matters, but too prone to becoming diverted from the goal by them.

Punishment and Coercion

My impatience with my clients early in my career for not following through and being successful with our behavioral programs was similar to the feelings I detect in fathers in their interactions with mothers in my office. Being good behaviorists, fathers understand the concepts of reward and punishment, although too often they understand the concept of punishment a lot better than they do the concept of reward!

Rewards and punishments, to fathers, are often black and white, right and wrong sorts of issues. They appear to be simplified, binary decisions. The strictest behavioral plans are supported by the fathers and then left to the mothers to enforce, since the mother is the one who usually spends more time with the child. Then the father blames the mother when the program fails. What fathers frequently overlook is how they make the process more messy and unpredictable because of their difficulty recognizing their own inconsistencies and emotional reactions that interfere with the plan's proceeding in a straightforward linear manner. Mothers have an easier time recognizing when they have contributed to a plan's failure by their own inconsistencies and difficulties in carrying out the plan. The problem is, with the mother more likely to feel guilty and admit her responsibility and the father more likely to blame the mother, the mother ends up with the blame and the guilt when things do not work out as planned.

Stan and Sheila agreed that whenever Sheila's ADHD son or his non-ADHD sister (who was almost as defiant as her brother) would defy their authority, they would immediately send the child to his or her room for a half-hour, and revoke telephone privileges and going outside for the rest of the day. They had arrived at such a plan after a year of steadily escalating behaviors from both children.

Sheila was able to tolerate more negotiation than Stan could. If she told one of the children to clean up his or her mess, and the child answered "Not now, later," Sheila would discuss with the child the need to do it, how much more time the child needed to finish what he or she was doing at the moment, and when the clean up would take place. As long as the child was respectful to her, Sheila was satisfied with this approach.

Stan found it difficult to tolerate any challenge to his authority and would blow up when the children did not jump at his command. He felt that Sheila was too flexible, which he felt encouraged the children to question his authority. When Stan came home from work, not knowing what had been transpiring in the house before he walked through the door, he usually saw something out of place that he wanted straightened up. He typically told the first child that he saw to take care of it, no matter what the child was engaged in at the moment. This led to some resistance on the child's part, which Stan interpreted as defiance.

Stan responded by yelling at the child to go to his or her room, and suspending privileges for the rest of the day. An argument then ensued between Stan and Sheila over whether the child actually had done anything wrong. Sheila felt that Stan had overreacted, and Stan blamed his overreaction on Sheila's lax discipline, which encouraged the children's defiance of parental authority.

Because fathers often see the value of punishment better than they see the value of reward, they reason that if children do not behave, they should be punished until they exercise their free will to behave. It is what I have heard referred to as an Old Testament form of reasoning. It is based in the belief that children should know better. While I agree that children *should* know better, I do not believe that they automatically *do* know better, and that they must be taught to know better.

Punishing undesirable behavior might help to decrease or eliminate the behavior, but it does not teach the child what behavior to substitute in its place. The desirable behavior is not lurking just under the surface, waiting to come out as soon as the curtain of undesirable behavior that is covering it is removed. Nature does abhor a vacuum, and if the behavior that is punished is eliminated, other problems can arise in its place, such as more devious behaviors, more clever violations of the rules, or other behaviors based on the child's anger and resentment and his attempt to wrest control back from the parents. These latter developments often result in even more punitive reactions from the father, and the cycle continues, but in an escalated form. While we might see the child as making a choice to misbehave, for ADHD children we have to engineer the environment to give them the opportunity to make the right choices and to enable them to see the rewards and consequences of their choices.

To increase a child's compliance, it is therefore not sufficient to punish noncompliance, but to teach compliance. When compliance increases and desirable behavior occurs more frequently as a result of being rewarded, noncompliance has to decrease, because the two cannot exist at the same time (Forehand and McMahon 1981).

Another misuse of punishment is for retaliation, and it is important for parents to understand where this comes from and what it does to their relationship with their children. When parents feel punished by their children, they often want to punish back. Because children with ADHD can be particularly demanding, noncompliant, defiant, and aggressive, this increases the parents' sense of being controlled by their children, which is different from the stress they experience in being unjustly controlled by their bosses or their own parents. Feeling controlled by children is a reversal of the hierarchy, of the natural lines of authority, whereas being controlled by bosses or by parents is within the bounds of the hierarchy that we have come to expect and rely on in our lives. It is part of the world in which we feel we have a place.

Not only does the struggle for control with our children contain the normal stresses and strains of other control struggles in our lives, it also upsets what we see as the natural world order, and our place in it. Therefore, our experience, when involved in such struggles, takes on a desperation that other control struggles lack. This desperation is so emotionally charged that it blinds us to alternative solutions, disrupts our normally rational selves, and gets us to focus more on approaches based on punishment and coercion, even though they have not been working. In this irrational mind-set, we persist in doing things that have not worked in the past, and the more they continue not to work, the more we do them, until we just give up.

The entering of emotional desperation into parents' interaction with their children disrupts their rationality, but is usually not seen by fathers as irrational when it happens. Failing to recognize their own emotionality, fathers hold on to the black and white thinking that sees the child's behavior as bad, the father's authority as good, and punitive action as both corrective and morally justified. While this view of things might be worth testing, fathers tend to see this as the truth before it is put to the test, not as a hypothesis that needs to be tested. Once this worldview is put to the test and found wanting in terms of its results, it is often difficult for fathers to reexamine their assumptions and try something else. This worldview of fathers is incomplete in that it ignores important aspects of reality.

With their ADHD children, fathers often play into a cycle of coercive interactions, which comes to characterize the malfunctioning of the entire family. Coercive interaction cycles occur when both parties learn to control each other through aversive means. Aversive interactions occur when our behaviors in relationship with others are based on inflicting unpleasant, harmful, or undesirable (on the part of the recipient) consequences (in other words, punishment), or on avoiding the same from the other person.

Paterson (1976) describes parents who respond with coercive behaviors, such as yelling, to their child's noncompliance. If the child then complies, it reinforces the parent for yelling. The child, however, might not comply, and might respond with his own coercive behaviors to what he experiences as aversive stimulation—the parent's yelling or even the parent's giving him a command. The child's coercive behaviors, such as yelling, might be modeled on the parent's behavior. If the parent withdraws the command in the face of the child's coercive behavior, the child learns to repeat or escalate his coercive behaviors in order to terminate the parent's commands. If the parent develops more resolve to control the child the next time, and escalates his own coercive behavior (yelling, commanding) only to back down when the child responds with more intense, longer-lasting coercive behavior of his own, the parent will be reinforcing even stronger coercive behavior in the child. An orientation toward punishment to the exclusion of other forms of behavioral control and parent–child interaction at times of noncompliance reinforces this cycle (See Figure 3–1).

It has been my experience that fathers are especially likely to establish interaction patterns with their ADHD children based on punishment to the relative exclusion of other ways of interacting. However, research has also shown that families in which the father is absent tend to have rates of coercive interaction that are twice as high as in intact families (Paterson 1976). Fathers, therefore, have a profound effect on the interaction patterns and the atmosphere at home when they are present and even when they are absent.

It is also interesting that, although coercive interaction patterns create and perpetuate a great deal of family distress, fathers tend to

---

Figure 3–1: Two Coercive Interaction Sequences

1. Child does not comply → Parent yells → Child complies → Parent more likely to yell in future
2. Child does not comply → Parent yells → Child yells → Parent backs down → Child more likely to yell or not comply in future

---

be insulated from the effects of this stress more than mothers. Paterson's research found that the feelings of anxiety, depression, anger, and confusion that afflict the caregivers in distressed families are relatively absent from the self-perceptions of fathers in these families. This might be due to the fact that fathers tend to gain a great deal of positive feeling about themselves from work, and they do not see family management as a significant part of their responsibility and identity in life.

One implication of this finding is that, although fathers might contribute greatly to the stress in a family with an ADHD child, they might not be so affected by this stress that they would see a great need to change things at home. The mothers are left "holding the bag"—experiencing the distress and knowing that something is gravely wrong. Fathers can continue their coercive interaction patterns with their children and then go to work and feel good about themselves, while mothers are distressed and suffering from damaged self-esteem at home.

Families in which a child engages in frequent and intense antisocial behavior are more likely to rely heavily on punishment and aversive control than other families. However, punishment is often used by these families in inadequate ways that reinforce rather than punish the antisocial behavior. For example, Paterson (1976) points out that parents of children whose behavior is antisocial often fail to bring their punishment to a firm conclusion. These parents often threaten things that they do not follow through with, or they might institute a punishment and then remove it. Furthermore, these parents are likely to issue commands that are unclear. Thus, the child is given incomplete or incomprehensible instructions about what he is supposed to do.

Real punishment also takes time. It is highly unlikely that punishing a behavior once or twice will eliminate it. Fathers who rely solely on punishments, which means that they mainly respond to negative, not positive, behavior in their child, want their problems solved immediately. They are often impatient and frustrated with the consistency of time and effort that is required for true punishment, in which the father deprives the child in the same way each time the infraction occurs. With all the time and effort required to truly punish a child, the child is bound to exhibit the behavior again, leading many fathers to conclude that their punishment did not work. They fail to see punishment as the training of behavior, which requires time and repetition, and they fail to understand that the unwanted behavior will recur.

Impatient fathers, who may be more impulsive due to their own ADHD (diagnosed or undiagnosed), will then revert to yelling or spanking, which is more likely to be aversive than truly punishing. While yelling and spanking may be immediately tension relieving and emotionally satisfying for the father, they are short-term responses that are often based on the father's emotions rather than on a consistent long-range plan. The father opts for immediate emotional gratification rather than for the delayed gratification that is involved in planning and repetition. The paradox here is that the father is trying to teach the child how to delay gratification with methods that stem from the father's need for immediate gratification.

Furthermore, yelling and spanking the child are highly stimulating events. Children with ADHD crave stimulation. They seek out situations in which stimulation is available. Nonstimulating activities are boring for them. No matter how aversive being yelled at or spanked might be for a normal child, the stimulus value of these experiences might outweigh the aversive quality for an ADHD child. The yelling and spanking then actually provide the child with more stimulation, making it a situation he is more likely to be drawn to and seek out.

Fathers who opt for an overly punitive approach may overlook many instances of positive, prosocial behavior in their children. Other fathers may notice these behaviors, but are too angry at their child to reward them. These are opportunities missed, because a failure to reinforce prosocial behavior results in a child who does not have these skills, and therefore learns only antisocial behaviors.

Fathers who respond to their child based on their emotions, especially anger, are more likely to administer consequences noncontingently—when the father is angry, he is more likely to hit or yell; when he is pleased, he is more likely to reward. However, he is not responding consistently in a way that is determined by the child's behavior, regardless of how he is feeling. This type of pattern is more likely to result in antisocial behavior in the child.

Distressed couples also spend less time discussing problem solving than do nondistressed couples. And when distressed couples whose families are marked by coercive control do problem solve, their discussion is marked by coercive interaction. This type of interaction tends to be self-reinforcing, pervasive, and very resistant to remediation.

Fathers have difficulty even thinking of rewarding a child who misbehaves and disrupts their control frequently. They associate reinforcement of specific behaviors with reward of the child as a whole. When they are at the height of frustration with their child, they will see giving any rewards, for any reason, as being "soft on crime." That is why fathers often punish children with grounding or restrictions for long periods of time, such as several weeks. Any rewards during that period will be seen by the father as allowing the child to get away with the infraction, no matter how removed the reward is in time from the infraction, and no matter what immediately precedes the reward in time.

Fathers who punish for prolonged periods of time have not mastered the concepts that (1) consequences should be administered immediately; (2) prolonging a punishment for a long period of time removes the consequence from immediately following the behavior, and therefore from being a true consequence to the behavior; (3) when the punishment is finally imposed, what actually gets punished is whatever the child was doing just before the punishment occurred, which might have been behaving appropriately; and (4) reinforcing good behaviors with rewards, if done correctly, does not reward misbehavior and noncompliance.

Fathers are correct in fearing that giving any reward to a child who is acting bad much of the time, might reward bad behavior or a bad attitude. This certainly happens when reinforcers are administered inappropriately, so these concerns need to be taken seriously. Some fathers say that setting up a reward, such as allowing their teenage sons to attend a dance at the school, gets their children to manipulatively behave just before the date of the dance, and once they get their reward, they return to the same undesirable behaviors as previously.

Children with ADHD can certainly become master manipulators, which leads many fathers to want to punish them all the time. This might seem logical, but it never works. Also, because fathers are naturally generous souls, they want to give their children the world. This is consistent with their own sense of identity—being the good provider, the protector, the role model, and the one the child looks up to. This part of the father's personality is in dynamic conflict with the punitive part. Again, the Old Testament parallel comes to mind—fatherhood modeled after the all-giving but harshly punishing Supreme Being.

The dynamic conflict between these poles of the personality often leads fathers to be inconsistent. They will impose a one-month punishment, and then in a moment of generosity allow the punishment to be lifted early, in time for the child to attend the dance. Fathers often end up feeling more guilty than mothers for depriving their children.

The Need for Immediate and Short-Term Consequences

Parents want to train their children to be well-socialized individuals: to respect authority, to negotiate for things in productive rather than destructive ways, to know right from wrong, and to be able to delay immediate gratification in order to obtain long-range goals. Children with ADHD have difficulty with these skills. They are resistant to ordinary rewards; they have difficulty following rules for extended periods of time; they have difficulty with behavioral persistence, such as planning and organizing behavior in order to meet a goal; and they resist complying with demands made on them because they feel they cannot master the expectations that others have of them.

Barkley's (1993, 1994, 1995a,b) reformulated theory of ADHD states that children with ADHD have difficulty holding a goal in their minds long enough to maintain the image of the goal beyond the immediate moment. They also have difficulty maintaining an image of past consequences for their actions in order to guide their behavior in the future. These ideas speak to the need for reinforcement to be immediate and brief.

Behavioral theory, which concerns itself with the control of consequences over behavior, is consistent with the implications of this reformulated theory of ADHD. *Reinforcement* is any event that immediately follows a behavior that increases the chance of the behavior occurring again in the future. *Reinforcement* and *reward* are terms that are often used interchangeably.

In my work with parents, I ask fathers to put aside their moralistic stances for a moment in order to focus on what our goal is and what works. I attempt to get parents to be scientific about child management. Being a scientific parent is very well articulated by Barkley (1995b). Appealing to a father's scientific side often puts me in conflict with his moralistic side. I do not challenge what the father believes to be morally right. I agree with his intent, align our goals, ask him to suspend his belief in what he is doing, and consider alternatives that might be effective in reaching his desired result. I acknowledge that my approach might prove to be wrong (because when it is, the fathers let me know it loudly and clearly!).

What controls behavior most effectively is whatever immediately follows the behavior. Whatever events follow the occurrence of a behavior will have a great hold on whether the behavior is likely to occur again. As people mature, long-term goals, morals, and values have more influence on their behavior. So even when a behavior is followed by a much desired reward, feelings of guilt, shame, or failure might override the pull of the immediate reward. However, it is still not possible to discount the influence of the immediate consequences. For ADHD children, as morally sound as they might be, the immediate consequence has even more of a pull and the long-term or more abstract consequences have less of a pull over their behavior. We cannot expect that this internal, long-term orientation will develop in the same way that it will in others as they age and gain more experience.

The principle that we have to work with in helping ADHD children with their behavior is that consequences (rewards and punishments) have to be immediate and short-term. This means abandoning the grand punishment for grand offenses, and substituting short-term but meaningful consequences for appropriate and inappropriate behavior. Since consequences are the most powerful (and are followed through with more consistency) when they immediately follow behavior, they should be imposed the day of the transgression when possible. The child should lose something meaningful for that day and then have the opportunity to earn privileges for good behavior the next day.

For example, if a child fails to complete his chores, or has not handed in his homework, it is reasonable to take away telephone and/or television privileges for the rest of that day. Taking away these privileges for two or more days gives him little incentive to behave well the next day, because even if he behaves well, his good behavior will be punished by the removal of privileges, since the deprivation of privileges will immediately follow his good behavior on the second day. It is generally more effective to give the child the chance to earn the privileges on the next day by doing his homework or chores. In this way, the child experiences a reward immediately following appropriate behavior.

There are responsibilities and behaviors that do not fit so neatly into this scheme. One such responsibility is that of getting good grades in school. Grades are reported periodically throughout the school year. Some school systems issue progress reports or warnings midway through each marking period. But grading is not done frequently enough to lend itself to the use of immediate and short-term consequences. If a child is punished for poor grades, he might have to wait several weeks before there is evidence that he is doing better. An ADHD child then has to do better day after day with no recognition or reward to help him sustain his efforts. Or a child might earn privileges for a good report card, and enjoy these privileges until the next report card comes out even if he has started to slack off.

These are not reasons to abandon an emphasis on school performance as a basis for rewards and privileges for the ADHD child. After all, schoolwork is the major responsibility of children and therefore must be included in determining their privileges. Grades are reflective of effort, task completion, and learning over a period of time. These factors can be monitored on a daily or weekly basis by the school and reported to the parents. A counselor in school can work with the child to collect a daily report from his teacher or teachers that charts the percentage of assignments and homework completed, the classroom behavior, and test and quiz grades. In the upper grades, the student can bring a checklist to his teachers each period and review it with a counselor at the end of each day before bringing it home to his parents. The chart can look something like this:

Date	% of Work Completed	Homework Done?	Behavior	Test Grades	Teacher Signature
English	100 75 50 25 0	Y N	Cooperative Uncooperative		
Math	100 75 50 25 0	Y N	Cooperative Uncooperative		
Social Studies	100 75 50 25 0	Y N	Cooperative Uncooperative		
Science	100 75 50 25 0	Y N	Cooperative Uncooperative		
Language	100 75 50 25 0	Y N	Cooperative Uncooperative		
Health	100 75 50 25 0	Y N	Cooperative Uncooperative		

In this way, the child can earn rewards and privileges daily for school performance that is consistent with earning good grades.

There are going to be privileges that the child desires that are not daily occurrences but that are available in the short term. For example, a teenager who is having problems in school or with his behavior at home might request permission to go to a school dance in two weeks. In this case, the parent can set minimum standards for the daily report card at school, establish a similar one for behavior at home, and require a certain number of days in which these standards are met in order for the child to go to the dance. One possible objection to this might be that the child might earn the points, but his behavior might be uncooperative and inappropriate the day before or the day of the dance, and allowing him to go might feel to the parent like he is being rewarded for bad behavior. One possible remedy to this is to require not only a certain number of days in which the criteria are met, but also to require that the criteria be met during the two days before the dance.

Another frequent objection is that the child will do what he has to do to earn this privilege, but revert to inappropriate behavior as soon as the dance is over. This might happen. The child has earned the dance through his appropriate behavior, which is as it should be. When he reverts to inappropriate behavior, the consequences will be in place so he will continue to lose privileges until his behavior improves. The consequences for inappropriate behavior following the dance should be meaningful to the child. The child is therefore still experiencing that appropriate behavior results in enjoying privileges and inappropriate behavior results in restrictions and losses of freedom. This may not proceed perfectly in its impact on the child, but it is important for the parents to expose the child to the idea that in order to enjoy the freedoms and pleasures that family life has to offer, the child is expected to be a "good citizen" of the household, just as we have to be good citizens of the community in order to enjoy our rights and privileges as adults.

Fathers often report, after punishing their child, that "nothing bothers him." Many children with ADHD have adapted to being punished so often that the only way they can feel in control of their parents is to act like they do not care. This is a very powerful tool for children. It is disturbing for parents to think that they can take away all of their child's privileges, use every weapon in their arsenal, and not make any impression on their child. Too many parents react to this stance by stopping their disciplinary efforts because they seem to do no good. This is a mistake. Even if the child acts like he does not care, it is very important that he experience consequences for his actions. Do courts fail to impose sentences on criminals because they do not seem to care? On the contrary, this attitude results in stiffer sentences.

Another possible root of this "I don't care" demeanor is that the parents have run out of creative approaches to limit setting.

Mr. and Mrs. Paulson were distraught that their 13-year-old ADHD son Karl was refusing to do his schoolwork, talking back to his teachers, refusing to do chores at home, and provoking and antagonizing his younger brother to the point of physical confrontation. Throughout the discussion, Karl sat silently with a superior smirk on his face. He responded to questions with shrugs of his shoulders, or by saying "I don't know" or "I don't care." He was silently defiant and a master of self-control and control of others. Mr. and Mrs. Paulson said that they had tried everything to punish Karl. He was now so restricted, they said, that there was nothing else to take away. When Karl was asked about his interests in going to an upcoming school dance, being able to play on the computer, or going over to a friend's house, his response was the same detached attitude with the claim that he could live without them. The Paulsons pointed to this as proof of just how powerless they were.

I noticed that Karl was wearing a fashionable pair of running shoes and a sports team logo windbreaker that was very popular at the time. I asked, "Who got Karl those nice shoes and that jacket?" The parents replied that they had bought them at Karl's request when they were school shopping. I then inquired about Karl's room. I asked the family to describe his room. The parents had already removed Karl's stereo, television, computer, and radio, and were using them as rewards for good behavior. In addition to containing the basic furniture and books, however, Karl's room was decorated with his favorite posters of rock stars and sports figures. I asked the parents whether they had considered making Karl's access to his favorite articles of clothing and the posters decorating his room contingent on his good behavior. As an analogy, I mentioned the use of zero-based budgeting for governmental departments. Under this method, each department would start with an assumption of having no assets, and develop a plan for expenditures and for obtaining resources from the ground up. I advocated this mind-set for thinking about the resources that they provided their child.

Mr. and Mrs. Paulson had never considered using Karl's clothing or posters as part of the deal because they had assumed that he came with these, that they were part of him. I urged them to strip Karl's possessions down to just the necessities, with everything else being negotiable.

For the first time that session, an audible, emotional protest came from Karl. He was animated, engaged, and angry, furiously negotiating what was fair and what was not. Suddenly, Mr. and Mrs. Paulson had power again, and began to work together as they had not done in a long time.

FATHERS USE AUTHORITY DIFFERENTLY

Fathers are often much more comfortable with their authority than are mothers. As Tannen (1990) has pointed out, men tend to establish relationships based on hierarchy, while women tend more often to establish relationships based on symmetry. Fathers are often more forceful than mothers when they are disciplining their children because fathers fit easily into a hierarchical world where there are superiors and subordinates. They communicate in ways that establish differences in power, or an asymmetry between individuals. Their communications to their children tend to be more commanding, briefer, and more instrumental. They focus on what the father needs the child to do rather than how the child feels or on the process of doing it.

However, in this hierarchical worldview, men are more comfortable working alone rather than coordinating their efforts with someone (such as the mother) who operates differently (Tannen 1990). To coordinate with another who does not necessarily share one's assumptions and methods requires a temporary diversion from the goal and a willingness to empathically understand a different point of view. It involves treating one's own point of view as relative rather than as absolute, and regarding another way of thinking as equal to one's own.

The ability to empathize with another's point of view and see another's perspective as equally valid as one's own is, however, an important component in effective disciplining. This is one that many fathers have difficulty appreciating and mastering. In focusing on the goal and on a no-nonsense approach, and in insisting that the child attune himself to the father's needs and wishes, fathers often fail to tune in to their children's emotional needs. There is plenty of opportunity for inefficient communication and therefore unsatisfying results from the father's discipline.

For example, a parent might have the following experience: you have the goal of having your child clean up all of his toys before bedtime. You are facing a common evening problem: a roomful of toys scattered all over the place, making the room a hazardous place to walk, and giving any sane person pause as to where to start. You give the child the command to "clean up this mess" and then leave the room, and you come back to see that nothing has been done. You then stand there to oversee the situation, but your child might see toys that interest him and might play with them, wandering from toy to toy. He might pick a toy up as if to put it away, and then put it down when a more interesting toy crosses his path. You even volunteer to help or work with the child, and get down on your knees and start cleaning up, only to find yourself being the only one accomplishing anything. You are now getting more and more aggravated, because you have told the child several times to clean up the mess.

The problem is that your command is clear from your point of view, but the goal is not clear to your child, or when it is to be accomplished, or that it is to be accomplished to the exclusion of all other goals (like playing with a toy if it appears to be more interesting at the moment), or what sequence of activities will be required to accomplish this goal. The child's understanding and attentional abilities do not conform to your point of view.

To communicate this command effectively, you have to become better at empathizing with your child's point of view. For example, it might be more effective for you to specify, step by step, what you want your child to do, and to offer immediate praise and reinforcement for each accomplishment. You might go to the blocks on the floor, get your child's attention, hold a block up, and say, "Now I want you to put the blocks in this crate." You can lead the child over to the blocks and praise him for what a good job he is doing as he is doing it. Then, you can give your child another specific command in the same way.

It is the mother who is more likely to pick up on how to communicate with the child so that the child will be able to comply with the parents' wishes. This is consistent with women's tendency to form connections with others based on symmetry rather than on hierarchy. Women are generally better able to put themselves in the place of another and to see the other's point of view, partly because a woman will strive to connect with others through their similarities rather than their differences.

A woman is less likely to feel a need to appear as an expert and is more likely to try to communicate that she has shared the other person's experience and that this experience is as valid as her own. Women are more inclined to make a connection with someone by putting themselves on the same level as that person rather than by proving that they know more than the other person, that they can solve the other's problems, or that they can be helpful by telling the other person what to do. Rather than insisting that the other person do what she wants him to do, understand the situation the way she understands it, feel the same way that she does about it, and go about doing the task in the same exact way that she would, a woman will intuitively understand that she has to work with someone, understanding the other's point of view and helping him to understand hers.

For these reasons, the mother will more likely understand that the child might need step-by-step guidance, a feeling of teamwork, and the experience of being given to in order to put forth effort. The mother might be better able to gauge the right balance of helping the child and having the child work independently. The combination of the mother's ability to communicate the goal and the process leading to it, her ability to interact with the child in a way that is conducive to meeting the goal, with the father's ability to assert authority and hierarchy and communicate that the child has to adapt to him, can achieve powerful results in accomplishing this and other tasks.

Fathers often see being an authority as being inseparable from fathering. Being an authority *is* inseparable from parenting, for both mothers and fathers. Fathers tend to take on the authority role more often as a core part of their parental identity. This orientation is handed down to men from generation to generation. Often, men who suffered under their own fathers' harsh punitiveness come to rely too much on punishment and harsh authoritarianism themselves. In fact, the use of punishment as a mode of parenting has been found to persist across generations. In one study, being the recipient of harsh paternal punishment was associated with aggressive behavior in males ten years later (Lefkowitz et al. 1978).

Using harsh punishment as the primary mode of discipline fosters aggressive tendencies in males. Since aggressive behavior is one of the most difficult behavior problems for many ADHD boys, and since it puts the ADHD child at greater risk for lifelong problems, punitive parental behavior can be seen as a serious risk factor contributing to later problems in ADHD children.

Fathers often feel that they must be the undisputed authority at home, and any questioning of their authority is unacceptable. Questioning the authority of the father often results in the father redoubling his efforts to exert undisputed authority over his children and he therefore becomes harsher and his authority becomes more dogmatic.

Many fathers become inflexible in their use of authority, as if being flexible in itself was incompatible with being an authority. However, there is more than one way to be an authority. There is an important difference between being *authoritarian* and being *authoritative* (Buri et al. 1988, Starrels 1994). *Authoritarian* fathers have definite standards of discipline, but do not tolerate verbal interchange with their children. They demand that their way of behavior be adhered to without question or comment. There is usually no discussion of their standards. *Authoritative* fathers also have definite standards of discipline and behavior that they enforce. However, they assert their authority with warmth and nurturance. They tolerate and even encourage verbal interchange with their children. Engaging in verbal give and take with their children does not threaten or undermine their authority. They are secure enough to engage their children in discussion and even argument, knowing that their authority will be stable even if they allow the opposition to be heard and even if they modify their decisions. But authoritative does not mean permissive (Table 3–1). Permissive parents believe that the child should have few if any restrictions, and are not demanding of the child (Starrels 1994).

It appears from the research that it is often difficult for fathers to be authoritative rather than authoritarian, to combine firm authority with nurturance. Starrels found that fathers tend to yell more than mothers. With their sons, fathers are less nurturant than are mothers, and when they are nurturant, their nurturance tends to take the form of buying their sons things or giving them money, rather than being nurturant in the emotional sense, including giving verbal praise, appreciation, and encouragement. This praise deficit on the part of fathers is also of concern, given the importance of the frequent verbal feedback that ADHD children need to maintain their desirable behaviors. With their daughters, fathers are less involved with discipline than are mothers.

Fathers lacking in the skills to nurture and praise their children should be concerned if they wish their children to model themselves after them and adopt their values. In reviewing the literature, Radin (1981) found that children tend to imitate models who are nurturant and rewarding, and that these characteristics are important determinants as to whether children adopt characteristics of their parents.

Authoritative parenting has other advantages that are especially relevant for children with ADHD. Research has found that children of authoritative fathers tend to have higher self-esteem compared with children of authoritarian fathers (Buri et al. 1988). This has been

Table 3–1. Characteristics of the Authoritarian, Authoritative, and Permissive Styles

Authoritarian style	Authoritative style	Permissive style
Goal focused	Goal focused	Not goal focused
Hierarchical	Hierarchical	Not hierarchical
Goal clear to father but might not be clear to child	Goal clear to father with empathy for child's needs, level of understanding, and attention span	Few goals, restrictions, or demands
Likely to be harsh, inflexible, and aggressive	Warm, nurturant, and flexible	May be warm and empathic, and flexible to the point of ineffectiveness
Intolerant of discussion	Tolerant of discussion	Tolerant of discussion at the expense of authority
Likely to be deficient in praise	Praise is an important part of disciplining	Praise may or may not be present
Might promote oppositional, defiant, and aggressive behavior in child	Promotes self-esteem in child	
	Promotes marital satisfaction	
	Promotes healthy psychological and scholastic development in child	

found to be especially true for girls. Furthermore, greater father authoritativeness has been linked to a greater feeling of marital satisfaction among wives (Starrels 1994). Starrels also found in reviewing the literature that adolescents who are raised in homes where their parents are both nurturant and firm do better psychologically and scholastically. She concludes that healthy child development is more likely to occur when authoritative parenting is employed.

In my clinical experience, I have often found that authoritarian fathering elicits oppositional and defiant reactions on the part of ADHD children. ADHD predisposes a child to learning oppositional behaviors as a way of coping with the demands and expectations of his parents. Being confronted with such defiance makes the authoritarian father become even more punitive and less nurturant, rather than approaching discipline differently. This occurs even though the authoritarian stance is not working and the situation, in fact, gets worse. I have seen the interaction between authoritarian fathers and ADHD/oppositional sons escalate to the point of court involvement for the sons. Furthermore, these fathers often see their wives as being too passive and ineffectual with their sons. The reality is that both parents are ineffectual, but it is easier for the tougher one (the father) to blame the softer one (the mother) for the problem. The father feels, "If only my wife were tougher, we wouldn't have a problem." This point of view often results in one of two reactions. The father might become more harsh, angry, and uncompromising, or he might, in his resentment, passively withdraw from active involvement in discipline, further weakening the parenting team.

The use of authority in a father's parenting style is very important in helping the child control his aggressive impulses. Controlling aggressive behavior is a major concern for parents of many ADHD children who have strong symptoms of impulsivity and hyperactivity. In reviewing the literature, Lamb (1981) found that aggressive boys come from families where their fathers were harsh and punitive, employed much physical punishment, were inconsistent in their discipline, and made little use of reasoning or praise.

It is important for fathers to learn that empathy and nurturance are not incompatible with firm authority. Empathy and nurturance in themselves are not sufficient to parent effectively. What fathers sometimes observe or perceive is their wives being understanding and caring without the requisite firmness and consistency in disciplining their child. This encourages them to take the opposite approach rather than an approach that integrates both aspects of parenting.

This integration is essential for raising an ADHD child. As reported above, self-esteem is enhanced in children by authoritative parenting. ADHD children start out with serious challenges to a healthy self-esteem because they experience peer rejection, school underachievement, and failure in meeting the expectations of the adults in their lives.

FATHERS PLAY AND SPEAK DIFFERENTLY

Differences in how parents adapt to the child and make the child adapt to the parent are evident in how mothers and fathers play with their children from an early age. James Herzog (1996) has been researching the differences in how mothers and fathers, in two-parent families, play with their children from the time the children are 2 years old. He has found that there are consistent and striking differences between mothers and fathers. Mothers are *homeostatically attuned* to the child, and fathers are *disruptively attuned*. Both respond to different needs in the child.

Fathers are likely to impose themselves into the world of the child and disrupt his play with the introduction of different themes and ideas that are out of synchrony with the child. As long as the differences are not jarring or overwhelming for the child (in which case they might be traumatizing), this type of interaction teaches him to adapt to the social environment around him. The child gains experience in having to match himself to another person rather than being matched by the other. This experience is vital in being able to cope with the outside world. These experiences with the father are also crucial in teaching the child the ability to tolerate disruptive, dissimilar, and unexpected experiences that are beyond his control. They provide the child with experience in regulating his own internal emotional state, which is a critical area of mastery for ADHD children. In addition, this style of play by the father is often more intense and exciting to the child than is the mother's play, as the father's style is not only different from the child's but at a greater intensity level. There is an interplay between this disruption in the child's world and the subsequent positive, harmonious interaction that Herzog describes as a "finding-and-being-found" quality. This cycle of interaction becomes the basis for the exciting element in future intimate relationships.

The above finding is consistent with the finding that fathers' play tends to be more physical than mothers' (MacDonald and Parke 1986, Power and Parke 1983). Fathers stimulate their children more by engaging in faster-paced play than do mothers (Arco 1983). Fathers also control and direct the play of their preschool children more than do mothers (Bright and Stockdale 1984). Infants have been found to respond to their fathers with higher rates of physiological arousal than to their mothers. Lamb (1981) cited research support for the observation that fathers encourage curiosity in their babies and try to motivate them to solve cognitive and motoric challenges, while mothers engage in more conventional and toy-mediated play.

Mothers are homeostatically attuned to the child in that they tend to follow the lead of their children, blending in with the child's play, allowing the child to be in control, and introducing new ideas that are in harmony with the child's play. There is an empathic understanding of the child in the mother's play, and an attempt to fit in with and adapt to the child. The mother tends to match the intensity level of her play to that of the child (which indicates that she is able to read her child's level of intensity and is interested in experiencing how the child is feeling). Mothers' interactions provide the child with an experience of safety and with the experience that the world understands him, that he is good and whole and makes sense, and that both his inner world and the outside world are trustworthy and stable. This experience is critical to future feelings of basic trust and love in another. It provides the experience of someone being consistently available and responsive and of a sense of safety in the world and in others.

While both types of interaction provide very different experiences that enrich the child's ability to deal with himself and the world around him, it would be a mistake to interpret these terms to mean that it is only the interaction with the mother that makes the child feel safe, comfortable, and nurtured, while the interaction with the father solely challenges the child to learn new things.

In both the disruptively attuned and the homeostatically attuned types of experiences, there must be a balance of safety and growth. The mother should not simply mirror the child's actions, making it safe for the child to express what he needs to express, but do so in such a way as to enrich the child's understanding of his internal world. Mechanically parroting the child's words and actions will not do. The mother must respond to the child's feelings, needs, wishes, and fears in her own way, and with her own words, demonstrating her understanding and acceptance, and helping her child see himself.

For his part, the father should not disrupt or intrude on the child's play in a way that is frightening or incomprehensible to the child. His interaction must be different enough that it forces the child to adapt but not too jarring that it disrupts the child's ability to cope. He must also come in and out of disruption, meeting the child and validating his experiences as he challenges the child. Too much anxiety, or stimulation that is too overwhelming or too difficult to comprehend, does not lead to learning and mastery.

Here is a good way for a father to learn to be homeostatically attuned, adapted from Barkley's (1987) parent training program. Sit with your child and observe him playing for short periods of time; make no comments, demands, questions, or interactions. Then practice observing your child, only commenting on what the child is doing, rather than changing the nature of the play. Do not ask questions or introduce change, such as by asking what will happen next. Simply make statements about what is happening. Your tone of voice should communicate interest and appreciation, without the need to comment about how much you appreciate what your child is doing. For example, if your child is enacting a scene with figures or puppets, you can make comments like "He's driving the car," or "She's building a big house," or "They're going someplace together." The next step would be to practice following your child's lead when playing with him, doing what he tells you to do. This exercise will train you in being an empathic observer, in being homeostatically attuned to your child in his play. They will help you to match your child and practice seeing things from his point of view. It can help you as the father achieve a balance in your interactions with your child.

Other research has been consistent with these findings. In contrast to the greater amount of physical play engaged in by fathers, mothers have been found to be more responsive to changes in what the child is looking at or attending to (Power 1985, Power and Parke 1983). Although mothers' play was slower-paced than fathers', mothers tended to interact for longer periods of time (Arco 1983).

Both of these types of interaction are healthy and necessary for the child to develop relationships with others that are based on love, trust, and excitement; a relationship with the world that is based on an ability both to adapt to reality and to change reality, or have a positive effect on the world; and a relationship with oneself in which one is experienced as stable, whole, effective, and passionate.

Since both types of experiences are healthy and necessary, it is also important for each parent to respect the style and the importance of the other. How the parents relate to each other is critical in the development of a stable sense of self in the child, as well as in each parent's availability to the child in helping him to regulate his internal emotional states of excitement and aggression.

Play is a way of interacting with children. It should not be surprising, therefore, that in another area of interaction—the use of language—mothers and fathers behave differently with their children. Malone and Guy (1982) found that fathers communicate in more controlling ways with their preschoolers than do mothers and involve the child's perspective less in their verbal interactions. Mothers' communications, on the other hand, are more child-centered.

McLaughlin and colleagues (1983) similarly found that mothers tend to adjust their language more to their child's needs and linguistic abilities, thereby providing more linguistic support to the child. Fathers, on the other hand, are less sensitive to their children's abilities, demand more from them, and thereby raise the level of their performance. Fathers challenge the skills that their children have already acquired and momentarily destabilize the children in order to help them achieve greater success (LeChanu and Marcos 1994).

McLaughlin (1983) and Bellinger and Gleason (1982) found that fathers use more imperative and directive verbalizations with their preschoolers than do mothers. Overall, McLaughlin found that children comply more with controls that are oriented to directing their attention than to controlling their behavior, which would argue against an exclusively male approach to behavioral control.

Fathers have been found to place more linguistic demands on their children than do mothers through the use of more "wh" questions (what, where, why), compared with mothers' use of yes/no questions, through being less able than mothers to adjust their language to their child's abilities (McLaughlin et al. 1983), and through their domination of conversations (Fash and Madison 1981).

Fathers also have been found to paraphrase what the child has just said in order to confirm what he meant more than do mothers, indicating that fathers might have more difficulty than mothers in understanding their child's speech (Walker and Armstrong 1995). This is consistent with the findings that communication breaks down more often between fathers and children and that fathers request clarification of the child's intent more often.

In one study, mothers and fathers were observed teaching their infants a visual-motor task. Fathers tried to control and direct their infants' behavior more (Brachfeld-Child et al. 1988), and to set limits on their child's behavior (Brachfeld-Child 1986). Mothers tolerated more mistakes by their children and permitted them to use a trial-and-error method, developing their own approach to the task rather than teaching them the right way to do it.

Fathers, therefore, provide their child with more challenges and frustrations in communication, forcing the child to use feedback from the other to revise and adapt his communications in order to be more effective. The child learns to adapt his language to that of the surrounding community. Mothers, on the other hand, adapt to their child's level of communication, providing him with the experience of having his messages received accurately and of being effective in conversational interactions with another (Gleason 1975, Walker and Armstrong 1995). The mother's style also allows the child to gradually develop his own mode of problem solving without as much interference as the father provides.

These findings concerning play, arousal, and language indicate that fathers and mothers play complementary roles in their interactions with their children (Table 3–2). Whereas fathers tend to introduce more novelty into the environment, to which children respond on a biological and social level, mothers make the world seem safe and predictable. Mothers provide a social world that adapts to the child, providing the safety necessary for growth, risk, and exploration, whereas

Table 3–2. Characteristics of Fathers' and Mothers' Interactions

Fathers' Interactions	Mothers' Interactions
Are more disruptively attuned	Are more homeostatically attuned
Teach child to adapt to others	Blend in with child
Control play interactions more	Let child be in control
Are more intense, exciting, and physical when playing	Are slower paced when playing
Create more breakdowns in verbal communication	Adjust language to child's level of understanding
Communicate in controlling ways	Are more responsive to what the child is attending to
Stimulate taking on challenges in play	Provide child with safety, empathy, sense of trust
Challenge the child to raise level of performance	
Introduce novelty	
Attempt to teach the right way to do things	Are more tolerant of mistakes and development of individual approach to problem solving
Force child to adapt to external reality	Adapt to child's internal world

fathers challenge the child to adapt to the demands of the community at large, demanding that the child understand and master what is unfamiliar to him. Mothers adapt to the internal world of the child, whereas fathers force the child to adapt to the external environment.

The humanistic psychologist Abraham Maslow (1968) discusses the need for a balance of safety and growth. To expand our awareness of things, learn new things, explore new ideas, and take risks, we must have our basic needs for safety and security taken care of. We need to feel that we have a secure jumping-off point and will have a safe place to land. Attempts at growth should not be traumatizing or fill us with unbearable anxiety. Without our safety needs being met, taking risks will be intolerably anxiety-provoking, preventing any learning from taking place. The corollary of this is that relying on safe choices denies our need for personal growth. A totally safe existence is profoundly unsatisfying and hardly makes life worth living. Within each type of parental interaction, both of these human needs must be respected.

Understanding the need to balance homeostatic and disruptive attunement and safety and growth in our interactions is essential in raising an ADHD child. On the one hand, the ADHD child needs to develop the ability to tune in to his internal state, to soothe himself, and to recognize the ups and downs of his moods and the vicissitudes of his attention, in order to exert better control over himself. On the other hand, the ADHD child needs to better recognize the expectations of others, to shape his behavior in response to feedback from the environment, to adapt to the demands of reality, and to control his behavior over time.

The struggle over understanding and nurturing the ADHD child versus making him adapt to the parents' expectations is a conflict that surfaces all the time in clinical work. Fathers often see "understanding" as being too permissive, as coddling the child, as not making him grow up, and as making excuses for him. They see mothers as doing too much for the child, therefore preventing him from becoming independent.

Mothers, on the other hand, often see fathers as failing to understand the true nature of ADHD—that their child actually has a disorder that makes him different from the other children. They fear that treating the child as if nothing is wrong interferes with the child's being able to achieve because his needs are not taken into account.

This debate often surfaces when the discussion centers on school-work, especially with adolescents. Adolescents with ADHD often have difficulty functioning independently when it comes to completing their schoolwork and homework.

Jared, a 15-year-old boy, would not do his homework unless his mother told him that it was time to sit down and do it. She would structure his time, planning with him what assignment to start with, checking his work after each assignment, and then directing him to the next one. If she did not do this, the homework would not get done. She had become accustomed to doing more for him than other mothers did for his classmates from the time Jared began school. She knew that Jared was bright, and she could not stand the thought of him failing, so she helped him as much as she could without doing the work for him, enabling him to pass each school year.

Jared's father wondered if she was doing too much for him. The mother was willing to entertain this notion because she was tired, and anticipated that, at this rate, she would be doing this for her son throughout high school and college. The school was also concerned because Jared, at age 15, should have been taking more responsibility, and should have been functioning more like an adult to prepare him for adult responsibilities.

Through listening to each other's concerns, Jared's parents agreed that if left to his own devices, Jared would complete little or no homework. They agreed that he needed help in structuring his time during homework and that he also needed to learn how to impose this structure on himself. They developed a plan in which one parent would sit down with Jared each night and map out his assignments, specifying the order in which they would be done, approximating the time he needed to complete each one, scheduling breaks, and scheduling time to check his work. Jared would gradually assume more of this responsibility each week, with the parents fading out the help that they gave him.

The understanding and empathy that mothers offer can be a very mixed blessing.

A fairly common situation was presented by 16-year-old Stewart, whose mother convinced him to seek professional help although he had no interest in discussing ADHD or hearing more about it. He saw his mother as a constant nag, who was always bringing up the issue of ADHD when they talked about chores or schoolwork. Although he was so angry at his mother that he did not want to talk to her, Stewart reported that he had more conflict with his father, because his mother was willing to listen to him and discuss things more but his father was more focused on getting things done. His father had little tolerance for the type of discussion that Stewart and his mother engaged in. So although Stewart seemed to value his mother's empathy, he did not want anything to do with her because of her nagging. There was so much conflict between Stewart and his mother that it was hard to imagine that there could be even more with his father. It is uncertain how much of a good thing Stewart's mother's listening and discussing was. Her willingness to take this approach left her open for serious conflict, criticism, and rejection, and she felt a great deal of distress in her relationship with her son. Stewart might have expressed resentment toward his father because his father would not be manipulated by him, but there might have actually been less overt conflict between them than between Stewart and his mother.

FATHERS' HELPLESSNESS AND ANGER

Some men are easily provoked to anger. Anger is both an expression of frustration and an attempt to gain control over the environment. It is an expression of power and of hierarchy. It is a reflection of feelings of helplessness and an attempt to obliterate the source of these feelings and to reestablish the man at the top of the hierarchy. However, anger without a rational plan of approach to solve a problem is only useful as intimidation and often perpetuates the failure to find a solution.

There are several ways in which anger can interfere with rational limit setting and problem solving with the ADHD child. Some men find it intolerable that a child would defy their authority. On the other hand, some women too often accept the disregard of their authority by their children. When men are faced with the unacceptable, some try to alter reality through sheer force of will. Unable to obliterate the source of their helplessness, they try to render the source itself helpless, humiliated, and defeated. They attempt to subjugate the other. This detracts from the ability to compromise and negotiate. Compromising and negotiation are perceived as dangerous because they disrupt the hierarchy from which the man derives a large part of his identity.

Therefore, in retaliation for the disruption of his authority, the father of the ADHD child may go overboard in punishing the child. The problems with taking away all privileges for a period of time have already been discussed. A related problem is that prolonged punishment takes away any leverage a parent might have to reward future good behavior or to punish future inappropriate behavior during that time period. It is difficult, in a fit of anger, for a father to see the benefit of inflicting punishment for a handful of hours or for only a day. However, providing an immediate consequence, such as taking away a privilege that is important to the child for the rest of the day, adequately punishes the child with ADHD, allows the parent to punish future misbehaviors, provides the child with the opportunity to be good, and provides the parent with the opportunity to reinforce the child for good behavior.

Anger also results in a distorted view of others. A person who is angry at another person is prone to attribute hostile motives to the other. Therefore, being chronically angry at one's ADHD child will lead a parent to attribute the noncompliance or nonperformance to purposeful, hostile actions on the child's part rather than to his disability. This can lead to a disastrous cycle of control struggles and mutual hostility. Therefore, it is not just the child's behavior that causes child management problems, but the attributions that parents form about that behavior that affect the behavior as well. When those attributions are grounded in reality, parents are better able to deal with them. When those attributions are based more on unexamined assumptions, parents lose the tools they need to deal productively with the problem.

FATHERS' DISBELIEF ABOUT ADHD

Fathers often react with disbelief to the suggestion that their child has ADHD. There can be several reasons for this: (1) fathers often have a greater acceptance of a high activity level and imperfect social behavior, and maintain a "boys will be boys" attitude; (2) fathers often identify with the ADHD child, seeing themselves in their children and needing to see themselves as "normal"; (3) the child's behavior and performance are highly variable, making the problem seem less severe or making it seem like the problem is due to willfulness or laziness; (4) fathers may want to avoid the narcissistic injury or shame they experience from seeing their own child as damaged or defective; (5) fathers have a normal parental wish not to have something wrong with their child; and (6) fathers often find it difficult to accept someone else's authority, especially when it involves control over their own child.

Fathers are often in a state of disbelief when their wives tell them that they want to have their child (usually their son) evaluated by a professional. They sit silently in the therapist's office as their wives report on the multitude of problems that they are having with their child. This might be the first time that the father has given his wife's concerns a fair hearing. Many fathers have said, "He's just like I was when I was a boy," implying that the behavior is normal because it is familiar. When the therapist subsequently inquires as to how things were when the father was a boy, the father responds with a colorful story about how much mischief and sometimes serious trouble he got in, or how he messed up in school, or ended up leaving home at a young age, or dropping out. These histories are often related with a twinkle in the father's eye, but frequently end with some real sadness about opportunities missed, the failure of adults to understand his needs, and his own failure to recognize his potential and achieve it. These fathers often leave the session with a determination not to allow the same thing to happen to their sons.

Other fathers end the session more skeptically. Well, maybe there is a problem, but the child will grow out of it, or it isn't so bad. Many balk at the idea that the problem is so serious that it will require medication. Many fathers react to the prospect of medication with the comment, "I'm not putting my child on *drugs*." Notice the emotionally loaded use of the word *drugs* rather than the more neutral and therapeutic term *medication*.

Even when the science behind the diagnosis of ADHD is explained, many fathers find it difficult to see the disorder as medical in nature, on a par with other medical conditions, such as diabetes. The analogy with diabetes is particularly useful given that diabetes is a problem with the regulation of one of the body's natural chemicals that might require medicine to correct. The management of diabetes also requires environmental and behavioral modifications in the form of diet and exercise, and a certain degree of structure in planning one's day. Parents who disparage the use of medication for their ADHD child would not hesitate to give their child medication if the child were diabetic. If parents can accept the medical analogy with diabetes but reject the consideration of medication because, unlike diabetes, ADHD is not life threatening, it is important that they be made aware of potential quality of life issues that result from persistent failure, underachievement, frustration, not fitting in, depression, and the related health and safety issues.

However, parents should not be frightened into giving their children medication. It is the parents' decision whether to medicate their child, and their judgment must be respected. However, it is the responsibility of the professionals involved to help the parents face whatever prejudices they might have that are influencing their judgment.

The fact that the symptoms of ADHD are so variable also makes it a difficult diagnosis to accept. The inconsistency leads to the question frequently asked about ADHD: Is it real? This question is not asked about other, more commonly accepted disorders that have as much variability in the symptom picture and inconsistency in presentation, such as depression, which covers a wide range of conditions that vary in frequency, severity, and duration. Like depression, inattention and hyperactivity are on a continuum. Children with ADHD can pay attention much of the time. They often do quite well, even for extended periods of time. Many are well above average in intelligence and achieve at an average to above-average level fairly consistently. Everyone, after all, experiences some variability in attention and concentration, performance and achievement. If a child is doing well most, much, or some of the time, how can we say that child has a deficit?

Although all children exhibit a certain degree of variability and inconsistency in their attention, activity level, and impulsivity, there are some who are hindered by this variability and inconsistency more than others. These children cannot regulate their behavior and attention consistently enough to achieve up to the level of their abilities much of the time. This is independent of how intelligent they are and of what their general level of functioning is. Because of problems regulating their attention, effort, focus, behavior, and impulsivity, what they are achieving is far below what they are capable of. This inability to regulate attention and behavior, to complete work and meet other expectations placed on them in the normal course of life, independent of their intelligence or their wishes, is the real, potentially disabling condition. If this is not attended to early on, the result can be chronic failure and disappointment in life, as well as misunderstanding what the cause of this failure is.

The father's disbelief is akin to denial, but it is not necessarily something that is negative. If we all accepted bad news or the judgments of others too easily, there would be no room for questioning. A state of disbelief in the father encourages the professional to justify the diagnosis, to educate the father about it, and to try to understand what it is like for a father to receive this news. The father's disbelief challenges the professional to justify his clinical judgment and sharpen his empathic skills. Working with the father's disbelief can also lead to better co-parenting by the father. The disbelieving father can be encouraged to acknowledge the severity of the problem. The believing mother can develop more of a healthy skepticism about proposed solutions and can learn to think critically about input from professionals. Working with the father's disbelief and forming an alliance with the disbelieving father, rather than only with the believing mother, helps the professional, and the parents, develop better ways of coping with the disorder. Allying with the father also helps the believing mother develop greater empathy for the father. Both parents need to understand each other's points of view, preferences, and vulnerabilities in order to work as a team in coping with their ADHD child.

Ezra's parents had divorced when he was 4. In the first grade, he was noted to be highly active and distractible. He was the class clown, although his teachers described him as bright and engaging. Ezra lived with his mother, stepfather, and stepbrother, who had ADHD. Ezra's mother was very concerned about his behavior, and thought that it significantly interfered with his ability to adapt to the demands of home and now of school. Familiar with the problems of ADHD children because of her stepson, Ezra's mother wanted to have Ezra evaluated and his problems addressed as quickly as possible.

Ezra's father and stepmother saw him on weekends and holidays, and more frequently during the summer. Their home environment was more structured and more low-key than Ezra's mother's home. Given the less frequent contact they had with Ezra, and the greater structure and lower level of stimulation in their home, they did not see the severity of the behavior problems that his mother observed. Ezra's father and stepmother attributed his difficulty complying with their more formal rules to the fact that he was accustomed to fewer limits at his mother's house and "got away with more there." His immaturity in school was attributed more to emotional issues and anxieties over his parents' divorce and his difficulty adapting to two sets of rules and multiple relationships.

Even before the evaluation was undertaken, Ezra's father stated his strong opposition to medication. At the same time, Ezra's mother advocated for medication, as she had seen its benefits, and she was also familiar with the difficulties of life with an ADHD child. She was also afraid of Ezra being frustrated in school and turning off to learning.

Ezra was diagnosed with ADHD, and his mother and father became very frustrated with each other because of their different stances. Their spouses joined in the debate on their respective sides, and wanted the therapist to understand their points of view and reason with the other party.

Ezra's mother saw each day of delay in medicating him as a violation of his needs. Ezra's father said that he wanted Ezra's emotional needs thoroughly taken into account before he would consider medication. Ezra's mother pushed the therapist to convince his father to agree to medication. The therapist had explained the potential benefits of medication to Ezra's father previously, and had given him an opportunity to discuss his concerns and preconceived notions. Rather than having this conversation again, the therapist cautioned Ezra's mother to be patient, discussed with the father and stepmother their emotional concerns, and agreed to meet with Ezra specifically to get a sense of these issues.

After the therapist addressed Ezra's emotional needs with his father and stepmother, and explored what might help him both at home and in a therapeutic relationship, Ezra's father was ready to consider allowing Ezra to be medicated.

The father's disbelief stems from an understandable wish for the child to be normal. In this sense, it can be seen not as denial, but as a healthy, protective parental wish that one's children have as successful and pain-free life as possible. The father's disbelief also reflects the difficulty we have in the field in making this diagnosis and being certain of it. We need to be humble. Since the diagnosis of ADHD, more than most other disorders, requires the sophisticated sorting out of complicated and confusing clinical information, there is much room for doubt in the diagnosis of many children. Confronting the clinician with his disbelief, the father is reflecting back to the clinician the uncertainties in the field.

A father of an ADHD child might also have difficulty accepting the diagnosis because of his difficulty accepting the authority of an outside person. Men tend to be oriented to relating to others in a hierarchical manner. They are accustomed to seeing themselves as "one up" or "one down" in relationship to others. When the organizational structure is clear, such as in one's family or in one's business, it is easy to adapt. However, it might be difficult for a father to accept the authority of someone telling him that there is something wrong with his child, especially when he does not observe that there is something wrong.

It is important for psychologists, physicians, and other professionals to recognize this and understand it, rather than try to impose authority on a resistant father, which will probably lead to more resistance. This form of control struggle is detrimental to the needs of the child. If the father is resistant, he has already taken a stand by stating that he is challenging the hierarchy of the doctor over the parent. Fathers often are just not that impressed that someone supposedly knows more than they do. In fact, this is often a challenge to the father to prove his own mettle and knowledge, especially in an area in which he is supposed to be expert—his own child. No matter what the professional supposedly knows psychologically or medically, a father is supposed to know his own child. This personal and paternal knowledge is now pitted against the clinical knowledge of the professional, which can stir up some rather deep-seated feelings of ownership, belonging, and protectiveness.

The professional must not challenge the authority of the father over the child (except in cases of suspected abuse or neglect). Responding to a challenge to one's authority with authoritarianism is counterproductive. Understanding the father's need to struggle with the hierarchy of himself and the professional is necessary. It is important for the father to recognize this need in himself and not let his hierarchical orientation to life get in the way of doing what is best for his child. His protectiveness about his child, and his need to maintain his position of authority over his child and his own expertness about his child, might stem from a natural protective instinct, but it can get in the way of respecting the greater knowledge of someone else. The point is not to eliminate the father's doubt and questions, but rather to recognize when personality and communication factors get in the way of considering the best decision.

SUMMARY

The discussion in this chapter can help fathers become more aware of their own parenting behavior with their ADHD children. Fathers should consider the following points:

- Fathers tend to see their child's behavior as being less serious than mothers do. Fathers need to be careful not to invalidate the mother's perceptions of and experiences with the child. The mother's beliefs are legitimate.

- Men tend to be instrumental and linear thinkers and problem solvers. This style is useful in defining goals and keeping track of progress. However, it can also result in overlooking emotional and interpersonal factors that make behavior management more complicated. Fathers also tend to overlook their own emotional reactions and conflicts with their child.

- Fathers often misuse punishment.
  - Punishment should not be used to the exclusion of praise and reward for desirable behavior.
  - Desirable behaviors should be specifically defined and reinforced frequently.
  - Punishment should be used as soon as possible after the undesirable behavior occurs and for short periods of time.
  - Fathers can identify all of the things in the child's life that they control in order to understand what they can make the child earn.
  - Punishment should not be used for retaliation.
  - It is not enough to punish noncompliance; one must also teach compliance.

- Fathers need to become aware of how their behavior promotes their child's coercive behavior, and how their child's behavior promotes coercive behavior from them.

- Authoritative discipline is generally more effective than authoritarian discipline. Nurturance mixed with authority is the best combination.

- Instructions to children should be geared to their level of under-standing and ability to pay attention.
  - Instructions should be concrete and specific.
  - Instructions should engage the child in interaction.
  - Instructions should guide the child one step at a time.

- Consequences should train behavior, which requires time, repe-tition, and the understanding that the unwanted behavior will recur.

- Yelling and spanking are often emotional, tension-reducing re-sponses by parents that provide immediate gratification but are not often consistent with long-range plans.

- Flexibility in the use of authority, and negotiating with one's child do not need to undermine the father's authority.

- Skepticism about ADHD can be useful in engaging profes-sionals in dialogue and questioning. There is a great deal for everyone to learn, and a father's doubts are useful for stimu-lating discussion.

- A father's issues with authority can interfere with his ability to listen to professionals and can be detrimental to the child.

The Assessment Process

KNOWING SOMETHING IS WRONG

The process of assessment begins with the feeling, often on the part of a parent but sometimes on the part of a teacher, that something is wrong in how the child is behaving or learning. This feeling is often an intuition, or it can be linked to specific behaviors that have been observed. Often, there are no hard-core academic difficulties that have been noted, especially in the earlier grades. The child has been passing every grade, and standardized testing has indicated average to above average intelligence and learning. But, there may be a pattern of teachers' comments over the years that is consistent with this feeling that something is not right.

Children who are later diagnosed with ADHD often have these types of teachers' comments on their report cards: "Inconsistent effort," "Incomplete assignments," "Missing homework," and "Let's try to have a better year next year." They are often described as being enthusiastic participants in class and being eager to show what they know (which can be a euphemism for not staying in their seats and blurting out answers), but having difficulty settling down. It is also common for these children, in spite of all the work that the teacher must do to manage their behavior, to be described as having great personalities.

The intuition part of the process is what disturbs fathers the most. The mothers might feel something is wrong without being able to put it into words. This reflects not a lack of knowledge, logic, or reason on the part of mothers, but merely a lack of specialized training. It also reflects a trust in intuition. The mothers take many pieces of subtle information, including emotional information from the child and their own internal, emotional responses, as a whole, without necessarily laying them out logically and putting them into words.

But fathers often cannot accept the idea that their child is different or impaired because they experience this impairment as a narcissistic injury to themselves, and thus they feel shame, confusing their sense of self with that of their child, attending to their own needs rather than the child's. So they chafe at basing conclusions, decisions, and diagnoses on intuition, which seems no better than a hunch. They prefer logic. Conclusions need to be derived from tangible supporting evidence, and all other possible explanations must be ruled out.

Fathers might regard the mothers as being overly concerned about or overprotective of their child. Fathers tell mothers that the child will "grow out of it," and that they should not worry. If fathers, or others, refer to the mothers' concerns with words such as *worried*, *overanxious parent, overprotective mother, impatient*, and *pushy*, this reinforces the impression that the mother is irrational, misguided, and acting out of some form of psychological deficiency. Then these value-laden messages to mothers may deter them from getting the help their child needs, thus hindering early intervention. And the mothers get subtly labeled as having something wrong with them. Interestingly, I have never heard of fathers being labeled overprotective of their children when they raise similar concerns. Of course mothers are protective, of course mothers worry about their children, of course mothers want their children to succeed. All the more reason to take what they have to say about their children seriously!

True, some parents may overreact, expressing concerns that are not in synchrony with reality. They may be anxious about things simply out of a lack of knowledge. There are mothers and fathers who unknowingly let their own psychological issues get in the way of perceiving their child's needs accurately. But too often assessment and intervention are delayed, sometimes for years, because a mother's concerns are not taken seriously.

Chris, a 15-year-old high school freshman, was getting B's, C's, and D's in school. His mother had a sense since elementary school that something was wrong. She was told that Chris was a little behind developmentally, and that he would catch up. Chris continued to be behind, making progress but never quite catching up in his mother's eyes. However, Chris was a bright boy, and musically talented. He maintained passing grades, although they never reflected what he thought was the effort he put in. He often failed to finish his work. He worked more slowly than the other students, and he often got low grades because he could not complete his quizzes and tests within the time period allotted. He would do his homework, often spending hours on it at home, and then receive a grade of zero for failing to pass it in. Chris's teachers believed that his problems with productivity reflected poor motivation and making poor "choices." As Chris became more frustrated with school, he became more argumentative with his teachers, reinforcing their impression that he suffered from emotional problems.

Over the years, Chris's mother's impressions were discounted, and this fed into the conflicts that Chris was having with his father and the conflicts between Chris's parents. Chris's father would come home from work and within fifteen minutes would be in a fight with him over homework. He would start off trying to be helpful, but the help would quickly deteriorate into frustration with Chris's slowness, his disorganization, and his difficulty producing the work independently, as when his father left him to do part of his homework and came back some time later to find little work completed. Chris's father would often throw up his hands in frustration, walk out of the room, and say something about Chris being lazy or being a failure.

Chris's mother took a different approach to helping him. She was as frustrated as his father, but she was also able to sense Chris's genuine frustration by his inability to produce work that was equal to his intellectual abilities. She understood the toll that the conflicts with his father and his teachers were having on him. Chris's father was more focused on the end product, and pushed Chris to produce, appealing to his motivation, his sense of responsibility, his pride, and his shame. He did not understand that no matter what one's motivation, work ethic, pride in achievement, or sense of responsibility, one cannot overcome a handicap unless one is aware of it and knows what to do about it.

Chris's mother, in perceiving his dilemma differently, tried to help him by doing some of the work with him, and by negotiating with him to do small amounts of work. She also helped him figure out how to organize his work. She tried to bolster his self-esteem by taking the blame off him for his difficulties.

Chris's mother was going through a difficult internal struggle of her own. She was constantly weighing whether she was doing too much or too little for him. Not having the problem diagnosed, she was left to guess whether she was helping or hurting Chris.

Chris's mother's actions understandably led to conflict with his father, who saw her as coddling their son. He believed that Chris was now at an age where he had to take responsibility for his actions, where he had to be made to sink or swim, and where success or failure was totally within Chris's hands. These were valid and reasonable beliefs for a parent of a typical, non-ADHD 15-year-old, which the parents had been told Chris was.

The issue of responsibility is a tricky one with ADHD children. Children and adolescents should be taught responsibility for their actions. However, this is not an excuse for parents and teachers to remain ignorant of handicaps that the child might have. A child cannot take responsibility for himself, and a parent cannot impart this to a child, if they both misunderstand the child's abilities and needs. It is knowledge about a problem that enables a person to take responsibility for himself. Knowing whether a child has an attention deficit, and knowing the nature of that particular child's attention deficit (all children with ADHD are different), enables a parent to judge whether the help that he is giving to the child is coddling him or is providing him with the tools that will help him take responsibility for his learning.

To complicate the situation in the above case example, Chris was becoming increasingly depressed and withdrawn. He was not hyperactive. Rather, he tended to be inattentive and moody. He was typical of many children with ADHD of the inattentive type. His self-esteem was poor. He wanted to believe his mother, that he was good and smart, but the lack of an explanation for his difficulties with schoolwork left nothing but his personality problems or lack of intelligence to explain them. Furthermore, the conflicts between his parents were hard to ignore, and he was aware that they were about him. He could not help feeling responsible for his parents' fights; if he was not a problem, his parents would get along.

Chris's problems illustrate the importance of seeking assessment. Accurate information is essential in order to plan effective intervention or treatment, and the earlier the better. Too much time is lost in children's lives by not doing an assessment when there is a feeling that there is a problem. I have seen too many parents proven to have been right in their awareness that something was wrong after too much damage was done to their child's self-esteem and after too many years of frustration and school failure.

Therefore, a parent's feeling that something is wrong should always be taken seriously. Fathers need to consider their wives' concerns enough to observe their child and at least do some reading on ADHD and then consult with a professional who is an expert in ADHD.

Parents often ask the schools to evaluate their child's problems. Signs of difficulty often first become apparent in the school setting, where the child is expected to sit still, follow the rules, and produce. Concerns are raised in parent–teacher conferences, or by the parent noticing that her child is not keeping up with his classmates, or by the child getting into trouble because of his behavior or his incomplete work.

The mother might have had some concerns before the child was of school age. With the more relaxed structure of home life, the greater forgiveness for violations of rules, the wider range of behaviors that are tolerated, and the acceptance of negotiation around rules, the child's behavior might have been considered somewhat problematic but normal. This is especially true if the child is a boy. The parents might have also blamed themselves for their difficulty in setting effective limits or for being too lax. Or the parents might have blamed each other for being too lenient, too harsh, or too inconsistent.

This focus on their own shortcomings can hinder the parents from seeing that abnormal characteristics of their child might be contributing to the problem. Fathers often see rambunctious boys as being like they were when they were younger, and some mothers also identify with their young ADHD children in that they recognize the irreverence toward authority, the headstrong nature and independence, the inconsistent performance, and the preference for social or physical activity as also having characterized themselves when they were children. Since the parents don't think that they were abnormal, they will not think their child is either. Nor do they see that the child might be suffering. Thus, they don't seek an evaluation.

REQUESTING AN EVALUATION FROM THE SCHOOL

It is a parent's right to request an evaluation from the school for an educational handicap. The laws and procedures vary from state to state, but the school generally forwards such a request to a child study team for evaluation. If the team agrees that an assessment is called for, such assessment might entail observations of the child, psychological testing, or referral to outside professionals.

It is my experience that schools are generally very good at evaluating some things but not others. A well-run school will acknowledge its areas of expertise and recognize the areas in which it is not expert. Teachers can provide expert observations on how the child is behaving in class; how easily the child seems to learn the material; the speed, accuracy, and thoroughness with which the child is able to complete his work; and the child's ability to conform to the rules and expectations of the class. Learning specialists can assess, through standardized tests, the child's percentile ranking on thinking skills, problem solving, speech and language development, gross and fine motor skills, and information processing. The school can assess abnormalities in learning that indicate the presence or absence of certain types of learning disabilities. The school can explore other possible factors that interfere with learning and that might warrant further evaluation from an outside health professional, such as a psychologist, psychiatrist, neurologist, pediatrician, ophthalmologist, optometrist, or audiologist.

Since the schools tend to have well-trained experts in the identification of learning disabilities, it may be natural to assume that the identification of ADHD would be included in this expertise. This is often not the case. The assessment of learning disabilities and the assessment of ADHD are different, although interrelated, skills. The assessment of learning disabilities involves psychometric testing as a major component of the evaluation. Although no diagnosis should ever be made or ruled out solely on the basis of psychometric testing, psychometric tests are often and appropriately the main tool in the accurate identification of learning disabilities.

In evaluating for ADHD, however, psychometric testing is just one component of the assessment, because the reliability of psychometric testing in identifying ADHD has not been clearly established. The identification of ADHD requires complex clinical judgment, which proscribes relying too heavily on test data in isolation from other sources of information. ADHD assessment requires specialized training in differential diagnosis, which entails differentiating ADHD from other disorders that might look like ADHD. It is generally trained health professionals, such as psychologists, social workers, psychiatrists, pediatricians, and neurologists who have this expertise.

An assessment of the child's learning problems by the school might not answer all the parents' questions about ADHD. The evaluation might state that there is no indication of ADHD. ADHD might also be ruled out by the school based on the child's scores on psychometric tests, or on the ratings by teachers on questionnaires or rating scales. The teacher might report his or her belief that the child does not have ADHD because he can concentrate on things that interest him, because he can achieve when he wants to, or because he is not getting in and out of his seat all the time. These observations might be true and the child could still have ADHD.

The symptoms of ADHD vary widely in individuals. As was discussed in Chapter 2, many children with ADHD are not hyperactive. They are very well behaved and may quietly tune out. Their tuning out may or may not be noticed by those around them. If the child is bright, he may be able to tune in and out and still catch enough of what he is expected to learn to do at least average work in school. The teacher and the classroom might also be highly structured, which might help the ADHD child compensate for his deficits and comply with the teacher's expectations often enough not to be a major problem.

It is also one of the characteristics of ADHD children that they can attend very well when they are interested in something. The term *attention deficit* is somewhat misleading, since children with ADHD have adequate attentional abilities much of the time, but they are inconsistent in using these abilities. They are often unable to sustain their attention when they are expected to do so or on tasks for which they have low interest or motivation. Therefore, it is not unusual for children who have ADHD to spend long periods of time being attentive in class, and then failing to complete an assignment or doing poorly on a test.

Therefore, there are reasons that the impressions and observations of the classroom teacher, as important as they might be in helping to understand a child's strengths and weaknesses and the type of learning environment that is best for him, might not be reliable indicators of whether or not a child has ADHD.

Many parents are told not to worry so much, or that it is too early to tell if a child has ADHD, or that the child is immature and will outgrow the problems. This might be true in some instances, but in too many cases the parents' concerns are not taken seriously, and the child continues having difficulties throughout his schooling.

Early assessment of ADHD is crucial to the child's well-being. If there is a problem, it is better to identify it in the first grade than to wait until junior high school. If appropriate intervention is not provided early on, the child will be at risk for underachievement in school, poor self-esteem, a negative view of school, a negative view of achievement in general, and failure in school.

It is in school that one's self-concept as a learner largely develops. Early success experiences in learning, mastering academic tasks, and receiving positive regard from one's teacher and fellow students orient a child to a lifelong love of learning, the self-confidence to handle new challenges and seek out new experiences, and the expectation that authority figures will judge him fairly and favorably.

The child with ADHD often tries hard, but in spite of his efforts, finds he cannot succeed and cannot understand why. If the problem is not identified, his parents and teachers do not understand why he cannot succeed either. He might seem to be as intelligent and as capable as the other students, so he will be expected to perform as well as they do. The teacher and the student will see no reason why he cannot meet these expectations, so the expectations will continue to be set, and the student will fail to meet them. The child might act up, becoming oppositional and defiant, in order to move the focus from the task demands to his disruptive behavior and the control struggle with the teacher. He might become the class clown and find his competence in entertaining the class and receiving approval from his peers rewarding, even at the expense of disapproval from his teacher. Whatever the child's coping strategy, he is not developing self-confidence as a learner and positive expectations of school and of productive accomplishments. He is at risk for failure, poor self-esteem, and difficulty becoming a productive member of society.

Once an evaluation is requested from the school, there is the temptation for the parents to let the school take over, out of deference to the school as the authority. The impression that the school is an authority is a powerful one. The school is, in the parents' minds, not just an authority in instruction and education, but an institution not to be questioned. So if the school deems that there is no problem, many parents are content to let the matter rest there, even if they still suspect that there is something wrong.

It is dangerous for parents to totally cede their authority over their child to the school, or to any institution. (The one exception to this might be in cases of child abuse or neglect.) Parents must remain the executive decision makers for their child (Barkley 1995b).

COMPREHENSIVE ASSESSMENTS

Basing a diagnosis on test scores alone is not a reliable way to assess for ADHD. A comprehensive assessment is required.

The *Diagnostic and Statistical Manual for Mental Disorders* diagnostic criteria for ADHD (see Chapter 2) are not quantified. They are descriptive in nature. All of them begin with or include the descriptor *often*, which is a highly subjective and inexact term. Although the criteria appear to be detailed and comprehensive, there is little guidance provided by the *DSM-IV* as to how to differentiate the severity of these symptoms from what is normal or typical for children at certain ages. Unlike many other medical and psychiatric conditions, ADHD does not involve the presence of some symptom that is exclusive to ADHD or to a small number of maladies. Most of the symptoms of ADHD can be observed in many normal children much of the time. It is not the behaviors themselves that make them unique to ADHD, but rather the severity, the chronicity, the early onset of these symptoms, and the interference in functioning that they cause.

The lack of specificity of the diagnostic criteria is also illustrated by the lack of developmental norms. No mention is made of the fact that the number and severity of these behaviors that involve a significant discrepancy from the norm change, depending on the age of the child. Using the diagnostic criteria from a former edition of the diagnostic manual (*DSM-III-R*) (American Psychiatric Association 1987), Barkley (1990) found that relying on the diagnostic criteria of eight out of fourteen symptoms of inattention and/or impulsivity-hyperactivity to make a diagnosis is appropriate for children ages 6 to 11, but for children ages 5 and below it is more meaningful to require that ten symptoms be present, because of the norms for that age group. For adolescents, on the other hand, it is appropriate to require only six symptoms to make the diagnosis, since the number and severity of these symptoms decrease in the normal population by that age. The symptom picture is not based on absolutes but on the relative interference in functioning that these behaviors represent, when comparing the child to his or her age peers.

Not only are the deficits of inattention, impulsivity, and hyperactivity hard to quantify, but these deficits are also common in several other psychiatric disorders. Many children are anxious and have problems separating from the parents. Anxiety interferes with the child's ability to focus on tasks and attend to the here and now. Children with separation problems are often preoccupied with what might be going on at home at the moment. Thus, a teacher might interpret a child's inattention as being anxiety related rather than ADHD related.

Children with ADHD use maladaptive ways of coping with the demands that are placed on them, which brings them into conflict with others. This maladaptive behavior of an ADHD child might be correctly understood as oppositional, but this oppositional behavior might be seen as evidence that the child does not have ADHD. If a child is avoidant and oppositional, he will not be able to complete his work, and his efforts will be inconsistent. He might tend to slack off. A teacher or parent observing the child might say, "He does not have ADHD, he's just being defiant," as if the two were mutually exclusive. It is common for a child to be oppositional *and* have ADHD.

To make matters more confusing, there is a high degree of *comorbidity*, that is, overlap, between ADHD and other psychiatric disorders, such as learning disabilities, behavior disorders, and affective disorders. A diagnosis of ADHD can unfortunately obscure the existence of these other problems, which are just as serious.

ADHD is difficult to diagnose. There is no blood test for it. There is no one psychometric test, symptom cluster, or rating scale that can be used to diagnose ADHD. Diagnosis requires the skilled accumulation of a great deal of information and the ability to sift through it and judge the relative relevance of all of it.

In some cases, however, diagnosis is easily made, such as for a child whose behavior is so clearly outside the norm, and has been for a long time, and in whom there is an absence of evidence of other disorders.

Seven-year-old Michael, a first grader, sat in my office with his parents, fidgeting with his arms and legs, squirming in his seat, and making fleeting eye contact. He would get up and look out the window any time he heard noise coming from outside. He frequently interrupted his parents and often brought up subjects irrelevant to what was being discussed at the moment. His parents had been concerned about his behavior since he was 3. He was always "wound up," had difficulty playing quietly, and was much more active than most of his peers. Since he started first grade, his teacher was concerned that he just was not tuned in enough. He usually looked around the room in a seemingly random manner when she was giving instructions to the class. In arts and crafts projects or hands-on activities, he often did not know what to do next. He was observed watching his neighbors for cues as to the next step in these activities. He frequently asked to go to the bathroom. There were no positive medical findings.

On rating scales from home and school, the Attention problem scales were consistently clinically significant. Other scales that would have indicated emotional problems were not clinically significant, although some signs of anxiety were noted. There were no reports from the parents or the teacher of bizarre or repetitive behaviors or of difficulty learning once his attention was engaged. A classroom observation found Michael to be off-task much of the time, making frequent requests to sharpen his pencil, and talking in class. He responded well to the teacher's attempts to refocus him on his work.

Michael's behavior had been fairly consistent over a number of years. The family had been quite stable, with no moves, financial difficulties, or trouble in the parents' marriage. There was no history of major psychiatric disturbance in the immediate family or in the grandparents' generation. However, Michael's mother had a history of underachievement during childhood due to inattentiveness, with a lot of daydreaming behavior reported by her teachers.

Based on the behaviors present in my office, the mother's history of attention problems, the absence of other significant family history, the developmental history, the teacher's report and classroom observation, and the home and school rating scales, a diagnosis of ADHD was clear.

There are many other cases, however, in which even a clear attention problem is not simply ADHD.

Jimmy, a 17-year-old high school junior, was referred for an evaluation for ADHD by his counselor and his psychiatrist. For many years Jimmy had severe behavior and attention problems both in and out of school.

Since elementary school, he had difficulty staying in school for the complete day because he felt trapped. He had been very active and aggressive, and in the eighth grade he threatened one of his teachers. He received good grades throughout most of elementary school, and he seemed to be bright. In junior high school, his attention problems worsened. He had more difficulty completing his work. He would become very agitated and was easily provoked to anger. He found school intolerable and the school found him intolerable. The school arranged for him to be tutored at home.

Jimmy had not been getting much work done in school. He was increasingly given to angry outbursts. He would harbor angry feelings that festered inside of him. When he encountered someone on the street against whom he had been holding a grudge for over a year, he threatened and intimidated the person. He had been in trouble with the police for getting into a shouting and shoving match with his best friend's father, which he justified by blaming this man for being unfairly punitive with his friend.

Jimmy's therapist and psychiatrist thought that he met the criteria for ADHD, and that the number of symptoms of both inattention and of impulsivity-hyperactivity were highly significant. On rating scales and questionnaires, Jimmy's parents' reports supported these findings. His tutor reported that Jimmy had had difficulty settling down to work, and when he was seated he often poked holes with his pencils in his paper and in the cloth upholstery of chairs, and left many broken pencils around him, but that more recently Jimmy had been consistently self-motivated, and he was able to sit and work for an hour at a time without being fidgety or distracted. He worked best when alone. When the tutor was present, Jimmy tended to talk to him and not complete his work.

Although Jimmy seemed to meet the criteria for a diagnosis of ADHD, his emotional volatility and severe behavior problems warranted a fuller assessment. During the testing, Jimmy had great difficulty providing concise answers to verbal questions. His responses were long, tangential, and emotional in nature when brief, factual answers were called for. For example, on a question of general knowledge, when Jimmy was asked who a fairly well-known heroic historical figure was, he correctly identified the man, but continued on a diatribe about how this man was actually evil because of his associations with exploitative institutions and secret dealings with intelligence agencies. His responses were frequently angry and suspicious in content.

When responding to these verbal items, Jimmy's speech had a pressured quality to it; he seemed to have difficulty inhibiting his speech production. The content of his speech was not always clear, and was often illogical, as if he were saying something that had a special meaning to him that was not discernible to others. The more emotionally carried away he became by what he was saying, the more pressured, tangential, and illogical his speech became.

On tasks that measured attention, with both auditory and visual information, Jimmy performed quite well and was consistently above average.

Based on the totality of the evaluation, it was my impression that Jimmy was suffering from Manic-Depressive Disorder, also known as Bipolar Disorder. After receiving this information, his psychiatrist prescribed a mood-stabilizing medication for him that is commonly used for Manic-Depressive Illness, rather than a stimulant, which is commonly used for ADHD. Jimmy began to do much better, whereas a stimulant might have worsened his condition.

Avi, 7 years old, met the criteria for a diagnosis of ADHD. Not only did he exhibit most of the eighteen symptoms listed in Table 2–1 in Chapter 2, but he had done so from a very early age, and his problems were interfering with his functioning at school and at home. Avi was a first grader who had great difficulty following rules and listening to directions. He would typically start what he was told to do, but drop it for something else within thirty seconds. He could not stay seated for more than thirty seconds. If attempts were made to set limits on him, he would have a tantrum and hide under a desk or a chair.

Intelligence testing revealed highly inconsistent functioning and several areas of weakness that did not fit into any clear pattern of learning disability or attention deficit. In responding to the demands of the testing, Avi engaged in many repetitive, self-stimulatory, and regressive behaviors. He often became lost in fantasy, and his responses to factual questions involved fantasy characters about which he had been thinking. He would repeat these answers in a perseverative manner on several consecutive questions. Avi's speech was not always clear, and it seemed that he made up his own words at times. Personality testing indicated poor reality perception and impaired reality testing. Avi did not see the world the way that others typically did, and he had difficulty using feedback to modify his behavior.

Avi's testing, therefore, revealed not just symptoms of ADHD, but serious problems with information processing and disturbances in his thinking. He was dissimilar to children with ADHD, and he did not seem to have a learning disability that fit any commonly known pattern. A previous trial of stimulant medication had resulted in extreme anxiety, crying, and emotional volatility. The best way of conceptualizing his behavior was not as ADHD, but of a variant of Pervasive Developmental Disorder. Pervasive Developmental Disorders are severe impairments that affect several areas of development, such as social interaction, communication, and intellectual functioning, with the presence of un- usual and repetitive behaviors. The prescribing psychiatrist was able to find medication that controlled his mood better, and the school was able to develop a plan to focus on his learning needs, to provide struc- ture, to set goals relative to his abilities, and to develop his social skills.

These case examples demonstrate the importance of a comprehen- sive assessment for ADHD. One interview that covers the parents' report of the symptom picture, with the possible addition of contact with the school, is usually not enough. Getting additional informa- tion from checklists and rating scales is crucial, but even that is not always enough. Assessing a child's attention span and concentration and judging how much they deviate from what is typical for his age are not clear-cut. There are many conditions that affect a child's at- tention and concentration. Having the required number of behavioral symptoms of ADHD is necessary to make a diagnosis, but it is not sufficient, since other conditions might mimic the symptom picture.

An article in *Newsweek* magazine (Hancock 1996), stated: "This would all be a lot easier if science could isolate a flaw in the brain to aid diagnosis" (p. 54). The wish for a simple solution to the problem of ADHD is tempting. However, even if a "flaw in the brain" could be isolated, even if the brains of ADHD individuals could be shown to be different from those of non-ADHD individuals in ways that positively identified those with the disorder, all ADHD individuals would still be different. ADHD is not an all-or-nothing thing. Identifying an individual with ADHD is just the beginning of the process of diagnosing and assessing the problem and helping the individual.

The fact that ADHD is an *organically* based disorder does not mean that identifying the biological marker or indicator will lead to a universal treatment. This is because ADHD is, and will remain, a *functional* disorder. It affects how people function—how they carry out the tasks and responsibilities of their daily lives, such as working, planning, and communicating. The symptoms of ADHD vary so greatly between individuals that questions need to be raised for each individual diagnosed: What is the nature of the impairment in attention? Is it mild, moderate, or severe? A "mild" attention deficit is not a mild or insignificant thing; the child still is more impaired than about 95% of his age mates.

The other part of this question relates to the type of attention that is impaired and the conditions under which it is impaired. This has enormous significance for designing school and home interventions to help the child. Many children with ADHD have problems with *sustained attention*—they can focus their attention on something but only for a short period of time. Setting up a reward/monitoring program to develop longer periods of task-related work (Garber et al. 1995), or making the tasks more stimulating by adding color (Zentall et al. 1993) for example, might be helpful. Other children might be more distractible, or have problems with *selective attention*. For these children, reducing distractions, such as by using cubicles, might be worthwhile.

As discussed in Chapter 2, some children have difficulty attending to auditory stimulation but do very well with visual stimulation. These children would have great difficulty attending to lectures in class and being able to remember the important information. They might, however, do quite well with printed outlines or study guides that they can use while listening to the teacher. Other children show the opposite tendency. That is, they attend well to auditory and not to visual stimuli. They might do well remembering what was just said to them, but might have difficulty copying things correctly from the board.

These considerations are important from an assessment point of view because there are instruments that are supposedly sensitive to diagnosing ADHD, but that rely on only one modality—visual or auditory. Just because a child does well on one of these tests does not mean he does not have ADHD.

Anastopoulos and colleagues (1994) have found that while the Freedom From Distractibility Index on the Wechsler Intelligence Scale for Children–Third Edition (WISC-III), which assesses auditory distractibility, shows a correlation with ADHD when data are analyzed for a large number of people, this index is not predictive of ADHD for any specific individual.

There are other tests that assess attentional problems on visual tasks. These tests are often computerized and referred to as continuous performance tests (CPTs). They assess attention by requiring the individual to look at a computer screen and wait for a letter, number, or other stimulus or sequence of stimuli to appear on the screen. When this stimulus appears, the individual is required to quickly press a key on the computer. The tests assess several measures of attention: the accuracy of the response, the speed with which the individual responded, and whether he responded as quickly when he had to wait for a longer interval, thereby maintaining a state of attentiveness in the absence of stimulation. Because the tests are repetitive and not very stimulating or interesting, and because they take about fifteen minutes to complete, they can measure whether the individual responded as consistently near the end of the time period compared with the beginning of the test, to see if attention was sustained over time. These tests can also include the instruction that when a different letter, number, or stimulus is presented, the individual is to refrain from responding, thereby obtaining a measure of response inhibition or impulsivity.

The degree to which impulsivity or hyperactivity is a problem is also highly variable. Some children are severely inattentive, but sit still and keep to themselves. They do not disrupt the class and are often not noticed by their teachers as having a problem. Although their work might be inconsistent or mediocre, they do not attract attention from others because they are not active. They might sit in their seats and daydream and drift in and out of mental participation in class. Teachers might see them as quiet, or perhaps depressed. However, without the symptoms of hyperactivity or impulsivity, the diagnosis of ADHD might be ruled out. Girls with ADHD often do not show prominent signs of hyperactivity and impulsivity, and therefore are at risk for being underdiagnosed.

Hyperactivity can range from being in constant motion—getting out of one's seat and running around the room—to sitting in one's chair and restlessly tapping the arm of the chair or shaking one's foot. It is not true that the child has to be "bouncing off the walls" to be considered hyperactive.

Impulsivity can vary from situation to situation. Some children are more impulsive when there is less structure. They might do relatively well in a classroom with a very structured and firm teacher, but have great difficulty waiting their turn and cooperating with peers on the playground. Other children might do better in the unstructured environment of the playground or the loosely structured environment of their home, but have difficulty complying with the stricter rules of the classroom.

Another issue is the extent to which the child's attention and activity problems interfere with intellectual functioning and academic achievement. That is, what is the impact of ADHD on the child? Giving the child an intelligence test under standardized conditions can provide some important information regarding how impaired the child's attention problems are relative to his overall intelligence. For example, the intelligence test looks at discrepancies between abilities, not just at absolute ability levels. A child with average intelligence who scores in the average range on the subtests on the IQ test that assess attention, unless other factors are present, cannot be said to demonstrate impaired attention on this test. However, a child who scores in the average range (25th to 75th percentile) on the attention-sensitive subtests who has superior intellectual abilities (91st to 98th percentile) can be said to exhibit impaired attentional abilities. The comparison of the child's overall intellectual abilities and his performance on specific subtests that assess attention is therefore very useful.

It is also useful to look at the consistency of attention and the interference of inattention and activity level on performance. Most of the subtests on the IQ test are structured so the items gradually increase in difficulty. The child is given points for each item that is completed or answered correctly, and the score on that subtest is dependent on the total number of points earned. Therefore, if a child is intelligent enough to get the most difficult items correct, but fails to get many of the easier ones correct, his score will be low and might not reflect his true intellectual abilities. This is called *scatter*. Why would a child get more difficult items correct and fail much easier items? One possibility could be inattention, where the child's focus vacillates so much during the testing that his attention comes and goes. Another possibility is that, because of his hyperactivity, the child fails to look at some items, or does not consistently take in the information that is being presented to him. The child is not available for the information because his body or his eyes and ears are not "there" at the moment. Another possible reason is that, although the child might have attended adequately during the testing session, his learning in school or at home has been compromised because of his inattention, and he has retained only scattered bits of information and developed erratic proficiencies, which are reflected in his erratic test performance.

For these reasons, intelligence test data enable the psychologist to make a professional judgment as to the extent to which the child's inattention or hyperactivity is interfering with his learning, and on what types of learning tasks this interference is to be expected.

The issue of interference in learning raises the question of what type of learning is interfered with, and of whether there are learning problems in addition to or instead of ADHD that might be interfering with the child's functioning.

The WISC-III (Wechsler 1991) clusters intellectual functioning into four broad areas, each representing a different type of learning:

verbal comprehension—learning that is based on the understanding and use of language; perceptual organization—nonverbal learning that affects the organization of information as well as visual and motor information processing; freedom from distractibility—attention, concentration, and short-term retention of auditory information; and processing speed—the ability to quickly and accurately scan new, repetitive information visually, and quickly and accurately learn and copy previously unfamiliar, repetitive information.

Deficits in perceptual organization and in processing speed can often result in problems that are similar to those caused by ADHD. Children with these problems have difficulty organizing information and physical belongings, and difficulty completing their work in a timely and efficient manner. These children might take in or think through information more slowly than does the typical child. These deficits often coexist with ADHD.

Deficits in language-based processing can also give the child the appearance of being inattentive and can result in the child's demonstrating variable success in completing his work accurately. Children with these deficits often misinterpret instructions and factual information, and often have trouble communicating to others what they know. They therefore perform more poorly than one would expect, given their intelligence. They often fail to complete their work because they do not understand it fully. A comprehensive assessment that includes an intellectual assessment helps to differentiate these issues.

ERRONEOUS ASSESSMENT METHODS

The assessment of ADHD is fraught with so many uncertainties, contradictions, and ambiguities that it is tempting to try to simplify it. A quick-and-easy approach to diagnosis is often taken that does not serve the parent or the child well.

Interpreting test data in the absence of a thorough history of the child's symptoms, development, and family background is insufficient to assess ADHD. All possible factors influencing the child's behaviors must be assessed. The symptoms must be consistent with a diagnosis of ADHD. The history should support such a diagnosis as opposed to some other explanation for the symptoms. In addition, if the child does have ADHD, there might still be some other problem that is contributing to his difficulties, as described earlier. A skillful, well-trained clinician knows what questions to ask to get a thorough picture of the child's symptoms and the relevant developmental and family background. Psychological testing, although important in obtaining measures of some aspects of attention in children, should never be the sole or even the main element in making the diagnosis of ADHD.

Unfortunately, test data are often misused in the diagnostic process. Most well-developed psychological tests report numerical scores. These tests compare the child to his or her age peers. They reveal meaningful discrepancies between different abilities that the child has, such as his attentional abilities compared with his overall intelligence, by allowing us to compare the child's scores on different tests or different parts of the same test. There are statistical tests that assess whether differences between one individual and his peers, or differences between two different skills and abilities, are so outside the typical range that they are probably due to a real deficit in the child. These numbers are often used to rule in or rule out a diagnosis of ADHD. Some educators may debate whether the differences between certain standardized scores are great enough to be statistically significant. But the diagnosis of any individual cannot be made based on a test score. The numbers are important sources of information that should be used to inform our clinical judgment, but it is a mistake to substitute them for the big picture.

The big picture involves taking all the information about an individual into account: his current test scores, his previous test scores, his history, the family history, his behavior, his learning strengths and weaknesses, his personality, and the frequency, intensity, and duration of specific symptoms. One piece of information cannot determine whether a child has ADHD.

Another erroneous method of diagnosing ADHD is relying on the child's response to medication to make the diagnosis. This is a dangerous practice. Many insurers and health care professionals say, "Just give him Ritalin and see how he responds. That will tell you whether or not he has ADHD." The response to Ritalin is considered by many to be diagnostic in itself.

Stimulant medication is highly effective with a very large percentage of children who have ADHD. However, given the number of disorders or behavior patterns that mimic ADHD, and given the number of children who have ADHD along with other psychological problems, such as bipolar disorder, prescribing medication before doing a comprehensive assessment can lead to medicating a child inappropriately. The child's problems might worsen, which can cause a great deal of pain and distress for the child and his family.

ACCEPTING THE RESULTS OF THE ASSESSMENT

Both parents should be present when the assessment results are discussed. The information that has been sorted through is so complex that the process of understanding the diagnosis and coming to terms with it is greatly aided when both parents are involved. If the fathers cannot attend, they might question the validity of the diagnosis without having adequate information and they thus may be less supportive of the remedies that have been proposed. Many mothers report feeling invalidated and unsupported by their husbands.

When both parents are present during the diagnostic process, their reactions can be out of synchrony with each other. Parents often experience something akin to a mourning process when they receive a diagnosis of a disability like ADHD in their child (Lavoie 1995). This process involves letting go of the image that they held of their child and accepting a reality that is different from what they had hoped for. This process can involve several strong emotional experiences that can change unpredictably. There is no preordained sequence of these reactions and no way of telling how long each will last. These emotions are part of the process of eventual acceptance of the diagnosis. They can include *denial*, in which the parent refuses to admit that there is anything wrong with the child, or continues to believe that he will grow out of it; *blame*, in which the parent attributes the child's problems to the spouse or to others; *bargaining*, in which the parent tries to make the problem go away by taking some action, such as spending more time with the child, or helping him more with his schoolwork; *guilt*, in which the parent blames himself; *isolation*, in which the parent cuts off contact with potential supports; and *flight*, in which the parent runs away from the problem by trying unrealistic remedies.

Each parent might experience a succession of different feelings. The feelings of the two parents might conflict with each other. This calls for a great deal of tolerance on each parent's part. It is important to understand that any of these reactions are normal, and might be necessary steps in the eventual acceptance of the diagnosis and in coping with it productively.

Sarah and Brian reacted very differently to the confirmation that their son, Kyle, had ADHD. Sarah had suspected it for some time, was relieved to get the diagnosis, and eager to get Kyle started on medication. She felt guilty about not having detected sooner that there was a problem, and therefore felt responsible for the years that Kyle spent frustrated in school. Furthermore, her family history was positive for ADHD, and she felt that she must have "given" it to him.

Brian, on the other hand, was not yet willing to believe that Kyle had ADHD. The past few years had been very stressful for the family, and Kyle might have been reacting to the turmoil with a fair amount of anxiety. He wanted to give Kyle some more time, and work with him more. Sarah correctly saw that Brian was reacting with denial. In her own anxiety about solving Kyle's problems without delay, it was hard for her to have the patience that Brian needed in order to cope with the diagnosis.

The therapist convinced Sarah to give Brian's concerns a fair hearing. Meetings with the family and with Kyle were set up to examine any anxieties that Kyle might have and to begin looking at how Sarah and Brian could structure Kyle's homework better. Sarah, however, continued to be impatient, and Brian reacted with more anger and isolation. Brian eventually sought the opinion of another psychologist, and, over time, eventually agreed to a trial of medication for Kyle. Fortunately, the medication was effective, as were Brian and Sarah's efforts to work with Kyle and the school, and Kyle began to do much better.

The involvement of both parents is also invaluable when there is resistance from the school in accepting the diagnosis. The father of one ADHD child found that the most difficult aspect for him of raising his ADHD child was the process of educating teachers that ADHD was a real disorder and was not just being used as an excuse for his son's problems. The process of educating others as to the reality of ADHD, of laying out objective facts and logical evidence, is a valuable contribution that fathers can make.

In contrast to the problems of accepting a diagnosis of ADHD, some parents have difficulty accepting the finding that their child does *not* have ADHD. Many children have difficulty concentrating, attending, and behaving well because they are anxious, bored with school, have learned inappropriate ways of coping with conflict, or have parents who find it difficult to meet their needs and communicate with them. Finding out that a child does not have ADHD means that there might be no clear explanation for his difficulties and the search for answers has to begin anew. The parents have to decide if the assessment process stops there, or if they should seek a second opinion. The child's attention problems still must be dealt with. Behaviorally, the methods used with a non-ADHD child with attention and behavior problems might not differ much from those used with an ADHD child. However, there might be other factors contributing to the problem that need to be explored.

SUMMARY

- The assessment process begins when someone feels that something is wrong with the way the child is functioning or learning.
- There might be a pattern of teachers' comments over the years indicating missing or incomplete work, inattentiveness, or underachievement.

- Fathers are often skeptical of mothers' intuition that something is wrong. They look for scientific facts. They also tend to discount indicators that there is something wrong with their child.

- Mothers are often characterized as overprotective or overanxious when they voice concerns about their children.

- Dismissing the concerns of mothers often leads to a delay in recognizing the child's problems and getting him help.

- Fathers often identify with their child's rambunctiousness and individuality and deny that there is a problem with the child's behavior.

- In requesting an evaluation through the school, parents should be aware that the school district might be expert at evaluating learning disabilities but might not have the expertise to evaluate ADHD.

- The evaluation of ADHD involves complex clinical judgment, of which psychological testing might be a part. But no assessment should be based solely on testing.

- The symptoms of ADHD are so variable, that any individual ADHD child might not fit any one teacher's idea of ADHD.

- Early assessment and identification are very important, and can have long-lasting implications for a child's self-esteem, achievement, and attitude toward school and learning. If a child is not identified and continues to experience frustration, he might avoid demands on him and seek negative attention.

- Whatever the school's findings, the parents must remain the advocates for their child.

- Comprehensive assessments are important to determine not just the presence of ADHD, but its severity, the types of attention that are affected, the conditions under which attention is impaired, the degree to which it interferes with different areas of learning, the relationship to the child's intellectual level, the complications introduced by emotional factors like anxiety and depression and the child's personality, and the possible presence of other disorders that might look like or coexist with ADHD.

- An assessment should always include a thorough individual and family history.

- A diagnosis should not be based on the child's response to medication.

- Accepting the diagnosis is easier if both parents process the assessment information together.

- Parents often experience a mourning process, and must go through stages of feelings, such as denial, anger, guilt, blame, bargaining, isolation, and flight, in order to eventually accept the diagnosis. In this process, two parents' reactions might be in conflict, and understanding and tolerance are needed.

The Intelligent Child with ADHD

Many parents know that their child is intelligent and does well in school. A son might struggle sometimes or act up in class. But kids normally do that, especially boys. A daughter might daydream at times and miss some important information. But her grades are usually, although not always, very good. All children have good and bad days. Therefore, the parent might conclude that there could not be anything to worry about. Or could there be?

There are many highly intelligent children who have ADHD. These children often do well in school despite their attentional problems. In fact, they often do above average work. They are usually liked by their teachers (teachers love high achievers), and they are also often personable and verbal. Much is forgiven in high achievers.

The high intelligence can be both a blessing and a curse. It is a blessing because, in spite of a problem that would be disabling to many children, the highly intelligent child with ADHD can still learn and succeed relative to his peers. The intelligence can be a curse because the child's ability to achieve obscures the ADHD, thereby preventing or delaying it from being recognized, and forestalling the help that the child needs (Faigel et al. 1985, Silver 1991). Furthermore, if the condition is not recognized by the parents, it is less likely that it will be recognized by the school.

Fathers often celebrate their children's achievements and minimize their behavioral or academic difficulties, especially if the child is a boy. It is the mothers who worry more about these difficulties. Mothers usually have more of a sense of what other children are doing—developmentally, academically, and socially. Mothers are often more attuned to how their child fits in with the group, since women tend to be more adept at understanding social networks and symmetrical, reciprocal connections with others.

Fathers are more likely than mothers not to be so concerned about their child being like others. With their sons, fathers often adopt a "boys will be boys" attitude toward somewhat wild and nonconforming behavior, and may even be pleased at these signs of independence and rebelliousness. For the father who was somewhat rebellious himself (which may have been related to his own undiagnosed ADHD), seeing his son defy authority might give him secret, vicarious pleasure.

Fathers, therefore, might be more comfortable with their child being different and not fitting in as well as others, and might see this as a sign of individuality and independence. Mothers might be more concerned about the child's relationship with his peer group. When the child is brighter than average, it might be harder for the father to feel that there is a problem, because not only is the child getting away with defying authority, but he is also succeeding in school. It may be difficult for the father of an ADHD child to see that his child is not really getting away with anything, and that he is not really succeeding.

Jessica was a bright, attractive, verbal 10-year-old fourth grader, whose teachers found her to be delightful but "a handful" at times. Since the first grade, her grades had always been "good" or "very good," the two highest designations in her school's grading system. Most of the time, Jessica's work was among the best in her class. Her homework, however, was inconsistent. Sometimes it was complete and accurate, and other times she did not bring it in, although she claimed to have done it. Her classwork, although generally good, was at times poor. There were quizzes and class assignments where she did not seem to understand what was being asked of her. She also spent too much time talking with the girls seated around her in class, and she frequently had to be reprimanded. Her seat had to be changed twice during the year.

Jessica's kindergarten and first-grade teachers had thought that there might be a problem. They noted that Jessica seemed to tune out or daydream much of the time, and that she was often off-task. However, since her obvious strengths outweighed her difficulties, the school did not pursue an evaluation, preferring to wait and see if serious problems developed. Her parents did not push for an evaluation and decided to follow the school's lead. By the fourth grade, however, the problems had not gone away, and homework was becoming more of a struggle between Jessica and her mother. Jessica took a very long time to do her homework, and it was a struggle for her mother to get her to sit down and complete it in a reasonable amount of time.

The school decided to do a preliminary evaluation to see if there were signs of a learning disability. Included in this evaluation were an intelligence test and tests of academic achievement. Jessica's Full Scale IQ tested at 115, which was in the High Average range. Her Verbal IQ, which is generally an indication of language-based intellectual abilities, was also in the High Average range. Her Performance IQ, which is generally an indication of visual-perceptual learning and organization, was in the Average range. Although there was a statistically significant difference between these two IQ factors, it was not large enough to be considered unusually great or indicative of a learning disability. It did indicate a relative weakness in her ability to organize information visually and spatially, to process visual information efficiently and quickly, and to write and copy quickly and efficiently. These are common problems that accompany ADHD in many children.

Jessica's achievement tests were all in the Average to High Average range, with some abilities falling at the low end of the Average range, and some falling at the high end of the High Average range. In other words, there was a large spread between her best score and her weakest score, but all of her tested abilities were at least average.

The school interpreted this information to indicate that there was not a learning disability, that Jessica was clearly a very bright girl, and that she was achieving at grade level or above. The school concluded that there was no reason to be concerned about her learning or to provide remedial services.

But Jessica's mother was troubled. After hearing his wife's concerns for years, and often feeling that she was overreacting, Jessica's father began to grant some legitimacy to these concerns when he witnessed some of the struggles over homework. This was reinforced when Jessica's mother showed him the teachers' comments on Jessica's report cards over the years that consistently said things like "A delight to have in class, but talks too much," "Adds a lot to class discussions but effort is inconsistent," "Many homework assignments missing," "Inconsistent effort," and "Does not appear to be motivated at times."

Jessica's parents expressed their concerns to their pediatrician who recommended that they consult with a child psychologist. The psychologist took a detailed history, met with Jessica, reviewed the school record, and did some of his own testing, and concluded that Jessica did not have a learning disability, but did have ADHD. The fact that she was bright was the reason that she was learning, but she did not seem to be learning up to her potential.

Since she was a well-liked girl who was not failing academically, and did not have any apparent learning disability, the school did not find a reason to commit extra resources to her. There were so many other children who were obviously struggling just to pass and with whom the teachers were struggling on a daily basis to control their behavior, that Jessica's problems seemed minor in comparison.

Although Jessica appeared to be succeeding academically, signs of frustration were beginning to show. To her parents and teachers, she was obviously very bright. They related to her in the way that parents and teachers relate to children who are intelligent and verbal—they communicated high expectations of her understanding things, remembering things, and performing well. These expectations and assumptions were not necessarily consciously stated; some were communicated nonverbally and unconsciously.

Fortunately, the school was willing to consider the psychologist's report. The school team developed a plan to structure Jessica's work in class. They agreed to give Jessica preferential seating, close to where the teacher stood. The teacher also agreed to list for Jessica the work that she expected her to complete each time a new subject was started. She would have Jessica contract to complete her work. Jessica was also to have a piece of paper on her desk on which the teacher would place a check each time a subject was finished to which Jessica had attended. At the end of the day, if Jessica earned a specified number of points, she would earn a privilege, such as time on the computer or being the teacher's helper. The teacher also agreed to break down classroom assignments into smaller units, in which Jessica would be expected to complete a small amount of work at a time, and be allowed a short break and an opportunity to check her work before proceeding to the next chunk of work. A system of tracking Jessica's homework was also agreed to. Her teacher would check to see that her homework assignments were recorded accurately before she went home. The teacher would sign the notebook if the work was accurate. Jessica's parents would then have accurate information as to her homework assignments for the evening. They would also check to see that Jessica had her completed homework with her before leaving for school the next morning.

The child experiences these high expectations from adults, and when the child is intelligent and unencumbered with a handicap like ADHD, he usually enjoys rising to the expectations of his elders. The child with ADHD, however, experiences these expectations, but is painfully aware that he often does not succeed in meeting them. He does not know why this is so, and he is also unable to predict when he will respond in a way that pleases the adult and himself and when he will not.

The intelligent ADHD child, therefore, develops ways to avoid the high expectations of others. He might blame external factors for his failures, such as a sibling. Or he might develop a habit of not telling the truth, such as denying that he did not do his homework or complete a chore. Not knowing that something is wrong, adults will continue to expect the child to perform up to the level of his perceived intelligence, continuing the frustrating cycle of expectations and avoidance.

Therefore, performing adequately in school is still frustrating for the intelligent ADHD child even if he is capable of performing more than adequately. The expectations will still be there. So will the disappointment of others when he fails to live up to those expectations. Because his ADHD will have been undetected, this underachievement will be attributed to lack of effort, laziness, lack of caring, or some other personal attribute, which will be communicated to the child. Children also know when they are not doing as well as they are capable of doing. They tend to have interests that match their intellectual levels. They take on challenges and find things interesting and engaging that are commensurate with their abilities to understand and problem solve. An intelligent ADHD child will tend to be drawn to things that children of above average intelligence are drawn to, but he will have difficulty mastering the challenges that he creates for himself or that others pose for him.

The other problem that intelligent ADHD children have is one of not being challenged enough academically. Combine this with the restlessness often experienced by children with ADHD, and their constant need for stimulation, and they will become easily bored with the daily curriculum. These children often have difficulty performing consistently up to the level of their abilities, and their performance is often at an average level, so they might not be seen by their teachers as eligible for an enriched academic program. They are therefore stuck in the regular classroom, without receiving the special help that they need for their attentional problems, and without being provided with the academic enrichment that would make school more stimulating for them.

The intelligent child with ADHD needs to know that he is intelligent *and* that he has a problem for which he needs help. If the attentional problems are not attended to, this child might continue to do adequately in school, but will probably experience increasing frustration as he reaches higher grades and fails to live up to his potential. It might be the school's job to ensure that each child receives an education, but it is the parents' job to see to it that their child is provided with every opportunity to realize his potential in life.

Although these children are more intelligent than the typical child, they still need basic help in the form of behavior management and structure. It is not insulting to their intelligence to repeat instructions, write them down, give them directions one step at a time, or break down their work into small units, because their organizational and attentional abilities are *not* above average and may in fact be well below average in spite of their intelligence. These structures, which make things more simple and predictable for these children, are often greeted with relief. It is these structures that enable the child to demonstrate his competence and therefore feel a sense of satisfaction in both the experience of achievement and the knowledge that he is pleasing others.

Advocating for an intelligent child with ADHD is complicated. The parent is often advocating for special help and for academic enrichment at the same time. The school might question the child's ability or readiness for enrichment because of his inconsistencies in meeting the demands of the normal curriculum. At the same time, the school might question the need to provide the child with special help because he is meeting most of the demands of the normal curriculum adequately. This seems contradictory, and it is. Neither viewpoint alone takes the whole child into account. The child's difficulty achieving and producing consistently is related both to his ADHD and to his need for greater intellectual stimulation.

The position of the parents as advocates for their child is complicated in these cases. Not only are they at a disadvantage talking with school personnel who are better versed in the concepts and language of education than they are, but now there are two areas of need that they have to address. One of the most important things for parents to keep in mind is that they are speaking about the whole child—not just an ADHD child, and not just an intelligent child. Parents have knowledge of their own child—what makes him happy, frustrated, excited, fulfilled—beyond the knowledge of any of the school personnel.

It is vitally important that both parents, whether or not they are together, work as a team in this advocacy, and not allow the focus on one part of the child's needs—his ADHD or his intelligence—to obscure the focus on all of his needs. One parent should not be left to negotiate these complex matters alone.

SUMMARY

- There are many highly intelligent children with ADHD who do reasonably well in school and are liked by their teachers.

- Average school achievement can prevent or delay attention problems from being recognized.

- Fathers often are less alarmed than mothers about problems in school, and often are more tolerant about their child not fitting in or defying authority.

- Even the bright child with ADHD is aware that he fails to live up to the expectations of others, and that he does not perform up to the level of his abilities.

- School can be very frustrating without the special help that the child needs and without the academic enrichment that would make school more stimulating.

- Advocating for the bright ADHD child is complicated, and involves convincing the school to provide special help for a child who is passing, and enrichment for a child who might not be excelling.

What Fathers Can Teach Their ADHD Children

TRANSITIONS

Transitions, which involve changes in routine or in the environmental expectations on the child, are often difficult for children with ADHD. Being able to cope with the world effectively involves being able to adapt to the flow of events as they take place over time. This involves the ability to predict changes and anticipate them before they happen, and to change one's behavior to conform to sometimes subtle and sometimes radical changes in rules, expectations, reinforcers, and reinforcement schedules (the frequency and consistency with which rewards are available to the child).

Two views of ADHD that Barkley (1990, 1993, 1994, 1995a,b) discusses are those of a deficit in rule-governed behavior, and a deficit in the ability to anticipate the future and orient one's thoughts and behavior to that future. ADHD is a deficit in rule-governed behavior in that the individual with ADHD has difficulty conforming his behavior to externally imposed or socially agreed upon rules of conduct. What we refer to as *structure* is actually the set of rules that creates consistent and repeated expectations on our behavior, and provides reinforcement for adjusting our behavior to these expectations and negative consequences for not conforming. Allowing our behavior to be governed by rules means that we do not allow our actions to be dictated by internal needs and impulses when they conflict with the rules. We defer to the rules of conduct that are agreed upon communally. This is the opposite of being impulsive. Hyperactive children fail to conform to the rules when the rules call for sitting quietly or staying in one place; the child's activity level makes this impossible. Impulsive children often fail to think before they act or speak, and therefore violate rules of appropriate social behavior. Inattentive children fail to attend to tasks on which they are required to work and instead attend to other, often extraneous, things. They thus fail to complete their work.

Orienting one's thoughts and behavior to the future implies an ability to delay gratification and to keep in mind a future goal that will guide one's behavior more powerfully than will immediate reinforcement. Therefore, one's behavior can be controlled by long-range reinforcement, which is removed in time from present circumstances.

Given these perspectives on ADHD, it is easy to see why transitions would be difficult for these children. Transitions within the same environment are especially difficult. In each situation in which one functions, there are different behaviors that are reinforced and punished. Attributes of the physical environment cue us as to which behaviors will be rewarded and which will not. This is why people behave differently in different situations. For example, the setting of the classroom might cue children that this is a place where sitting quietly and raising your hand are rewarded and shouting is punished. But at home, raising your hand is inappropriate and might actually be ridiculed. At school, children are cued that their jokes might be laughed at by their peers; this might be much more reinforcing for a child than the cues that his behavior will be punished by the teacher. But the same child might never make a joke in church.

Sometimes, similar behaviors are shown in different situations, but at different frequencies or intensities. For example, talking to peers might take place at school and at home, but the frequency might be much less at school. Disobedience to authority is often different at school and at home, depending on the disciplining skills of the authorities, the emotional relationship between the child and the authority figure(s), the clarity of the rules, and the amount of structure provided in each situation.

When the activity changes in an environment (for example, putting away the art projects in class and getting out reading worksheets), or when the people in the environment change (such as when Dad comes home from work), we have a transition within the same environment. ADHD children, who often have trouble adapting to any set of rules, find it especially confusing when the environment that was cueing them to behave in one way now reinforces and punishes different behaviors. In a matter of seconds, the reinforcement that the child was receiving and could anticipate receiving for drawing a picture is now gone, and the same behavior is met with punishment (a reprimand, an annoyed glance). Or a child who was having fun running around the house with his mother home now finds that he is yelled at for the same behavior when his father, tired and stressed out, comes home from work.

Father coming home from work is a particularly difficult transition for many families, and especially for families with ADHD children. When Mom is already home with the children, Dad walks into an ongoing scene without knowing what behaviors, experiences, or feelings had set up the scene. It is somewhat like walking into the middle of a movie and trying to figure out what is happening. At home there is a mood that Dad did not share in creating. Dad comes home and expects certain behaviors and reactions and tries to impose his own needs and wants onto the family, with little knowledge of the context in which he is operating. The movie script suddenly changes. Everyone might experience some confusion and a loss of control.

Fathers of ADHD children notice the chaos going on when they come home from work. Still, like the conquering hero home from the war, they anticipate a warm greeting from their wives and children. Hope springs eternal for some fathers, followed by continued disappointment. Some fathers of ADHD children have become conditioned to cringe when they turn the handle on the door and leave their private thoughts and the solitude that the drive home from work afforded them, to step into a chaos that they can barely manage.

If Mother gets home before Dad, or has been home most of the day with the children, she might eagerly anticipate the father's homecoming as a chance to get some relief from the responsibilities of child management. She is overwhelmed at this point with the children's behavior and would like some down time. Or Dad can now take over the care of the children while she makes dinner or attends to other chores. Or Mom would like Dad to make dinner or do the laundry so that she can attend to the children's needs. Whatever the mother's needs or expectations, there is an immediacy about them that bombards the father the second he steps in the door.

Children with ADHD are likely to see Dad's entrance as a disruption of the environment. There is confusion as to how to act, whether to continue doing what they were doing before Dad's arrival, thereby denying his presence, or to act differently, thereby accommodating to different expectations. Dad is thrust into a maelstrom of activity and noise, and not accommodated to (not greeted or listened to). His presence can be so disrupting that the children's behavior worsens, which leads to his increased efforts to exert control, which causes greater opposition in the children.

Furthermore, the increased disruption that follows the father's arrival, and his inability to control it, is often accompanied by Mom telling Dad what needs to be done and being critical of him (overtly or covertly) for failing to do it well. This understandably creates friction between them. Dad feels ineffectual, and is told that he is, if not in so many words. Dad feels more angry and reacts by silently withdrawing. Without much understanding between the parents, the children either run the household or become the targets of their parents' anger and heavy-handed attempts to exert control. Thus, Dad's homecoming is dissatisfying to everyone in the family. This scenario might sound like an exaggeration, but it is not an exaggeration for ADHD families.

The transition to father coming home is often a reflection of the quality of the parenting teamwork of the two parents. Improving this transition time in the family's day is a good jumping-off point to improving the teamwork and parenting skills in general of the parents. It also illustrates many of the principles of child management with ADHD children cited in this and other books. This particular transition is also one in which many fathers can make a very significant contribution.

How can we use this transition to help ADHD children manage their behavior and help fathers and mothers function more effectively as a team? We can begin with helping the children to prepare for and anticipate the changes in stimulation and rules that come with this transition.

It is helpful to provide the ADHD child with a schedule for the day, in which the sequence of the major activities is written clearly, perhaps in large print with an illustration or two. This schedule can be posted where it is easily seen, and where the parents can use it to keep the child informed about what will happen next. The child, then, will already have been informed of Dad's expected arrival. He can also be reminded, about fifteen minutes before Dad is due to arrive, of the sequence of events that have been preplanned for when he walks in the door.

It is helpful if Mom and Dad write a script for Dad's return home. Rather than being forced and artificial, a planned sequence of events provides the structure that frees the child to be more natural, calm, and spontaneous. Not doing any planning or scripting leaves parents doomed to repeat the same series of dysfunctional interactions and behaviors time after time. These interactions might not be consciously scripted, but they are as predictable as if they were. Therefore, a script does exist, but not one that the parents would desire. Parents can substitute a script that is of their conscious creation and under their control.

Charlie, the father of very aggressive, twin ADHD 8-year-old boys, and a 12-year-old boy who was very oppositional and defiant, felt beaten down every time he returned home from work. The boys were so aggressive that they hit and kicked him. By the time he arrived home, his wife had spent almost the entire day "putting out fires," with nothing working very well. She expected her husband to come home and "take charge," set limits, and provide her with some relief. The home situation was so chaotic that Charlie was not even able to speak to his wife without interruption. Therefore, he was unable to catch up on the day's events and orient himself to what was needed from him at the moment.

Confronted with the external chaos when he came home, and with the knowledge that his wife expected him, and desperately needed him, to master it, Charlie responded with a feeling of internal chaos—confusion and not knowing what to do. He felt like a failure before he even walked in the door. His response was either to give up and do little to control the children, which enraged and disappointed his wife, or to become enraged and discipline them in a heavy-handed, angry way, further alienating his children from him.

At this time of day, his children usually had finished dinner, and were expected to be working on their homework. Charlie was pulled in three directions at once, as each child wanted his help, in an exclusive, almost desperate way, evocative of the father hunger mentioned earlier. As the children competed for their father's attention, their behavior became increasingly out of control, noncompliant, and aggressive. Charlie became more frustrated at his inability to meet anyone's needs. Relations became more strained between him and his wife.

Situations such as this are common. The children need help in anticipating what will happen and what will be expected of them, with the sequence of events being clearly under the parents' control but responsive to the children's needs.

A situation such as this can be scripted as follows: Dad will come home and greet everyone, and then spend ten minutes talking to Mom, during which he will not talk to the children and will ignore their attempts to interrupt their conversation. The children will be provided with something interesting and stimulating to do in order to decrease the chance that they will want to interrupt their parents. Interruptions that are aggressive in nature or otherwise impossible to ignore will be responded to with a consequence such as a time-out. Next, Dad will spend fifteen minutes with each child on his homework, in a predetermined order, and then be freed up to spend additional time with any child who needs extra help.

About fifteen minutes before Dad is expected to walk through the door, Mother (assuming she is home with the children) can inform the children that soon Dad will come home, and remind them of the sequence of events to follow and the behavior that is expected of them. She can then have the children repeat this back to her, making sure that they are making eye contact with her as they do. In situations where the father comes home before dinner, she can tell the children that they are expected to clean up their toys, or set the table, or do some task that signals to the children that a change in routine is to be expected and that allows the children to participate in that change.

Writing down the script is important not only for the ADHD child, but for the parents as well, especially if the parents have organization problems themselves. A chart can serve as a visual reminder or cue for the child and for the parents, and can help the parents be consistent with one another and decrease the chances for misunderstandings or differing interpretations. A written script for the situation above could look like this:

TRANSITION TIME	
5:15	Reminders from Mom
5:30	Dad comes home, says hello
5:35	Dad and Mom talk
	Children play or watch a video
5:45	Dad helps Philip with homework
6:00	Dad helps Jim with homework
6:15	Dad helps Steve with homework
6:30	Dad helps by request

This type of script was tried with the family mentioned above. It was simple and straightforward. It allowed the parents to agree on something and work on something together that was easy to monitor and not open to differing interpretations. It permitted the parents to experience some success in their parenting and their teamwork. It allowed the parents time to communicate, connect, and share information, opinions, and strategies relating to their children. It decreased some of the expectations of mind reading that had occurred, when Mom expected Dad to know what she and the children needed, although he had not been home all day. It decreased Dad's anticipation of his wife's disappointment in him, and decreased his view of himself as a failure. It allowed Dad to do something that was a strength of his—teach and impart information—as he was very intelligent and logical.

This type of planning can be used at home or at school. The parent or teacher can work with the child to develop a sequential list of events to anticipate and then to script the behaviors that are agreed upon. A point or token can be rewarded for listening to the sequence as it is previewed for the child before the transition, and for compliance during each step of the process.

ADHD children also need help transitioning to new situations. These transitions involve more of a radical change from the current environment and the cues that guide the child's behavior. While it may be easier for a child with ADHD to behave differently in very different situations, since the level of stimulation and the reinforcers and negative consequences for behavior are so different, getting the child to stop doing what he is doing and move to another situation in which he is expected to behave very differently can be quite difficult. Like the law of inertia that says a body in motion tends to stay in motion, ADHD children tend to keep doing what they are doing; they cannot easily stop or shift gears.

Although ADHD children often have problems sustaining their effort on one thing for a long period of time, these problems arise on tasks that they do not find very stimulating and for which they do not have much motivation. The other side of the coin is that when ADHD children are involved in something stimulating or intrinsically rewarding, such as fooling around, creating a disturbance, or playing a video game, they have difficulty shifting attention at someone's command.

Just as in transitioning within the same setting, the ADHD child needs preparation for transitioning from one situation to another. If the transition is a normal part of the daily routine, this routine should be written out on a schedule. The child should be given a five-minute warning before the transition, in order to finish what he is doing and prepare himself. The child should also be cued as to what behaviors will be expected of him in the new situation, such as keeping his hands to himself, staying near his parent, or doing what he is told. The adult should cue him to respond by asking him to repeat what he is going to do in five minutes (such as put away his paints or toys, get up, and walk to the kitchen). The child should be given verbal praise for responding correctly, and then more praise for behaving correctly when he is reminded. Failure to comply after one warning should result in a consequence, such as having the play material taken away for a day, or the loss of some privilege that day. If the child is on a point system, points should be given for ready compliance with the command.

SEQUENCING SKILLS

Helping an ADHD child cope with transitions is also helping him with sequencing skills. This helps him to develop more of a future orientation, which ADHD children need. Sequencing is an important component of intellectual functioning and one of the basic modes of learning and processing information. The process of sequencing easily lends itself to linear and logical thinking and to reducing a process to its simple component parts. This seems to be compatible with the reasoning style that is typical of many men. This is therefore an area in which fathers can make an especially strong contribution to their ADHD child's development. In addition, many children with ADHD have coexisting learning disabilities, which often involve a weakness in sequential processing.

Sequential processing is also important in the child's ability to interpret and respond to social cues. One subtest of the Wechsler Intelligence Scale for Children, an IQ test, consists of several series of pictures that tell a story, but they are in mixed-up order. Most of these stories involve people in interaction with each other. The child is instructed to put the pictures in the right order so they make a story.

The ability to understand a logical sequence of social events is critical to the understanding of cause and effect and to the ability to plan and react to events effectively.

Developing better sequencing skills is also important to the child's ability to take responsibility for his actions. For example, a child who gets into fights often might blame the other children for getting him angry. He might cite a remark that another child made to justify his own aggressive behavior. A closer examination of the event might reveal that the other child called him a name after being pushed. The child might also overlook something that took place the day before, in which he did something that got the other child mad at him, but which he forgot about by the next day. Not having events in their proper sequence permits the child to escape responsibility for the conflict.

The father can suggest going over the fight step by step, eliciting from his child the sequence of events slowly and calmly. A useful aid might be to take a marker and a large piece of paper to make a chart, filling in the spaces as the events are clarified. Spaces should be left between lines in order to fill in additional events in the sequence as they are recalled. After the events in the recent past are recalled (that day, for example) attention can be focused on the previous day or days as to what transpired between the two boys. The father can then show the child the sequence as it was recorded, and can question the child on any inconsistencies or missing information.

The father can help the child identify instances where an alternative response might have been better, and can help the child think through what the other child might have been thinking or feeling.

ARGUING AND FIGHTING

Endless arguments, bickering, and fighting too often characterize families affected with ADHD. This is especially true when more than one family member has ADHD, or when the ADHD child has developed a pattern of learned oppositional, defiant, and argumentative behaviors.

Arguing and fighting take on consistent forms over time. It is as if the interaction was scripted from the beginning. The specific words and content of the arguments might vary, but the format of the arguments, the pattern of intensity, interaction, build-up, crescendo, and resolution usually fit into predictable patterns. Family members might think that the argument is really over the specific issue being discussed, such as bedtime, cleaning up, discipline, or work schedules, but examining the pattern reveals that the sequence of events is usually the same regardless of the subject matter. Arguments, therefore, usually have more to do with the need to engage in a control struggle than with any specific issue.

Families in which ADHD or aggressive behavior is present in one of the children often have parent–child interactions that fit into certain patterns and have certain characteristics. It is reasonable to speculate that parent–parent interactions would also fit into certain patterns. Examining these patterns can provide a greater understanding of the traps that parents fall into. If a parent's goal is to teach his children better self-monitoring skills, it is important for the parent to learn these skills as well.

It is important that parents be aware of their own role in initiating and continuing control struggles with their children and their spouses. This means that it is important that parents look at the *process* of their arguments, not just at their *content*. This is a separate issue from who is right. Men seem to become preoccupied with rightness and wrongness, justice and fairness: children should do what they are told to do because the father is the authority and knows best. When this does not happen, many fathers persist in repeating responses that have already proven to be ineffective.

I often say to fathers, "Let's be scientific about this." I point out that they have come to me because what they are doing is not working. Although I might agree with them about what *should* happen, what *is* happening is quite different. They have tried to force their will on their child repeatedly, and the results are usually the same. In fact, we could probably predict the next struggle fairly accurately. Why, then, repeat behaviors that result in frustration and failure?

Parents get trapped in old patterns and in the mind-set of self-righteousness. Until parents take responsibility for the control struggles they get into with their children, they are doomed to repeat the same frustrations and failures and to see the problems escalate as they try more heavy-handed or desperate measures.

GIVING THE CHILD CONTROL

Sometimes it is helpful to give the child control over something that the parent so desperately wants him to change and that he seems unable to change. The parent can, under some circumstances, give the child control and give up the control struggle. I have used this technique when all of my attempts at insight, reinforcement control, and behavioral contracts have failed. It is simple, but, I think, very elegant. I adapted it from techniques that are recommended by Garber and colleagues (1995).

I say to the child, "You and your mother [or father or parents] fight all the time. Every day there seem to be so many fights, too many to keep track of. I do not know how they start or who does what. I want you to do something important for me over the next week. I want you to keep a chart of the number of fights between you and your parent(s) every day. The chart looks like this":

I continue, "Mark an X for each fight. Your goal is to have a lower number of fights each day than on the day before. If you go over the number of fights from the previous day, don't worry, just keep as your goal having fewer fights the next day."

This suggestion is almost always met with loud and vehement protests from the child: "But I don't start the fights!" "It's not my fault!" "You're saying it's all my fault." "My parents get off easy, they don't have to change!" "I'm not going to change unless my parents do something different, too." "Nothing's going to change unless my parents stop . . . or let me . . ." "What are you going to make me do differently?"

I reassure the child that I am not blaming him for the fights, and I am not letting his parents off the hook. I agree that everyone has to

	SUN	MON	TUES	WED	THURS	FRI	SAT
20							
19							
18							
17							
16							
15							
14							
13							
12							
11							
10							
9							
8							
7							
6							
5							
4							
3							
2							
1							

do things differently. I also do not want to get into specifics about the fighting right now. I am only asking him to keep track of the fights, since I value his perspective and judgment and want to take him seriously. I want him to do whatever he needs to do to reach the goal of decreasing the number of fights each day.

These instructions are similar to those traditionally given in bio-feedback training; the patient is told the goal, but not told how to reach it. For example, a biofeedback patient might have electrical sensors attached to his forehead that measure the tension or relax-ation in the muscles of his forehead. When he is in a relaxed state, there is less electrical discharge recorded by the electrodes, which transmit a signal to a monitor and keep a green light illuminated. When the muscles tense beyond a certain degree, the higher electric output causes a red light to illuminate. The individual is instructed to keep the green light lit. He is not instructed as to how to keep it lit. He is not told to relax his muscles, to arch his eyebrows in a cer-tain way, or anything specific. The feedback from the machine—the illumination of the red or green light, and the maintenance of the green light—is somehow enough for the patient to do whatever he needs to do to keep the green light illuminated.

Similarly, children who are told to decrease the number of fights they have each day with their parents are capable of doing just that. It is my impression that, with these children, with whom interven-tions into specific behaviors have not worked, specifying the goal without prescribing or proscribing specific behaviors is very benefi-cial. As can be seen from the comments cited above, these children already feel blamed for everything. Not specifying behaviors that they have to change removes some of this message. It says to them, "Just get the number of fights down. I won't tell you how to do it." They might imagine that their parents are responsible for the fights, and that they will decrease the fights by not engaging their parents in their problematic behaviors. I do not know what they are thinking. What appears to be true, however, is that this method leaves the attribu-tion up to the child, so he is free to attribute the fighting and the improvement in this interaction to whatever is useful to him, and whatever makes it possible for him to stop it. Prescribing specific be-havior, on the other hand, limits the possible attributions for the be-havior and the behavior change. For some children and adolescents, this might get in the way.

I have seen this method work time and again with children of la-tency age through the teen years. I have recently begun employing it with adults. Within two weeks, arguments between child and parents have typically decreased to one or two a day, and that gain has been maintained over several months. The child receives much praise for providing a useful service for the family, and for successfully bringing down the number of arguments. Note that the child is not blamed for the fights, but he receives credit for decreasing their frequency. When the child protests that his parents have not gotten any better, and that this has not changed him, I wholeheartedly agree with the child, and let him know that he is even more worthy of praise for persisting in the face of such difficult and unchanging parents. I point out that whereas we have not succeeded in changing his parents, the decrease in the number of arguments has certainly made his life saner, and we can discuss what he now is freed up to do because of his extra time and energy.

Having the child keep track of the number of fights also trains the child in self-monitoring skills. Children with ADHD are notoriously bad at social awareness; they don't know how often problematic incidents occur. Parents and teachers become frustrated about the frequency of disruptive behavior, and the child has no awareness that there is a problem.

Timmy, a junior high school student, complained about his teachers treating him harshly and unfairly. Although he was bright, he was resentful of having to sit in school all day and catch flak from his teachers. He tended to be the class clown, much to the amusement of his peers and the scorn of his teachers.

In therapy, Timmy related an incident in his Spanish class in which the teacher sent him out of the room. He thought her response was extreme and that she punished him harshly merely for talking out in class. Spanish was a very difficult subject for him, so it was particularly hard for him to pay attention. However, on closer questioning, it turned out that this was the second time that he had been asked to leave the class that week, and he had been kicked out of three other classes by three other teachers. He minimized each separate incident, and he was not aware that this was an unusually high number of "minor" incidents in a one-week period, covering several different situations and people.

When he was confronted with the quantity and frequency of these incidents, he began to see that the problem might be more serious than
he had assumed, and that he might have a part in creating the problem as well as an investment in stopping it.

Often, children with ADHD rope their fathers into arguments and
control struggles in which the father ends up struggling as much as
the child, and no matter what the consequences for the child, the
child ends up "winning" by the fact that he has achieved power and
control over his father. In my experience, children tend to be control
freaks. They seek out opportunities to be in control of adults, even at
great cost to themselves. They tolerate all sorts of deprivation and
punishment just to be able to control their parents' moods and actions. If a child succeeds in getting a parent angry at him, he has won.
If he succeeds in getting his parent to lose control of his temper, if he
controls what his parent does with his time, he has won, no matter
the cost to him. A father's loss of control can be reinforcing to the
child. Children, being smaller, weaker, and more dependent than
adults, have a need to exercise their control over the world, whether
or not it is good for them. The screaming and hitting and the chaos
can be very reinforcing for the ADHD child, because it is highly
stimulating.

Just as it is helpful to focus the child on decreasing the behavior
rather than determining who is right, it is important for fathers not
always to be so concerned with proving themselves right. It is usually more important for fathers to be helpful to the child than to get
the child to agree that the father is right. Being helpful with an ADHD
child often means helping the child to decrease undesirable behaviors and conform to the expectations of the environment. For example,
a father might insist on certain rules if his ADHD adolescent goes
over to a friend's house. The father might require that he call home
from the friend's house, that a parent be in the home, and that he be
back at a certain time. Certain privileges might depend on his following through on these expectations.

The child might question the rationale for these rules. He might
turn the discussion around from the issue of rules, limits, structure,

and predictability to one of whether his father trusts him, whether the father is adequate, or whether a child of his age should have more freedom. If the father's goal is to provide structure and consistency for the ADHD child, these other issues might be irrelevant. However, teenagers are notorious for being able to argue issues on their terms. The father might find himself arguing to justify his expectations on the basis of the child's criteria, and lose sight of the reasons the parent instituted the rules in the first place. It might be sufficient to hear the adolescent out, and then enforce the rules without having to justify them on the child's terms, and without falling into the trap of having to prove to the adolescent that the parent is reasonable and wonderful.

A similar situation occurs when the adolescent and parent see the same incident or behavior differently, and the adolescent ropes the parent into an argument over the reality of their different recollections.

Stephen's mother, Connie, who was mentioned earlier, cited several incidents in which Stephen lost control and became belligerent to the point that it frightened her. Stephen would become explosively angry and follow Connie around the house, badgering her, knocking on her bedroom door, and refusing to let her get away from him. In discussing these incidents, Stephen diverted Connie into a struggle over whether his behavior was that bad. He accused her of exaggerating. Connie would slip into very frustrating arguments with Stephen over how bad his behavior was, which went nowhere because Stephen would never admit that his behavior was so bad.

A similar scenario occurs when the parent insists that the child clean up his room, and then gets into a struggle with the child over whether the end result is adequate. Since the child and parent have different criteria for neatness, and the issue is of far greater importance to the parent, it is impossible for the parent to convince the child to adopt his criteria.

It is not necessarily important for the father to get the child to agree with him. The point is to help the child bring his behavior into conformity with the expectations of others and, by extension, society.

For example, no child likes to do homework, just as most adults do not like to do the paperwork their jobs entail. But liking or disliking homework or paperwork is irrelevant to whether people do it. They do it because it is expected of them; they are required to do it to succeed in school and at work.

A child is entitled to his perceptions that his behavior is not out of control, or that homework makes no sense, or that his parents' rules are obsolete. There is merit in helping a child learn to monitor whether his behavior meets the expectations of others just for the sake of being able to follow rules, to be aware of the expectations of others, and to be able to fit in with the environment. It is valuable for a child to learn that certain behavior is not allowed, or not appreciated by others, or could get him into trouble, no matter what he thinks about his behavior.

> Jerry, a 10-year-old boy with ADHD, refused to do his schoolwork or his homework. When I asked him why, he said, "Because I don't like school." My reply to him was, "So what?" What I was trying to communicate to Jerry was that not liking school was irrelevant to whether he should do his work. While we could try to make his schoolwork more "likable," that is, more stimulating, schoolwork was not necessarily there to be liked but to be done, and the long-term consequences of doing or not doing his schoolwork were being overlooked. I was not going to get into an argument with Jerry over whether he should or should not do his work based on whether it was in fact boring or interesting, or whether he should find school interesting. He had already decided that it was not. The issue was the long-term consequences, his ability to follow rules and meet his obligations, and how we could engineer consequences to be immediate and important to help him complete his work.

HELPING THE CHILD WITH HOMEWORK

Monitoring the homework of an ADHD child is usually a thankless but necessary job. Homework usually does not get done without an adult monitoring the process because ADHD children have a difficult time producing. Barkley's concept of ADHD being primarily a deficit in behavioral persistence is very applicable when it comes to homework.

Fathers often become very frustrated when they know that their child knows the material or is intelligent enough to learn it, but the child is more interested in playing video games or talking on the phone. Moreover, the child will not get his homework done in a timely way even though it would mean more time available for recreational pursuits! So, even when it is in the child's best interest to get his homework done, he fails to complete it in a timely way. This inefficiency is often not matched in other pursuits, as the child very easily figures out how to win at video games.

The ADHD child's failure to complete his homework often involves the father and child in control struggles. Since there is this emotionally charged atmosphere that develops around homework, the child's failure often becomes attributed to emotional factors, such as laziness or defiance, which in turn makes the father more emotional. This adds to the emotional stress and further removes the focus from ADHD.

Even more distressing to fathers are the ADHD children who do their homework but fail to hand it in. They lose their homework in the dark recesses of their desks or backpacks. These crumpled pieces of paper surface weeks later or at the end of the school term, when their desks and backpacks get cleaned out.

In contrast, a child who is merely oppositional and defiant would just not do his homework in the first place. This is not to say that oppositional and defiant behaviors are not part of the ADHD-homework picture. The greater the conflict between the child and his parents, the more these behaviors will develop. Homework represents a demand on the child to do work for which he has a low motivation, which is often uninteresting and unstimulating, and at a time in which he would much rather be doing other things. It is a demand to produce something within a time limit, with heavy demands on the child's organizational abilities. The child with ADHD has learned that avoiding the demands made on him saves him from humiliation and failure. He is expected to produce and achieve up to the level of his talents and intellectual abilities, which he cannot do on his own because of his deficits. Demands and expectations are made on him according to his talents and abilities, without equal consideration given to his attentional and organizational deficits. He is therefore given a message that addresses only part of him, and ignores an equally important part of who he is. Since he gets the message that he should be able to do what is expected of him, and he experiences great difficulty doing it, he has only himself to blame since there is no other "out" that he is allowed. Rather than subjecting himself to certain failure and embarrassment, he develops behaviors that help to avoid these unpleasant experiences.

It is therefore necessary to help the ADHD child with homework, not just to expect him to do it. The trick is to understand what sort of help is actually helpful. Different children have different capabilities for sustaining their attention and persisting in their work. It is unlikely that a child with ADHD will be able to complete all of his homework assignments in one sitting. Setting aside a half-hour or an hour after school as "homework time" without providing additional structure is likely to be unproductive.

Fathers might be especially well equipped to help their children with homework. Research on father–daughter relationships has shown that fathers take more consistently action-oriented roles with children than do mothers, and that their daughters respond with behavior that is more specific to the task at hand (Lamb 1981). Therefore, fathers might be especially adept at defining the tasks that need to be accomplished and monitoring their children's production. In reviewing the literature, Lewis and colleagues (1981) found that girls spent more time working on a task when they were with their fathers than when they were with their mothers.

Children with ADHD are most likely to work at the peak of efficiency and interest when a task is new. Novelty attracts the attention of the ADHD child, but its effect is short-lived. It is more productive to expect the child to work for ten minutes and then take a break, even if he is working productively, than to expect him to push on until he is tired or bored. If the child stops when he is still attentive, productive, energetic, and still has some more to give, he will be more motivated to return to the work after a short break. If the child works until he is bored, tired, and distracted, no matter how he felt at the beginning of the task, he will associate the task with negative feelings and will resist returning to it. The mention of homework will then elicit a negative psychological and physiological reaction in the child.

Therefore, it makes sense to set a timer for a limited amount of time, ten- or fifteen-minute increments, for example, depending on the child's ability to sustain his attention and effort, and expect him to do his homework in these small increments, with short breaks in between. Not only will the child stop working while he still feels productive and efficient, but there will also be a short-term reward available (in the form of a break) for his efforts.

ADHD children need help with the initial setup of homework time. This assistance can be regarded not as doing the work *for* the child, but as working *with* him to organize his work and make him more efficient. This is best done when the child gets home from school, after allowing for a short break. Planning an adequate amount of time for homework into the schedule should therefore occur before the child embarks on his after-school fun activities. In this way, engaging in recreational activities can serve as a reward for completing homework in an efficient manner. The child will also get the message that time for homework has to be budgeted in as a priority before recreation is considered.

A good first step is to sit down with the child where he will be working, make a list of all his homework assignments, and review any long-term responsibilities, such as book reports, projects, or tests for which he has to study. For long-term assignments and studying, establish daily goals and list them in measurable terms, such as "Read Chapters I and II," or "Review class notes from April 4 through 12."

The parent and child can estimate the amount of time that each assignment or study period will take. The time can then be totaled to get an approximation of the amount of work time required. Since many fathers complain about their ADHD children staying up too late to complete homework that they failed to anticipate would take so long, an ending time should be agreed upon. Taking into account other activities that the child might want to do, the parent can now plan on how much time to allow for breaks.

The next step is to discuss with the child the amount of time that he can be expected to work efficiently before tiring. The parent's observations will be important here, as might be his teachers' opinions, since the child might not have a realistic idea of his attentional limits. This is a good opportunity to engage the child in discussion. The child's perspective will reflect his skills in self-observation and time estimation. After deciding on the length of time for each period of work, the parent and child can set length of time for each break. Five or ten minutes might be an adequate amount of time for a break.

Next, list the assignments to be completed in the sequence in which they will be done. Ask the child whether it would be better to begin with the more challenging assignment, in order to have the most energy for the assignment that will require the most concentration, or with the easiest assignment, in order to get it out of the way and have an early experience of success. Or the child might be more organized if he followed the same sequence of subjects every night. In that case, a list would still be useful. Study periods and long-term assignments can be inserted. The chart can look something like this:

PAUL'S HOMEWORK CHART

Date: Length of work periods:

Start Time: Length of breaks:

End Time:

Assignment 1:   End time:

Assignment 2:   End time:

Assignment 3:   End time:

Assignment 4:   End time:

Assignment 5:   End time:

Assignment 6:   End time:

A buzzer or an alarm can then be set to the amount of time that the child should work before taking a break, and it can be left where the child can hear it when it goes off. Setting and resetting the timer can be the child's responsibility.

At first, the parent can sit down with the child and cue him to list his assignments, approximate the work time he will need, plan the length of the breaks, prioritize the assignments, and set the timer. After that, the parent can start with cueing the child to do one thing, and then each day or every two days, make him responsible for one additional step. The child can gradually take over more of the responsibility for management.

In planning the child's approach to completing his homework, the parent should understand and empathize with the child's feelings about the homework. In fact, empathizing with his feelings will eliminate one potential area of control struggle—the issue of how the child *should* be feeling. Empathy with feelings does not indicate agreement with a course of action. The parent can acknowledge that homework is boring while still maintaining that the child has to do it. It often helps to agree that the situation is aversive, and join with the child in developing the best way to deal with this unfortunate situation.

The parent can write comments on the assignment sheet or on a separate piece of paper when a certain piece of work was exemplary, or when the child put forth good effort. These comments can be kept in a separate folder for the child (Buchoff 1990).

HELPING THE CHILD WITH ORGANIZATION

Physical Organization

"Everything has a place" is a concept that needs to be heavily reinforced in an ADHD child's mind. Physical organization is often an underdeveloped skill. Not knowing where he placed things, putting things away in different places each time they are used, and looking for missing things are tremendous wastes of time and sources of frustration for these children and the adults who care for them. The child's relationship to the physical world often reflects the disorganization in his mind, and the disorganization he creates around himself makes his own disorganization worse.

Zentall and colleagues (1993) found that fathers of hyperactive children are more likely than mothers to teach their children to establish routines in putting away their belongings in consistent places, and are more likely to help the child retrace his steps to systematically search for lost objects. Fathers are also more likely to help their hyperactive children be more organized by suggesting that they make lists when they have multiple tasks to perform. A father's ability to help his child be more organized is especially helpful to children with ADHD, as they do not respond to more indirect or subtle approaches to managing their behavior (Fowler 1980).

Tom, a junior high school student, would do his homework and then fail to hand it in. Since his teachers counted his homework as a major part of his grade, this boy of above-average intelligence was failing some subjects and getting D's in others, despite reasonably good grades on tests and quizzes. If Tom's interest was in being oppositional, he simply would have refused to do his homework. However, his unaccounted-for homework assignments often turned up months later in his backpack, when it was too late to get any credit for them.

I suggested to Tom that he bring in his backpack and that we go through it together. Tom was very willing to do this, and the next week he brought in an enormous and heavy knapsack, which he carried around in school every day, and dumped its contents on my desk. He began by pulling out his large textbooks and notebooks, all of which he carried around the entire day in school. He was not organized enough to store what he did not need in his locker, because going to his locker between classes resulted in his being late for class. He was not able to take this detour efficiently. After the large and small books came the thin folders holding handouts and worksheets from various subjects. After that came a number of smaller items: outdated memos and notices from the school to be brought home, crumpled up worksheets and missing homework assignments that made it to the bottom of the bag and got crushed by the weight of everything else, and sundry other items like combs, keychains, pencils, and paper clips. I nicknamed the knapsack "the Black Hole," where anything that entered got sucked up and disappeared.

Tom threw out a lot of papers. We also examined the contents of his notebooks. There were few notes and lots of doodles. In the pockets that were supposed to be organized by subject were many misplaced assignments. In fact a piece of Language Arts homework that he had failed to hand in turned up in his Spanish folder.

Tom and I then began by finding a place for everything: homework, handouts, class notes, take-home notices. We color coded each of his folders according to subject and function (such as things to bring home to parents). We designated the front of each folder to be the place where homework for the next day was to be placed. We also developed a set order in which to place his folders into his backpack. I instructed Tom to lay out all of his folders each night, and to make sure that each homework assignment was placed in the front of the right folder. He was also to clean out his backpack each day.

A written checklist of these steps helped Tom to make sure that he was organized each night before going to bed. Another checklist served to remind him of what he had to walk out the door with in the morning.

One of the hardest things for Tom to do was to stop and file his papers in the right place before leaving each class when the bell rang. Tom was always in such a rush and so afraid of being late that he typically threw his papers into his backpack and ran out the door. Training Tom to stop and organize himself for even a fraction of a minute took a lot of work.

Tom agreed to bring his backpack in for inspections every month. We went through the same ritual each time, but his backpack was never as messy as it had been that first time. It became more organized and we spent a lot less time on it than at the beginning. Although it was clearly important for me to be monitoring the bag with Tom, he was doing the organizing all by himself during the school week without any active involvement by me or anyone else.

Verbal Mediation and Rules

Even when ADHD children are informed of the rules that they are expected to follow in a situation, they have difficulty remembering and following them without reminders (Maag and Reid 1994). In addition, these children have been found to be deficient in short-term memory when they have been exposed to information just once, whether that exposure was visual or verbal (Robins 1992). It is not surprising, therefore, that their memory for rules is impaired. Repeated exposure, however, can often improve memory (Robins 1992). Increasing the degree of semantic, or meaningful linguistic, content of the instructions also improves retention.

The ADHD child's impulsivity also interferes with his ability to conform to rules. Driven by impulsivity, his behavior is often governed by immediate needs and stimuli, rather than by more long-range awareness of consequences and social convention (Giddan 1991).

Given the deficits in short-term memory and the tendency toward impulse-governed behavior, it is understandable that the ADHD child can be helped to follow rules by using repetition and by teaching him verbal mediation, which is also called verbal self-guidance. Repetition is simple to understand, but takes discipline to practice. Parents often feel burdened by having to repeat themselves, because this should be unnecessary, and it makes them feel that they are not in control. When the parents are guiding their child through his evening routine, and they have to tell him ten times to brush his teeth while he ignores the parents, jumps on his bed, reads a book, or dawdles in putting on his pajamas, the parents are being controlled by the child, and the repetition commands are proof of the parents' helplessness.

Planning the repetition makes it useful, under the parents' control, strategic rather than nagging, and responsive to the child's ADHD. This takes more work up front, but if the parents consider the time and energy that go into repeatedly nagging the child, they will realize that they are doing a considerable amount of work anyway, only not in a way that is under their control and planning.

When telling the child the rules or expectations, it is helpful to remind him several times. For example, as bedtime approaches, it is a good idea to remind the child that in five minutes, he will be expected to put away his toys and go to his bedroom to change. You can then announce the sequence of activities, even if they are the same every night. If there is a severe deficit in following even well-rehearsed routines, it might be helpful to have the child repeat the routine back to the parent. Then, when actually following the routine, it might be helpful to remind the child each step of the way.

For example, you can tell your child to go to his room and put on his pajamas, or give him a cue that indicates that it is time to do this. When he is putting on his pajamas, you can tell him that brushing his teeth is next. It may seem silly to be saying the same things over and over, and your child might even protest, but he will let you know when this repetition is unnecessary when he begins to follow the routine on his own or with minimal cues.

Verbal mediation helps a child learn to provide this guidance to himself through teaching him to talk to himself as he is doing something. This technique might be familiar from times that we have tried to remember something that we were in danger of forgetting unless we repeated it, or when we have had to learn a new procedure. For example, if we are trying to memorize a telephone number that we are unable to write down, we might say the number to ourselves repeatedly until we call it. Or, if we are driving to an unfamiliar destination and following directions with which we are unfamiliar, we might repeat them to ourselves as we follow them.

This is a skill that can be taught. For example, you might want to introduce your child to a new peer, such as a child who has recently moved next door, with the hope that he can begin a new friendship on a positive note. You can tell him to keep in mind a series of things to do when they meet, such as say "Hello, I'm Adam," smile, and ask him what he likes to play with. Your child can practice this and repeatedly say it to himself.

Another useful application is in teaching the child to organize his homework. You can work with him on a sequence of behaviors, such as getting out his math folder, taking out his assignment sheet, doing the assigned worksheet, putting the completed assignment into the front pocket of the notebook, and putting the notebook into his backpack. You can coach him on saying this to himself in a low tone of voice as he does it the first couple of times.

REINFORCING THE PARENTS'
RELATIONSHIP WITH THE CHILD

Fathers often are not home as much as mothers are, even when both parents work full time. Fathers spend more time away from home than at home. It is therefore important for the father of the ADHD child to help his child keep their relationship "alive" when the father is not around.

There are several reasons why this is important: (1) The ADHD child is much more attuned to his immediate environment—the stimulation, the rewards, and the consequences—than to future events and anticipated changes in the environment. ADHD children seem to have a deficit in their ability to anticipate the future and hold it in mind. Helping the ADHD child to keep in mind his relationship with his father might help to preserve the benefits of that relationship, whether that be in the form of the control the child exercises in the presence of his father, the self-esteem the child gains from the relationship, or the sense of consistency and stability that this relationship reinforces. (2) The ADHD child has difficulty with transitions, such as when his father comes home. It is difficult for the child to adjust to his father's presence and change his behavior to accommodate his father's way of doing things, the things that he approves of and disapproves of (the things that the father rewards and punishes in the child), and the rules he enforces. The child experiences a loss of behavioral and emotional control. (3) The ADHD child has difficulty holding things in mind, maintaining a consistent picture of all the complex relationships, rules, and situations in his life and having them guide his behavior. What is immediately rewarding in a particular situation might not be as productive a guide for his behavior as something he has learned from his relationship with his father. For example, a boy might be teased at recess, and the most immediately satisfying thing for him to do in front of his peers might be to hit the boy who is teasing him. However, his father might have communicated to him not to escalate conflicts with peers and to walk away from such incidents. In the presence of his father, he might win his father's approval by handling the situation in a nonconfrontational manner. However, without his father present, hitting the other child might be more reinforcing. The more his father is mentally present, the more likely it is that what the father values and reinforces will influence the boy's behavior. (4) If the mother is home with the child more than the father, it bolsters the mother's position of authority to be seen as part of a co-parenting team. This prevents control struggles from focusing on one individual versus another.

One tool for helping the child to keep the relationship with his father in mind is to give the child a concrete way to represent what the father is doing and where he is when he is not present. This is also a useful tool for children whose fathers travel a lot on business.

Alan, the father of two ADHD boys, was in sales and traveled part of each month. To reinforce his relationship with the boys, and to help maintain the active presence of their relationship in their minds, Alan and his wife made index cards depicting what Alan was doing at different moments of each day. The cards might have had pictures cut out from magazines, such as an airplane for when Alan was flying to his destination, between destinations, or returning home, or a map depicting the cities in which Alan would be staying. The cards could also have drawings made by the children or by one of the parents. The drawings, for example, could have a picture of Alan wearing the favorite tie of one of his children, or a tie given to him by his child as a gift that he will be wearing to one of his meetings.

Another possibility is for the father to make a recording of his voice for the child. This could contain a message for the child to play each day that the father is away, wishing the child good morning, wishing him luck on some activity he will engage in that day (a baseball game, a dance class, a school project), and reminding him of important behavioral rules and expectations. The father might also record himself reading a story to the child, which the child and the mother can read along with at bedtime.

The father can also leave a note for the child to find each day, with the same types of messages that he would leave on a recorded message. The note can also remind the child of special activities that they will do together when the father returns. Even ordinary activities that the father and child do together regularly can be special to a child, such as going out to breakfast on the weekend, or taking a weekly trip to the town recycling station or to the local hardware or home supply store, or cutting the grass.

Parents can also make a calendar on which they can depict the places in which the father will be and his activities, as they might do on the index cards mentioned above. The calendar can also be used to count the number of days until the father's return.

It is also helpful if the father calls home every day to review the day with his child, as well as to reinforce compliance with the rules at home. If there is a computer in the home, the father could send the child a daily e-mail.

TEACHING THE CHILD SELF-SOOTHING

Maintaining control over his emotional state is often difficult for the child with ADHD. In fact, many parents initially suspect that something is wrong not because of the child's poor attention span or hyperactivity, but because of his extreme anger, emotional volatility, and exaggerated or prolonged responses even to minor incidents. The child finds it hard to let go and move on to other things.

Jeff and Peggy were concerned because their son Sammy would become so upset over minor squabbles with classmates that he would be unable to concentrate on his schoolwork for hours afterward, and would instead be preoccupied with getting back at the other student. They could not understand this behavior because Sammy was usually a kind, loving, and fun child. They were concerned that he had some unresolved anger or psychological conflict that they could not account for.

The history revealed that Sammy was a highly intelligent boy who had difficulty completing his work and following multistep directions. His teachers were concerned about his variable school performance and inconsistent grades. Psychological testing revealed deficits on tests that assessed attention on auditory and visual tasks. There were no

indicators from the family history to suspect a serious emotional problem. The child had ADHD and its attendant problem with emotional and
behavioral self-control.

This problem has often been referred to as a difficulty with self-
soothing, which can be conceptualized as the child's ability to calm
himself when under stress. It is the ability to control and regulate one's
internal emotional and physiological state when that state is disrupted
from its normal balance (homeostasis).

Events that are upsetting, anxiety-provoking, anger-provoking, or
disappointing to us set off an emotional reaction that in most cases is
immediately and automatically modulated internally. This ability
develops at a very young age by the repeated actions of parents and
caregivers in responding to our distress and soothing us by holding
us, speaking to us calmly, or responding with clear and firm limits, as
is appropriate to our age and the situation. Children vary constitu-
tionally in their own abilities to be soothed. Some children are naturally easy to soothe and some are much more difficult. Before this
self-soothing ability develops, the infant experiences being flooded
with distress when his internal regulation is thrown off, such as when
he is hungry, uncomfortable, tired, or frightened. Over time, through
repeated experiences of frustration and soothing by his caregivers,
the child develops the ability to regulate his own internal state. He
develops fine gradations of feelings according to the situation and the
disruption the situation causes. Anger can be experienced as mild
irritation or annoyance, hostility, or intense rage. Depression can be
experienced as sadness and disappointment or as an intense, consum-
ing mood disruption.

Past infancy, emotions are normally no longer an all-or-nothing
event—either on or off. However, children with ADHD still seem
to experience their emotions in this way. They may be particularly
vulnerable to temper tantrums or intense rage reactions, or, at the
other end of the spectrum, unrestrained happiness that becomes
manifested as giddiness or silliness and therefore is experienced by
others as inappropriate and annoying. As adults, many of these individuals have poor frustration tolerance and are easily annoyed and

irritated. They are often quick to anger, and minor annoyances will be experienced internally with the same intensity as strong anger. They often have trouble dealing with co-workers and others. At home, their family members have to walk on eggshells out of fear of upsetting them. Their anger often seems to come out of the blue. Family members cannot understand what would get the individual so upset, and the individual with ADHD cannot understand why those around him do not see that they are upsetting him.

It is therefore often necessary for fathers to teach their children emotional self-control rather than just enforcing limits. When a father sets limits on an upset child with ADHD, the child's emotional reaction might escalate and continue escalating until he is out of control and may present a danger to himself or to property. Furthermore, his inability to calm himself keeps him socially immature and makes him disruptive to others around him. His failure to control his emotions might occur when he is not violating limits, but just reacting to minor annoyances, such as an article of clothing not fitting the right way.

When the child loses control, the father must judge whether to set a limit or intervene to help the child regain control. To be effective, it is very important for the father to understand what calms or soothes the child and what escalates the intensity of his emotional reaction. Men tend to be very good at understanding the notions of control and self-control and at helping a child gain self-control, but they may have trouble with empathy, that is, experiencing things the way the child experiences them.

Some parents find that sitting with their child and holding him firmly in an all-enveloping hug works to calm him down. However, many children have a strong need for personal space, and holding and hugging them when they are out of control will further agitate them.

In helping a child with ADHD calm himself, it is important to take a direct rather than a distant approach. It is not enough to ask or to tell the child to calm down. It is not enough to talk to the child from across the room.

Brandon, the father of Adam, a 10-year-old with ADHD, tried to intervene whenever Adam became loud and aggressive, which he did when he experienced frustration playing a game with a peer or a sibling.

Brandon had variable success, although he placed himself close to Adam and spoke in a loud, commanding voice. I suggested that he squat down to get to Adam's level physically, place his hands gently on Adam's shoulders, look him in the eye, and tell him firmly but gently to calm down. In this way, Brandon would make sure that Adam was attending to him, that other distractions were eliminated, and that he could make Adam focus on the one goal—regaining his composure.

It is important to gauge what personal distance is optimal for each child. Getting too close physically might agitate him more. Maintaining too much of a distance might not allow him to attend to the message. This is a trial-and-error process, but it is very important to listen to the child and respect his verbal and nonverbal cues about when Dad is too close or too far away.

A child might not want to be held or even touched. It might be sufficient to get right in front of the child, face to face, and tell him repeatedly in a calm but firm voice, "Calm down," and refuse to discuss anything else with him until he has regained control. The primary focus should be on regaining self-control rather than on any activity or any disagreement to be resolved.

Many children do not initially understand that their behavior is out of control, unusual, or unacceptable to others, no matter how obvious it may be to the parents and everyone else. They are just being themselves, reacting as their bodies trigger them to. It is therefore important to label this behavior for them, to be objective outside observers of their behavior, and to give them the language with which to understand themselves. It is useful to use a word to label the behavior in a descriptive but nonpunitive way. Describing the child's behavior as "fussing," or "busy," and using this repeatedly, can help the child to identify patterns in his behavioral and emotional responses so they no longer seem like disconnected, random events. Parents often tell their children, "Your behavior is inappropriate." The word *inappropriate* feels like an antiseptic, abstract, adult word, that might not be meaningful to a child.

Just as it is necessary to teach the ADHD child to soothe himself, it is very important for parents to help each other soothe themselves and keep their emotions in check. Life with a child with ADHD can become so chaotic, frustrating, unpredictable, and emotionally intense that it taxes the coping skills of even the most composed and mature parent. There is the danger, at certain moments (such as homework time or dinner time) of the household becoming a free-for-all with everyone yelling and screaming in frustration. It does not help the child to maintain self-control if the parents are out of control. The parents' intensity just serves as a further stimulus for the child.

MAKING THE CHILD A PARTNER IN BEHAVIOR MANAGEMENT

Managing an ADHD child's behavior involves things that we do *for* the child. Much of what is effective in working with these children involves managing the physical and social environment, including the rewards and consequences for the child's behavior. But how valuable will this be in the long run if the child does not learn how to monitor and control his own behavior independently? It is important for the child to learn to internalize the rules, limits, and values that his parents are imposing on him, so that he can establish an effective way of responding to the demands of the environment on his own by the time he is an adolescent.

It is important to try to make the child an active participant in managing his behavior. Even young children can make meaningful choices about their behavior when the options are clearly laid out for them by the parent. Three-year-olds can respond to "yes or no" questions and make choices accordingly. The younger the age at which a child participates in his own behavior management, the better.

> Bob, a 9-year-old ADHD boy, had several chronic behavior problems. He often fought or was bossy with peers, and in spite of being intelligent and athletic, he had few friends. He did not comply with his parents' commands most of the time, and delayed doing chores. He had a poor sense of time. In addition, he often got into control struggles with one or both parents during his morning and evening routines,

when there was more of an emphasis on doing things quickly and efficiently in a short period of time.

Bob's father, Phil, sat down with him one weekend day when there was no performance pressure. He said, "Bob, you know that you and I, and you and Mom get into fights and arguments a lot." Bob readily agreed with that. Phil stated the problem without assigning blame, and in a way that posed it as a problem in Bob's life. He continued, "I don't imagine that these fights are pleasant for you. They don't make you happy, do they?" Bob easily agreed with his father on these points. "I am going to try some things to help us all to fight less, and I would like your cooperation," Phil continued.

Phil introduced the idea of a solution that would help Bob with something that bothered Bob, and he did not give Bob a choice over whether this new method would be implemented. As Bob's father, Phil did not need to ask his permission to implement a new disciplinary method. This was clear in the way that he communicated the idea to Bob.

The idea was to label or identify the areas of difficulty: "There are a few things that we get into fights or disagreements about. What things can you think of?" Bob mentioned chores and homework. Phil asked him if he could think of anything else, and Bob did not offer other instances. Phil said, "I can think of some others. In the morning we often argue about whether you are getting ready on time, and at night we fight about your brushing your teeth and getting into your pajamas when you are supposed to."

After Bob and Phil identified four or five problem areas, Phil suggested working on just one of these areas in order to decrease the amount of fighting. He asked Bob to name the situation that bothered him the most, and then asked him to choose one to work on first. When Bob selected one, Phil discussed with him how difficult Bob thought it would be to change this situation, and they discussed whether it was a realistic one to tackle first.

Bob and Phil agreed to work on the morning routine first. Phil identified the problem as the fact that he and Bob's mother had to constantly remind him of what he was supposed to do and to keep after him to do these things quickly enough so that he would make the school bus on time. Bob and Phil agreed on a standard sequence of events in the morning that Bob would be responsible for: getting himself up and out of bed, getting washed, getting dressed, eating breakfast, brushing his teeth, and getting his books together. They also agreed that Bob would get his clothes out the night before to make the morning go more efficiently. Phil made sure that Bob had a working alarm clock. They also agreed that there would be no other activity allowed, such as watching TV, until the entire morning routine was completed.

Bob and Phil agreed on a checklist that contained each of the items to be completed, in sequence, with time goals written next to the item to identify the time by which each should be finished. They then discussed an appropriate reward for completing the entire sequence on time with no more than one reminder. The reward they agreed on was a fifteen minute later bedtime for that night, provided that Bob's homework was completed. But if Bob failed to complete his morning routine, his bedtime would be fifteen minutes earlier for that night. Given the time constraints in the morning, it was not possible to have a reward available immediately for Bob. The best that they could do was to have a reward that Bob could use that same day.

Phil also listed the natural rewards that would come with success, such as Bob's earning the good will and trust of his parents, having a more peaceful household, and having more time for the things Bob liked to do because less time would be spent on arguing, time-out, and grounding.

Phil agreed to give Bob one free reminder during the morning, including getting him out of bed if Bob did not respond to the alarm. He also made it clear that after two reminders there would be no more, and Bob would have to go to school late if need be and suffer the consequences in school, which usually meant serving a detention after school. Phil also wrote down the other natural negative consequences for failure, such as losing the trust and good will of his parents, a tense household, wasted time, and a decreased likelihood that his parents would give him greater freedom and liberty in the near future.

As Bob completed each step of his morning routine, Phil checked this item off on the checklist. Bob eventually took over this responsibility. His parents started dealing with Bob more calmly in the morning, and realized that they were setting up clear choices for him that would result in his either getting himself to school on time or late.

Phil realized that Bob's ADHD prevented him from structuring himself adequately to get himself out of the house on time. He needed to set up the structure for Bob, which would train him to monitor how he was fitting into what Phil defined as a reasonable time frame for doing things. Phil imposed his own sense of time on Bob, and gave him the tools with which to measure the adequacy of his performance within that structure.

When the morning routine was going more smoothly for two months, Phil introduced the idea of working on another problem area. Phil and Bob identified keeping friends as the next problem to tackle. Phil asked Bob what he thought went wrong with him and his friends. Bob's responses mostly involved wrongs that he felt that his friends had committed toward him. He said that certain kids were selfish, would not do what he wanted to do, and would not give him a turn. The latter complaint was related to Bob's need to always go first and his anger when his friends would not permit him to do so on every occasion.

Phil told Bob that he understood why these things would get him upset, and while he could not guarantee that the other children would change, he had some ideas of things that Bob might do differently that might make his friends treat him better. Again, he appealed to Bob's own sense of unhappiness with the way things were going with his friends. He also did not argue with Bob's perception that his friends did things that made him mad.

Phil asked Bob for some ideas about what would make a child liked by his friends—what traits or behaviors would help a child get along with his peers better. Phil was on a productive track here, since research has shown that children with ADHD tend to *know* the correct behaviors to do, they just have difficulty *doing* them when the situation calls for it.

With his father's help, Bob was able to name a number of behaviors that were important in making friends: waiting your turn, being willing to do what someone else wants to do even if it is not your first choice, saying "please" and "thank you," and stopping yourself from fighting when you are angry. Among these behaviors, Phil recognized several that were a problem for Bob. He suggested that he and Bob keep track of how often Bob did two of these behaviors, to help him with friends and to help him be a better role model or teacher for his friends. This latter idea was particularly appealing to Bob. Many children with ADHD are natural leaders, or try to be leaders in that they want to get their way all of the time and be in charge. He liked the idea that he could do something that the other kids would want to follow.

The two behaviors that Bob and Phil selected were (1) agreeing to follow someone else's suggestion without complaining, which was labeled "Letting others have their way," and (2) stopping himself from fighting when angry, which was labeled "Stop yourself from fighting."

It is important to label behaviors in the positive terms that you want to promote, rather than just telling the child to stop doing the undesirable behaviors. For example, for the first behavior identified, Phil was concerned that Bob butted in line to get in front of others, that he became argumentative when others wanted a turn before him, and that he yelled at other kids when they made him wait. Phil could have defined the goal in terms of what he did not want Bob to do, such as "Don't butt in," "Don't argue," or "Don't yell." However, telling a child what not to do does not inform him about what the parent wants him to do instead. Unless the child has an understanding of what he should do in place of what he is doing, simply stopping what he is doing leaves a vacuum. The easiest thing for a child to do to fill the vacuum is to do what he has been doing all along—the very behavior that the parent wants him to stop.

The second identified behavior, stopping himself from fighting, might seem at first glance to contradict this principle. It would be possible to identify the goal as "Cooperate," or "Keep your hands and feet to yourself," or several other descriptors, many of which would be adequate. However, Phil was trying to teach Bob to do something positive in learning to inhibit his aggressive responses. Therefore, he was not only trying to get Bob to *stop* fighting, he was trying to help him learn how to *stop himself* from fighting. In other words, it was not just the elimination of the fighting behavior that he was trying to communicate to Bob, it was the substitution of inhibitory responses.

For each of these behaviors, Phil worked with Bob at identifying when these situations occurred with his peers, as well as identifying similar situations when they were together.

For example, for "Follow someone's suggestion," Phil asked Bob to think of times when a friend wanted to do something and Bob did not. He reviewed how Bob felt and what he did, what the friend did, what the outcome was, and how Bob felt about the outcome. He asked Bob to think of a more desirable outcome and then work backward to figure out how to get there.

Phil then told Bob that he would point out to Bob examples of his following someone else's suggestion when he observed it happening. During the coming weeks, Phil pointed out to Bob whenever there was an occasion in the family in which Bob's preferences differed from those of others in the family, and how Bob handled it.

Stopping Bob from fighting when he was angry was a bit more difficult. When Bob exploded in anger, it seemed to come on him suddenly, without warning, and in full force. Phil began by helping him identify those situations that made him angry, and certain peers who were more likely to elicit an angry reaction in him than others. He then talked to Bob about recognizing the signs of anger building up in him. He and Bob identified things like feeling tension in his hands, having thoughts of running away or hurting the other child, or having the urge to yell or insult the other child.

Then Phil coached Bob on how to calm himself when he began to have these sensations. He practiced with Bob physically turning away from the situation and counting to ten, taking several deep breaths, and saying to himself "Stay calm, walk away, don't fight."

Phil then suggested a report card by which they could rate Bob's behavior on these two dimensions each day. He made a chart:

	LETTING OTHERS HAVE THEIR WAY	STOP YOURSELF FROM FIGHTING
BOB'S GRADE		
DAD'S GRADE		

Each time that Bob interacted with his peers and Phil observed the interaction, such as when Bob had a friend over, or when he had a soccer game, they would sit down together afterward and independently give Bob a letter grade as to how he did on each of the behaviors. Bob and Phil would grade Bob without revealing their grades to each other. Then they would let the other see the grades and discuss their reasons for giving the grades they did.

One early discussion occurred after Bob gave himself an A for letting others have their way, and Phil gave him a C. When Phil asked Bob why he gave himself an A, Bob replied that he let his friend have a turn hitting the baseball while Bob pitched. Phil agreed that Bob had done that, and praised Bob for it. He also pointed out that Bob had been reluctant to give up hitting and switch with his friend, and finally did so only after his friend became quite angry and threatened to leave. Also, Bob resisted changing activities when his friend got tired of what they were doing.

There were also occasions where Bob was a very harsh critic of himself. On the other dimension, "stop yourself from fighting," Bob once gave himself a D because he lost his cool with a friend and called him a name. Phil had given Bob a B on that occasion, and pointed out to Bob that his friend had provoked him for a long time, and that Bob had kept his cool throughout most of the taunting, and had even tried unsuccessfully to change the subject several times. Bob's outburst was actually milder than his previous outbursts had been under more minor provocations.

ADHD children are often poor judges of their own behavior in social settings. They tend to lose sight of the big picture, and often exaggerate the importance of one event or of something minor. They often perceive things in ways that others do not, so their interpretation of events differs from that of peers. This has been borne out in research on how ADHD children respond to a well-known personality measure, the Rorschach inkblot test. Children with ADHD respond in atypical or unusual ways. Their perceptions are of things that the typical, non-ADHD child would not commonly see when looking at these inkblots. These findings indicate that ADHD children tend to have poor reality perception. That is, they fail to see the world in the same way as their peers, and their perceptions or interpretations of events often do not correlate with those of others.

In reviewing the literature on aggressive boys, Whalen and Henker (1985) found that aggressive boys collect less information before they judge a peer, and that they remember fewer specific details of the interaction. This results in inaccurate interpretations of events, leading to inappropriate reactions, and more negative opinions of them by their peers. This increases the social rejection that they experience and the number of fights that they get into.

The report card technique can also be used to train ADHD children to see their behavior more objectively, as others see them. Phil was helping Bob to gain the perspective on his own behavior that Phil had and that Bob lacked. He was helping Bob to step back and get a sense of the big picture, instead of focusing on one detail that might have been emotionally important to Bob. Given Bob's low self-esteem and history of social failures, it was also often difficult for him to recognize when he was successful.

Parent involvement in teaching their children skills in social competence has been found to work. Bhavnagri and Parke (1991) found that children exhibited greater social competence with their peers when their parents facilitated their social interaction. Unfortunately, fathers were less likely than mothers to adopt this role of social facilitator, indicating that this is an area in which fathers can become more involved.

THE PARENTS' AWARENESS OF THEIR OWN THOUGHTS AND FEELINGS

We all develop patterns of thinking and feeling about things that are often outside of our awareness. Children with ADHD often develop long-lasting reputations of being troublemakers that follow them from grade to grade and class to class. These reputations can instill expectations in teachers who hardly know the child, so that when a group of children is being talkative or disruptive, the child with the bad reputation will be the one who gets caught or punished. The teacher might be unaware of treating the child any differently, but the preconceived expectations that he has for this child influence his emotional reaction and his interpretation of events when he observes the child acting inappropriately.

These unstated expectations also influence how fathers feel about and react to their own children. This might be easier to see if there are two or more children in the home. It is useful for fathers to consider the most difficult time of the day in their interaction with the child. Perhaps it is the bedtime routine, because there is so much to do, because the father wants some time alone, and because the father is exhausted after a long day at work or with the children.

Most children dawdle in doing their bedtime routine. But if the parent expects a hard time, any minor annoyance is likely to trigger feelings of "Here we go again!"

You might start the evening routine with the expectation that things will go wrong, and might be geared up for a struggle, waiting for something to happen. Or if the child is generally pleasant and cooperative, you will have the opposite expectations. When this easygoing child does something to delay the routine, which might be as challenging or worse than something that the ADHD child has done, it might be easier to tolerate it and react with humor. When two children fight, you might automatically assume that it is the ADHD child who started the fight, even as you consciously struggle to be fair.

While feelings of frustration, anger, and humor might seem to come automatically, they are related to an internal dialogue that fathers carry out with themselves. Examining your immediate emotional reactions to things that your child does enables you to recognize things that you are saying to yourself that are outside of your awareness.

For example, when you hear your child and a peer or sibling screaming at each other, and you rush in to referee the fight, you might be saying to yourself, "He always ruins his play dates," or "I can't leave him alone with anyone," or "He's always causing trouble," or some other statement that communicates a negative belief or expectation about the child. You can also examine your statements to yourself as you approach any interaction with your child, such as the bedtime routine. You might be calm on the outside, but be saying to yourself, "He'll give me a hard time at some point before he goes to bed."

These thoughts and beliefs influence your feelings and expectations of your child, as well as your interpretation of events in which your child is involved. Although these thoughts might be realistically based on numerous negative interactions with and observations of your child, they also set you up to make negative interactions more likely, and decrease the possibility that you will find opportunities to observe and enjoy your child behaving positively. Your assumptions also make it more likely that you will react more negatively or punitively to undesirable behavior than you would with another child, causing your relationship with your child to be even more negative. Your child might come to expect mostly negative interactions with you, which will detract from his seeing you as a possible source of positive reinforcement. He will then be less likely to behave positively when he is around you.

As Braswell and Bloomquist (1991) point out, it is important to examine these negative beliefs, and to recognize how they affect a parent's relationship with his child, and the messages that the parent is sending to the child about who he is and what the world expects from him.

AGGRESSION

Hyperactive boys are often prone to highly aggressive behavior. Their impulsivity, poorly controlled activity, and poorly regulated emotions create a volatile mix that leads them to react aggressively when frustrated, instead of finding alternative solutions.

Fathers are often ambivalent about aggressive behavior in their sons. Although many fathers communicate that fighting is wrong, and that starting a fight is unacceptable, they will be less clear about how their sons should handle provocations from peers.

Fathers give a variety of messages to sons about aggression. They range from telling the boy to walk away from any fight and tell an adult, to ignoring a provocation three times before he retaliates, to "never start a fight but if someone starts with you fight back with all you've got." Boys take the messages that their fathers give them about aggression very seriously. A father might get some satisfaction from knowing that his son is tough and can beat his peers in a fight. Although he might caution his son against fighting, it might be hard for him to hide his pride in his son for physically besting his rivals and not being a wimp.

Permission to be aggressive, even if it is qualified, is difficult to ignore. This does not mean that children should be taught never to defend themselves. It is important that fathers be aware of their own feelings about aggression, because these get communicated to their sons. Fostering aggression in one's son because it gives Dad a feeling of satisfaction might not be doing the son any good.

Fathers often counsel their sons either to fight back or walk away. Their choices of strategies for dealing with aggression tend to be more limited than are mothers' (Mills and Rubin 1990). Although fathers often see dealing with aggression as a "male thing," mothers tend to have more knowledge about their children's behavior because they delve into the complexities of their children's relationships with others. They seek more information about their children and about the context in which their behavior occurs. Mothers can therefore be good resources for generating alternative strategies for dealing with aggression.

The mother is more likely to know the history of her child's relationship with the antagonist because of her more extensive experience with her child and her greater interest in these matters. Mothers might be better able to instruct their children as to what children to avoid because of their history, and thereby prevent aggressive interchanges from occurring. When provocations do occur, mothers might be better able to guide their child as to what to say to the other child or what to do to de-escalate the conflict, because of their knowledge about the subtleties of the relationship of the two children.

Mothers can help fathers guide their children to react differently with different peers, and to understand with whom they can joke around, with whom they can be physical, and with whom they can play competitive games. They can guide their children as to how to back away from an escalating interaction with different peers. They can also make their children more aware of the signs that other children give off when they are angry, through their knowledge of the nuances of other children's personalities.

Children can also be taught to recognize anger building up in themselves. A preventive measure is to teach the child which peers are most likely to elicit feelings of anger and aggressive behavior in them, and to avoid these children or make their interactions with them brief or very structured. Parents can also review with the child signs that he is getting angry, so there is an awareness prior to the explosion of rage. For example, a child might come to recognize certain physiological signs, such as his heart beating faster, or his face feeling warm, or physical signs such as clenching his teeth or a tightening in his stomach. He might also become aware that his voice rises when he is getting frustrated, or that he suddenly feels like leaving but does not. Recognizing the warning signs of anger is the first step to planning what to do about it. It is then that a father can coach his child on whether to walk away or say something to his peer. With this coaching in self-awareness and strategizing about behavior, many fights can be avoided.

HELPING THE CHILD UNDERSTAND ANOTHER PERSON'S FEELINGS

The term *empathy* is mentioned several times in this book. It is vitally important in human relationships that individuals attempt to understand how other people experience situations, how they feel about things, and how they understand things. It is important that individuals understand that other people experience, feel, and think about situations in ways that might be very different from their own, but that are equally as valid as their own. It is also important that individuals take the additional step of trying to experience events in the way that other people do.

Empathy is important in the relationships between husband and wife and between parent and child. With the differences between men and women that are discussed in this book, it seems likely that women would find it easier or more natural to be empathic with another person than would men. The easier empathic understanding achieved by women provides an important model for men from which to learn. It is important for men to develop this ability both for the purpose of understanding and working effectively with their spouses, and for the purpose of tuning in to their child in order to be a more effective authority. It is also an important skill for the ADHD child to develop in himself. ADHD teens in particular often lack a sense of empathy for other people. This lack of empathy often perpetuates the trouble that they get into.

Timmy, who was mentioned earlier, was frequently getting kicked out of class, and always had several of his teachers angry at him. This was in spite of his friendly demeanor and his good sense of humor. Timmy just could not understand why his teachers could not take a joke. When he made fun of them or of something they were teaching, the entire class was in stitches. Timmy was the center of attention, with the entire class, except the teacher, laughing at his antics. Timmy was not just quietly funny. He was loud and persistent, and frequently got out of his seat to provide "visuals" for his jokes. His attitude toward his teachers was that they were just too uptight and that they were unfair. Since he saw what he was doing as being perfectly reasonable, and the teachers' reactions as being unreasonable, he saw no reason to stop.

In my work with Timmy, instead of focusing on his intent to be funny, I focused on the sequence of behaviors that occurred when he got into trouble. We looked at the teachers' reactions in the context of what the teachers were trying to do, and the disruption of the classroom that made that impossible.

If Timmy had trouble grasping this point, I had him look at the teachers' anger. I tried to help him to realize that, for a teacher to be that angry, she must have been feeling very frustrated or hurt herself. I took the focus off whether the teacher *should* have been angry (from Timmy's perspective) and on to the fact that she *was*, for whatever reason. This distinction was critical, because it helped to take Timmy out of his perspective and his justifications for his actions, and deal with the reality that the teacher *was* angry or hurt, and therefore could be expected to act a certain way. By understanding that the teacher had certain feelings, Timmy was able to make the connection with similar feelings that he had had himself.

Ryan, another adolescent, dismissed his younger sister's crying and complaining after he had lightly pushed her. Ryan's mother was very upset about her daughter's distress and about Ryan's difficulty understanding it. Ryan shrugged off his actions by claiming that his sister was overreacting, and that he had only tapped her lightly.

By getting the focus off how hard Ryan had pushed his sister, and whether or not he had intended to hurt her, we were able to focus on Ryan's sister's feelings instead, as facts that had as much legitimacy as observable actions. When Ryan defended himself by saying that his sister's feelings were overblown in relation to the incident, I was able to focus him on why someone might overreact or seemingly exaggerate an emotional response. Ryan was able to acknowledge that, although his sister might not have been physically hurt, perhaps she was feeling emotionally vulnerable in dealing with Ryan, who was older, bigger, and stronger than she was.

Empathy did not come easily to either of these two boys. It took repeated exercises like the ones described above to reinforce the point. To help these boys develop a better understanding of other people, it was necessary to break specific incidents down into their parts and look at the events in a step-by-step manner. Then it was necessary to take the focus off the boy's feelings, intentions, and opinions, and walk them step by step through the other person's point of view. This was aided by making the boys partners in the discovery process, by asking them questions: "What do you think she might have been feeling to act that way?" "How do you think she felt when she was trying to teach and the whole class was laughing, you were shouting, and you were out of your seat?"

Empathy is a skill that can be taught to or whose development can be nurtured in the ADHD child by breaking down the instructions into small components and discussing them while providing the child with concrete cues as to the possibilities to consider.

SUMMARY

- Fathers can help their ADHD children cope with transitions by developing a script for the transitional times. This can be used at home or at school.

- Fathers can help their children develop better sequencing skills through charting and reviewing events, which will help them to anticipate the future, and can help with the development of cause-and-effect knowledge in social interactions.

- Arguments and fights usually follow predictable patterns. Fathers can help their children take responsibility for monitoring these conflicts and for reducing their incidence.

- Specific ways of structuring homework can prevent control struggles and help the child be more productive and responsible. The child can be made a partner in homework organization.

- Fathers can help their children establish routines and procedures for the organization of their physical belongings.

- Teaching the child verbal mediation and using planned repetition of rules can help the child remember procedures and rules.

- Fathers can help their children keep their relationship with their father in mind when the father is not present through the use of index cards, pictures, and calendars that illustrate what the father is doing and when he will be returning home, and through the use of recordings of the father's voice.

- Fathers can teach their children to soothe or calm themselves in order to contain out-of-control emotional reactions.
    - The child's needs for personal space and his individual tolerance for physical closeness must be respected.

- Parents must help each other maintain calm when dealing with their children's upsets.
- Using words helps the child to label the problem.

- The child can become a partner in managing his behavior.
  - The father should appeal to the child's self-interest, discussing how his behavior creates problems for him. The father should outline the problem without assigning blame. The father should discuss this with the child during a nonstressful time.
  - The father should introduce the idea of finding a solution and request the child's cooperation.
  - With the father's help, the child can make a list of specific problem behaviors, and select one on which to work first that has a reasonable chance of success.
  - The desired behavior should be labeled in a positive, not a negative, way.
  - Father and child can develop sequences of behaviors and checklists, which are written down, to clearly define the desired behaviors to change, and rewards and consequences for compliance and noncompliance.
  - Rewards and consequences should be things that are enforced during that day, as soon after the behavior as possible.
  - What the parent will or will not do to help should be specified.
  - Natural consequences (like trust, respect, and good feelings) that accompany success should be listed.
  - Following success in one area, the next area to work on should be defined.

- For peer problems, a social skills report card can identify one or two social behaviors to develop in a child.
  - Father and child can give a letter or number grade to each of the target behaviors immediately after Dad observes a social interaction.
  - The reasons for each of the father's ratings should be discussed with the child, giving very specific examples of behaviors that influenced the father's rating.

- The goal is for the child to rate himself similarly to how his father rates him, over time.

- Fathers can help their ADHD children learn to be more under-standing of other people's feelings and points of view. Incidents in which other people have reacted to the child with anger and hurt can be used as teaching tools. The events can be broken down into sequences of actions. The child can be helped to understand how the other person might have been feeling as a separate matter from the child's feelings or intentions.

❖ C H A P T E R 7 ❖

Working as a Parenting Team

Teamwork is essential in raising children. This is especially true when raising an ADHD child, with his need for structure, consistency, predictability, and calming. ADHD children have less of an ability to make up for their parents' problems working together than do most other children. Teamwork is essential in implementing behavior management plans, enforcing expectations, limits, and discipline, and advocating for the child. Thus, the relationship between the mother and the father is crucial. Many well thought-out plans for addressing an ADHD child's behavior problems that were agreed upon by both parents have collapsed because of the inability of the parents to understand each other and overcome the problems in their relationship.

THE HIDDEN MEANINGS OF DISAGREEMENTS
AND THE NEED FOR EMPATHY

In Chapter 1 we examined the struggles of Cora and William James and their 5-year-old son Billy, over Billy's behavior during dinner. Each of Billy's parents thought that he or she was arguing over the right way to enforce proper eating behavior at meals, and that the other was being stubborn or unreasonable. Cora came from a family in which her mother had been very controlling and had difficulty letting her children grow up and make decisions independently. Now that her children were grown, she continued to criticize their choices of mates, homes, and occupations, as well as how they raised their children. She had announced that she did not believe in "this ADD stuff" and accused Cora and William of trying to take the easy way out by attributing many of Billy's problems to ADD (if only she knew how difficult it was!). Cora's father had died when she was a year old, and her stepfather, whom her mother had married when she was 5, had been superficially genial, but never very close or loving. He made little effort to visit Cora or to give to her or her son, while he was constantly bailing out Cora's brother from his financial and legal difficulties due to his drug habit.

William grew up with an alcoholic father who constantly ridiculed him. His passive mother failed to protect him from his father's emotional abuse. William grew up to be a very skilled and hard-working tradesman who was able to master carpentry, plumbing, electrical work, and heating and air conditioning. In spite of his abilities, William had poor self-esteem and he continued to work for a contractor who would not pay him what he was worth.

While William and Cora appeared to be locked in a struggle to determine the right way to manage Billy's behavior at dinner, their intransigence and emotionality about the issue suggested that there was something else going on. Knowing their histories, and the effect that their childhoods had on their self-esteem and their expectations of each other, in my work with them I decided to focus on their own control struggle before discussing a behavior management plan. It was important that each of them feel in control of a difficult-to-control situation, that neither was being controlled by the spouse as he or she had been controlled or infantilized by his or her parents, and that each was being listened to and respected.

It was the latter issue that may have been most important here. Both William and Cora experienced the other's disagreement and different way of dealing with family matters as a profound discounting of their self-worth. This was especially true given that the matter on which they were disagreeing was emotionally charged. Both William and Cora badly needed affirmation and understanding of who they were at the very core of their being. The profound disappointment they had each experienced as children in getting their emotional needs met had made them seek a great deal in their relationship with each other.

The psychoanalyst Heinz Kohut (1977) describes the young child as needing relationships with others that provide him with the experiences of being "mirrored," and of attaching himself psychologically to an idealized other. When parents mirror a child, they respond to him as an independent center of initiative, as a separate person with his own thoughts, feelings, needs, and experiences, who is not merely an extension of the parents. The parents attempt to experience the world in the way that the child does, rather than assuming that the child experiences things the way that the parents would, or the way that the parents think he should. The child's own experiences, thoughts, and feelings are therefore valued, affirmed, and validated. This promotes a healthy self-esteem in the child, a sense of initiative, a realistic sense of his own importance and abilities, and the ability to soothe himself.

As idealized attachment figures, the parents enable the child to develop wishes and aspirations for himself, to strive for productive participation in life, and to acquire skills that are consistent with his abilities and interests.

The child is initially dependent on the adults in his life to provide for his developing self what he cannot at the time provide independently. The parents function as attachment figures who supply for the child a sense of wholeness, goodness, stability, and calming. These are some of the functions they make available through mirroring and idealization. If these experiences are adequate, the child develops into an individual who can provide these functions for himself and who can provide them for others in emotionally intimate relationships—with adults or children.

If one is not fortunate enough to have adequate caregivers early in life, one will likely have deficits in one's self-esteem, initiative, goals and ambitions, regulation of emotions, frustration tolerance, and ability to engage in the give and take that occurs in intimate relationships. Small disagreements and minor disappointments may be experienced as major catastrophes, eliciting intense rage, depression, an inability to put the disagreements aside and get on with things, or an inability to compromise.

Mirroring provides the child with the experience of being valued and understood through the excitement, understanding, and validation that his parents experience in his presence. The parents must be capable of seeing the world through their child's eyes, of validating rather than dismissing their child's feelings and experiences. The child needs to experience his parents' genuine excitement about, interest in, and respect for him. The child needs his parents to suspend their perspective and enter his, to validate what he sees as exciting, interesting, funny, frustrating, and painful when it differs from how the parent experiences the same things. The child needs his grandiosity responded to in a positive, exciting way. When the child creates something or accomplishes something, he says to his parents, "Look at me!" He feels that he has accomplished the greatest thing in the world. At these moments, the child needs his parents to notice him and to respond with pride, appreciation, and encouragement. The child gains from this a sense of being valuable and important, a feeling of energy and initiative in dealing with the world and in accomplishing things. In addition, he develops an internal sense of cohesion; that he is whole; that he makes sense; that he is capable of mastering the world; that his internal state will hold together; that he will not be destroyed or torn apart or incapacitated by frustration, anxiety, anger, failure, or success; that his needs, wishes, and feelings will not destroy others; that he will be safe in the world and that the world will be safe with him in it.

By having a strong, powerful other with whom he can merge his identity, the child learns to channel his ambitions toward mastery and productivity. He learns that his goals and ambitions can be realized. He learns that he can make a difference, create change, and develop a sense of mastery and a sense of importance through what he does in life.

There is a continuum from fulfillment to frustration of these needs in childhood. If there is too much frustration or deprivation (and no one has figured out yet how to quantify this), the child looks to others to provide him with those functions that he cannot provide for himself. He relies on others for affirmation, admiration, appreciation, and for shoring up his sense of importance and value. This results in his being unable to provide these things for others. Relationships become one-sided, in which the person is constantly seeking approval or agreement, and focusing exclusively on his own needs. It is difficult for the person to see things from another's perspective.

In marriage, we look for someone who can provide these functions for us at times when we feel depleted or emotionally vulnerable. But in a good marriage, we can also provide these functions for the other, and each person is able to provide these functions for him- or herself most of the time (Jacobs 1991, Solomon 1989).

If two people have a one-sided relationship, where one person's needs are always being met at the expense of the other's, the marriage can be pathological. When each partner can provide these functions for the other, reciprocally, in times of undue stress, disappointment, anxiety, or challenge, this provides the foundation for a healthy marriage (Jacobs 1991).

When seen in this context, Cora and William's struggles with each other take on a much different cast than merely problem-solving some technical behavioral matter. Unknowingly, they were looking to each other to feel understood and valued. They so badly needed the other to see things from their perspective, and to feel their feelings, and they so craved the experience of empathy, that it was difficult for them to tolerate differentness in the other.

It was not that Cora and William were profoundly disturbed people. While it was true that they had more problems than many, including a history of alcoholism in William and depression in Cora, and chronically recurring marital difficulties, they were gainfully employed, hardworking, law-abiding citizens who were loving parents with a sense of spirituality and a concern for the well-being of their community. Dealing with an ADHD child did not create their problems with self-esteem and communication, but it did tax these vulnerabilities, and these vulnerabilities made coping with the challenges of an ADHD child much more difficult.

It was important for Cora and William to listen to each other and to understand that William's way of doing things came out of his experience with his own family of origin. It was also important for them to understand that the emotionally charged nature of their disagreement and their stubbornness in this matter did not arise from needing to be right, but from needing validation and empathy from the other. One thing for which they both needed empathy was their fear of losing control over their child.

Once Cora and William were able to discuss these feelings and needs openly, which took a great deal of patience, given the feelings of shame and humiliation that accompanied admitting these needs to themselves, they were able to see that there was more than one right way of solving the behavioral problem, as there always is. There is no one right way that applies to all situations. Each situation can be approached from a number of effective ways. It is important to be creative enough to think of and try alternatives.

There have been many occasions in which I have recommended a particular approach to an ADHD child's problem behavior, or have endorsed one parent's idea, only to have the other parent report that he or she just was not comfortable doing things that way. I might have been convinced that this was the best thing to try at the time, but rather than interpreting the parent's response as resistance, it was important for me and the other spouse to listen to and understand his or her discomfort.

Some people are not comfortable using money as rewards, or using certain types of punishments. If a behavioral plan is pushed through because of matters of expedience, and one or both parents' discomfort is ignored, the plan will not work. If a parent is uncomfortable with an approach being used, it is important that he or she discuss it with the spouse to enable the spouse to understand this point of view. This also enables the parent who feels uncomfortable to gain a better understanding of his or her own feelings, and encourages him or her to come up with more effective alternatives. Sometimes the uncomfortable spouse will endorse the approach after he understands his feelings and needs better.

THE PARENTAL TAG TEAM

When I suggest that parents work as a team I do not necessarily mean that both parents must approach the child at the same time or handle things the same way. It is more important that the parents share the same goals for their child (moral and behavioral), support each other as parents and as authorities, and respect each other's needs and opinions when they are with each other and when they communicate with the child. During the times in which the child struggles against them, the parents must work together to gain control over the child's behavior, or to help the child gain control over himself.

It is a common practice that when one parent is interacting with a child in enforcing discipline, the other parent does not interfere, but lets the parent involved complete the interaction. It is often believed that interference by the other parent only serves to undermine the involved parent's authority.

I believe that men, in particular, have a hard time not finishing something, particularly when that something involves a struggle for control. As discussed in a previous chapter, men are more likely to view relationships in terms of hierarchy. It is very important to establish who is up and who is down in relationships, and once that distinction is made it is important that those roles are secure.

Few roles are as clearly defined in terms of hierarchy as those of parent and child. Although the hierarchy in the mother–child relationship is also important to women, mothers are often comfortable negotiating around the periphery of that relationship in allowing their child some say in what goes on. Fathers tend to be more rigid in enforcing their authority, and more threatened when it is challenged. Mothers might respond with more flexibility to challenges to their authority, resulting in a less rigid response. At times this enhances their relationship with their child while leaving their authority intact, but at other times it undermines their authority. Fathers are often less willing to take the risk of their authority being undermined through their flexibility.

Men therefore find it much more difficult to give up their authority when it is being challenged, to walk away from a fight, or to call for help when they cannot handle things. It is like a gambler losing money at the table and refusing to leave, betting on one more roll of the dice or spin of the wheel, hoping that maybe this time he will recoup his losses, while getting more and more in the hole the longer he stays.

Disciplining an ADHD child, or interacting around rules, limits, and expectations, is often so trying that the longer the parent stays in the interaction, the more his or her frustration escalates into a yelling and screaming match. This in itself serves to undermine that parent's authority with the child. Even if the child ends up doing as he was told, the child often controls the parent's mood and behavior, and therefore wins a victory. At this point the parent needs to take a break and call in a replacement, as in tag-team wrestling. Sometimes a parent simply cannot finish an interaction productively in a way that leaves his authority intact and teaches the child what he wants to teach him. Wisdom involves knowing when you need help and how to ask for it. It involves not just knowing what to do, but also knowing when to stop.

A colleague of mine with an ADHD daughter who was prone to aggressive outbursts and uncontrollable temper tantrums, often got calls at work from his wife, who was overwhelmed and did not know what to do. They were trying to teach their daughter how to soothe herself when she was distressed. Their daughter was not always responsive, and as the mother used up more and more alternatives that she could think of and nothing worked, she became more distressed, overwhelmed, emotional, and argumentative with the child. This escalated the interaction, doing the opposite of soothing the child, and causing the mother to need soothing herself.

This mother's calls to her husband were often not for advice, but for soothing. Her husband, when he was able to, responded sympathetically and reassuringly, which often had the effect of calming her down and allowing her to think of a better solution. Sometimes the father simply gave her the advice to separate herself from their daughter, or put their daughter in her room, alternatives that the mother knew but was not able to implement until she calmed down. Sometimes we are like our ADHD children in that we know what we are supposed to do, but we cannot implement those behaviors at the time.

Another psychologist would care for his son while his wife worked part-time in the evenings. Although this psychologist prided himself on his skills with behavior management with children (he often gave behavior management advice to parents with very difficult children), he became overwhelmed and very angry when his son would not calm down and stop crying. He became angry not only at his child, but at his wife for abandoning him for her work. He often called his wife at work. Given the greater amount of time that his wife spent with their son, he deferred to his wife's expertise, granting her the status of being superior to him in the hierarchy of knowledge of and familiarity with their child. Although his wife could not do anything for him when she was at work, and although he was already trying all of the things they both tried in these situations, it was soothing to him to hear his wife ask him what he had tried and to discuss with him what to try next. It was also reassuring to hear that the tantrum might very well continue and the world would not end because of it.

"Tag team" parenting does not just work over the phone, but in person as well. It is important to know when to give up interacting with your child and to ask your spouse to take over. Sometimes you just cannot find a way to be right. This is not a sign of weakness but rather an indication of self-knowledge and wisdom. It takes a lot of self-control to say to your spouse: "Honey, you handle it," and get out of the way. After all, you are trying to teach your child self-control and nonimpulsive ways of dealing with conflict. Continuing an interaction that is escalating in intensity, nonproductive, and self-defeating, is a sign of impulsivity—the inability to stop doing something when we need to.

Maybe your spouse is better at helping your child to self-soothe, maybe she is better at negotiating a solution with your child, maybe she is just better at firmly enforcing limits, or maybe she is better with enforcing limits with this particular child. Or, maybe you just need a break because at this moment you are getting nowhere. Leave the interaction, let your spouse take over, calm yourself down.

If you do let your spouse take over, get out of the room! Do not supervise your spouse from the doorway, coaching or directing with your anger and desire for revenge. Leave, and let your spouse do what she will.

It is humiliating to be put into a position of being one-down to your child. Most fathers will fight hard to gain the upper hand in interactions with their children, if only to have the last word, and therefore come out on top. Often, the last word is in the form of a spanking, because, in the final analysis, the one area in which a young child cannot usurp power over his father is in sheer physical size and strength. Spankings are often the last resort for fathers who need their place in the family hierarchy reestablished. Yelling is another attempt to overpower the child, through the sheer physical power of one's voice and the emotional intimidation that accompanies yelling.

Many fathers will resort to one or both of these methods rather than walk away from the interaction. The need to establish oneself at the top of the hierarchy is strong and controlling. The paradox that exists here is that, if you allow the interaction to get to the point where your emotions are out of your control, then even if you yell or spank, you have gotten yourself into a position where your child has gained control of you through your emotional state.

Once your child has succeeded in getting you overwrought and has dragged out the interaction with you to the point where you are extremely frustrated, your escalating the interaction with yelling or spanking might silence the child, but the child has already won. Some children endure physical punishment, deprivation of desired privileges, and aversive responses from their parents in order to control their parents' moods. Children love to be in control. Although you might feel that ending your intense, contentious interaction with your child by yelling or spanking puts you on top, it really is an admission that your child has gained control over you, and your child knows it. It is much better to leave the interaction and let your spouse take over.

Allowing your spouse to take over establishes the primacy of the parenting *team*, rather than of one individual parent. It is more important for the parents as a team to be established at the top of the family hierarchy, than it is for either parent as an individual. By leaving the interaction and allowing your spouse to take over, by calling for reinforcements or relief in this way, you are establishing the family hierarchy in a very important way.

THE NEED FOR CONSISTENCY AND PREDICTABILITY

Consistency is difficult to achieve when two people are working together because no two people are the same. If we are empathic, we respect individual differences in the way that people feel, believe, and experience things in their lives. But the need for consistency seems to imply a negation of individual differences in favor of a collective view of reality. It is difficult for any one person to do things consistently as an individual. How then can we expect a couple to behave consistently as a duo? Add to this dilemma that fact that the subject in question is parenting an ADHD child. This is a highly emotionally charged issue that challenges the parents' own abilities to maintain emotional control, as well as their self-esteem and personal vulnerabilities, making consistency all the more impossible.

Consistency between two parents is touted as important in books on parenting and disciplining difficult children. Many mental health professionals, including myself, become irritated when parents have not been consistent in their discipline. Parents are thus reluctant to report their failures of consistency.

While I advocate for consistency, I have come to expect inconsistency. Inconsistency in following through with a behavioral plan that was agreed to by both parties can reflect one of several things:

1. an expression of each partner's individuality, which can be welcomed and worked with;
2. some unexpected or uncommunicated limitation of one parent in his or her ability to follow through with the plan (for example, the plan might call for skills in organization, memory, or sustained attention that the parent does not have);
3. some discomfort that the parent has with the plan that was not voiced or that the parent dismissed as unimportant (for example,

a parent might not be comfortable with giving a child money for good behavior, and might not have been given the opportunity to discuss and explore this further);
4. a problem with the design of the plan (for example, if the plan does not take into account the personality of the child and anticipate the challenges that the child might make to the plan's implementation, the parents will be forced to improvise, which is the opposite of planning, and therefore carries a high risk of failure).

To be consistent, parents must communicate with each other about the ways in which they are inconsistent. They must be honest about their disagreements, about their personal preferences, and about their discomforts, no matter how irrational they might be. Once they do this, they will be better able to work out a plan that they can both support and claim as their own.

To promote consistency, it is important that both parents develop the plan together, from the beginning. When I get called by a parent for an appointment concerning the behavior of an ADHD child, I inquire as to whether the other parent lives in the home and if he or she is available to come to the first appointment. Some families find this impossible, either because of the father's work schedule or because of the limitations of my schedule. However, plans tend to progress much more smoothly when both parents are involved from the beginning.

It is also important that both parents agree on which behavior to target for intervention as a priority. A choice has to be made between many possible problematic behaviors. There is ample room for disagreement about which behaviors are more serious, more intense, more long-standing, more frequent, or more disruptive of life at home or at school. A mother might be very concerned about her child's bossiness with peers, while the father might see this as an expression of individuality and assertiveness, and the conflicts with peers as being the price that one pays for having a strong personality. A mother might be most alarmed by her child's tendency to throw an object at her, although this occurs rarely, but the father might feel that it happens so infrequently that he will not observe it often enough to be of any help. A father might be most concerned about his child's failure to follow his coach's directions during soccer games, but the mother might feel that as long as the child is having fun and not being aggressive, he should be left alone.

There are some guidelines for identifying an appropriate initial behavior to target for intervention: (1) The behavior should be one that occurs frequently enough to observe and respond to on a daily basis. (2) The behavior should be observable by a parent, rather than one that is reported to the parent by an outside observer. (3) The parent should have control of the consequences of the behavior, rather than leaving praise and punishments in the hands of a teacher or a coach. (4) The behavior should be one that the parents have a good chance of modifying relatively easily in a short period of time. It does not have to be the worst behavior that the child exhibits. It is more important for the parents to have an initial experience of success.

In selecting a behavior for intervention, it is important for the father to understand that the behaviors that bother him the most might not be the same ones that most bother the mother. It might be important for the father to defer to the mother in the selection, as she spends more time with the child.

In following through on a behavioral plan, linearity, sequencing, logic, and cause and effect become important. These are often areas of strength for fathers. Fathers can often keep the focus simple. If the child exhibits a certain problem behavior one time, the negative consequences will be put into effect even if the child has done something laudable that day, even if the child promises not to do it again, and even if the father feels warmly or forgiving toward the child or guilty himself for depriving the child. Fathers can often be skilled at narrowing their focus and screening out other, complicating factors. They can be helpful at keeping the focus on one behavior at a time. This is useful not only in administering punishments, but in administering rewards, too. It is often hard to reward one behavior when the child has not been compliant with other behaviors. The parent's anger with the child over other behaviors might interfere with his plan to reward the child for a specific behavior that has been targeted for intervention. Keeping his emotional reactions about the other behaviors out of the decision to reward the targeted behavior is a strength that many fathers are able to contribute.

A parent's emotional reactions often threaten to take the focus off the planned reward or consequence for a specific targeted behavior. It is not easy to reward a child with whom you are angry. It is also not easy to punish or deprive a child toward whom you are feeling love, warmth, or gratitude at the moment. Guilt over punishing a child is common in all parents. The parent with whom the child is more emotionally involved, which is often the mother, might find it more difficult to detach herself from the guilt feelings and follow the plan. Unspoken emotional goals, that is, unconscious emotional reactions that control our behavior in spite of our conscious decisions to behave otherwise, can easily disrupt the focus on the behavioral goals that have been set.

When we set up a behavior management plan, we establish very clear connections between the child's behavior and the consequences that we control. We do this in ways that make logical sense, tying behaviors to consequences in linear fashion: "If you do this, then this happens at this time." However, in implementing these plans, we are in the flow of family life, caught up in our control struggles, wishes, needs, expectations, and disappointments. Emotions are often heated, and we often behave impulsively rather than rationally, according to plan.

Perhaps the parent grew up with an angry, controlling parent, and the challenge to authority and the emotionality of the ADHD child triggers this very early fear, anxiety, and sense of danger that the parent had when he or she was a child. Maybe the parent experienced severe emotional or material deprivation as a child, and depriving his or her child of anything triggers feelings of guilt, sorrow, and the parent's own sense of emptiness and loss.

We all have emotional triggers—situations that elicit strong emotions seemingly outside of our control and often without warning. When we are caught up in these emotional reactions, rationality goes out the window and we often do not realize until later that we have acted in an impulsive, counterproductive way.

Although fathers might be skilled at detaching themselves emotionally, one emotion that they often have difficulty detaching from is anger. Fathers often use anger to control others, including their children who are threatening their sense of control and authority. One of the reasons for this is that fathers were often controlled by their own father's anger, and they saw their father's anger control the family as they were growing up. Anger management can be a significant problem for men, and for all the objectivity and emotional detachment that men can muster, anger is often a glaring exception.

Spouses can be of enormous help to one another in coaching each other to detach emotionally so they can follow through on behavioral goals. Fathers can develop a verbal signal that they give to mothers, agreed to in advance, that lets their spouses know that it is time to back off. It helps if this verbal cue has some humorous association to it. The mother can then make room for the father to take over.

Fathers, on the other hand, might need help from their spouses at detaching emotionally when they are angry and trying to control the situation through their anger. The irrational display of anger often controls the child through fear, intimidation, and traumatization, which can have undesired emotional effects on the child.

It is important for fathers to talk to their spouses about their anger. When rage is elicited, there is a righteousness to it that nullifies all attempts at reasoning. Righteous anger demands rigid solutions. Force and intimidation are justified because only one outcome is acceptable. When one is caught up in anger and rage, it is not the time to be first discussing the merits of the anger. Prior planning works for the parents, just as it does for the ADHD child.

In discussing one's anger with one's spouse, it is important for the father to identify the emotional trigger points that elicit a rage reaction. Maybe it is open defiance by his child, or disrespectful language, or the child becoming physical with him or the child's mother that sends him into a rage. Or perhaps it is yelling and screaming, or the threat of being late, or being embarrassed in front of company. It is equally important for the spouse to understand how difficult this is emotionally for the father. One can understand the emotional difficulty the father has without condoning the behavior. Together, the father and mother, as a parenting team, can identify those high-risk situations and agree on a signal to let the mother take over the discipline at that point. In addition, if it becomes apparent that one of these situations is developing, they can agree to let the mother handle it in the first place. For example, if the father becomes enraged when his child defies him in front of others, the mother can agree to handle most of the discipline when visitors are in the home.

Linearity is also an important ingredient in consistent behavior management plans, and fathers can make an important contribution here as well. For example, behavioral plans are structured with a strong cause-and-effect orientation. The sequencing and timing of the parents' responses to their child's behavior are as important as the responses themselves. For example, rewards should be given only after desired behaviors have been performed, not beforehand in the mistaken belief that the reward will serve as an incentive. What this does is reward whatever behavior preceded the reward.

For example, a child might be watching TV when his parent asks him to clean up his room. The child then asks to play a video game first, promising to clean up his room immediately afterward. Acceding to the child's request rewards the child for watching TV (what he was doing immediately before he played with the video game), and not for cleaning his room. Similarly, buying a child a bicycle if he promises to behave in school during the coming year rewards him for asking for a bicycle or for doing things the way he has been doing them. The only way to reward a desired behavior is to provide the reward *after* the behavior has occurred. You "pay" the child after he has earned the pay. You reward retrospectively, not prospectively.

But rewards should be given soon after the desired behavior is performed, so that that particular behavior will be rewarded. If too much time intervenes, the reward will be reinforcing whatever behavior immediately preceded the reward. For example, if you are giving your child stickers for cooperative behavior, and he cooperates in the morning, it is important to put the sticker on the chart immediately. If you wait until the evening to place the sticker on the chart, and the child's behavior during the day has been horrendous, you will be reinforcing the horrendous behavior. Or if you then decide not to put a sticker on the chart because of this bad behavior, you will have missed the opportunity to reward your child for appropriate behavior.

Sometimes the mother asks the father to enforce a rule or a limit that she imposed. He might not have been present when the rule or limit was set, and whatever it was that upset his spouse to lead her to set the limit did not have any emotional impact on him. In this situation it is easy to become lax about follow-through. Parents often switch off who is home with the children while the other attends to work, errands, social or community obligations, or extended family responsibilities. It is common that both parents are rarely at home with the children at the same time, except when everyone is sleeping (unless parents work opposite shifts). Following through with rewards and consequences that are implemented by one's spouse is very important in maintaining consistency in behavior management. To do otherwise is to undermine the spouse's authority, which ultimately undermines the father's authority, as the parental subsystem in the family is weakened. But to do this effectively, communication is necessary. With one parent often rushing in as the other is rushing out of the house, parents often do not make time to communicate with care. Often communication is done by leaving each other notes. Parents must communicate with each other about what the behavioral infraction was, when it happened, what the consequence is, and why this is important to follow through on.

Behavioral rules should be as simple as possible, and defined in a way that is agreed to by both parents. When reminding your child of the rules, such as previewing them before entering into a situation that is risky (like going grocery shopping), or verbally rewarding your child for good behavior, it is important to use the same words consistently.

For example, if your child has a problem with hitting his peers, you set up a reward and feedback plan that emphasizes not hitting. You tell him that you want him to practice keeping his hands and feet to himself, or to talk, not hit, when he is angry. Either one of these messages emphasizes the behavior that you want him to ex-

188 ❖ FATHERING THE ADHD CHILD

hibit, in positive terms, rather than just telling him what you do not want him to do. Once you have established a consistent language for telling him what you want him to do, such as "keep your hands and feet to yourself," you can repetitively use this language to communicate with him. When he is waiting for a friend to come over, you can tell him, "Remember, the rule is keep your hands and feet to yourself. Now what is the rule?" When he is playing with his friend cooperatively, you can tell him periodically, "You're doing a great job of keeping your hands and feet to yourself." After his friend has left, you can tell him: "I'm proud of you. You kept your hands and feet to yourself."

Although this constant repetition might seem like overkill, it is important for the ADHD child. Rules that are given with the same words to him are the same rules, whereas varying the phrasing might be experienced by the child as two different rules or communications. The repetition helps the child to remember the rules, to anticipate them, and to internalize them and make them his own.

Consistency and repetition also provide predictability for the child. The more predictable things are for him, the more effective will be rewards and punishments. In addition, if you set up a predictable system in which your child knows that performing one behavior earns a reward and performing another behavior entails suffering a consequence, then the outcome becomes his choice. If you tell your teenage daughter, for example, that she has to hand in all of her homework for each marking period, or she has to earn a minimum grade of C in every subject in order to earn the right to go to the dances during the next marking period, and you consistently follow through with your stated consequences, then earning the right to attend the dances becomes her choice. She cannot blame her failure to attend the dances on your fickleness or meanness, since the criterion for attendance was clearly spelled out well in advance. By the same logic, if your daughter earns the right to go to the dances, it is then her accomplishment rather than something that you just gave to her. This can go a long way to helping her gain a sense of mastery and control over her life.

Simplicity is also important, and this is something with which fathers might need a little help. Fathers can become legalistic in critiquing a behavior plan. They are adept at finding the possible loopholes and the exceptions to rules. While this approach might uncover inconsistencies in the plan, and anticipate problems before they arise, too much of this can result in an overly detailed plan where every possibility is accounted for, and in which the rare exceptions end up overwhelming the common occurrences. The plan can then fall apart from its own weight, being too complex for any parent to carry out.

When a parent cannot settle on a plan, but instead has to keep asking "What if . . . ?" to anticipate everything that might go wrong, often the parent feels that he has lost his power over his child. He already anticipates that whatever he and his spouse try to do, the child will undo. Ultimately, he does not feel that he can be an authority over his child. Unfortunately, this belief often becomes a self-fulfilling prophecy. When a parent is doubtful about his authority over his child, the child senses this and defies the parent even more.

Darlene, a single mother of a very aggressive and belligerent teenage boy, felt guilty every time she said no to her son. Whenever she asked him to put away the dishes or clean up the kitchen, he challenged her as to why she was not doing more herself and told her how lazy she was. When she tried to establish rewards, such as driving him to his friend's house if he cooperated with chores, he criticized her for being an awful and selfish mother. When she walked away from him and refused to discuss things, he would follow her around the house demanding that she explain herself to him. She always felt on the defensive and inadequate.

Darlene grew up in a home in which she was constantly criticized by her parents and called stupid, while her sister was praised and doted on. She had married and divorced an abusive, angry man. In her work, she was always feeling short-changed and victimized, which was, in reality, what happened to her. Her guilt at depriving her son stemmed from her feeling that she was a "bad girl" who was always wrong and could not do anything right. She could only assert her authority so far, but she almost always gave in in the end. She stopped short of calling the police to back up her authority when she was being harassed by her son, and instead capitulated.

Other parents believe that they should be able to handle their family problems themselves without outside help. Needing help would be humiliating and make them feel like a failure. But parents are not provided with a training manual for raising children. And raising an ADHD child is even harder. No one could be expected to be prepared for this task.

When the parent's authority fails, it is a dangerous situation for the child. To continue to make the same mistakes and be repeatedly undermined is destructive to the family. It is better to find a way to use outside services—mental health professionals, the police, or the courts—to ensure the authority of the parent.

WHEN PARENTS CANNOT AGREE

It is frustrating for parents when they cannot agree on how to approach a situation, especially when each is convinced that he or she is right. But agreement is not always necessary. It is important, however, for parents not to get into a control struggle over how to respond to the child's behavior. No one can win this struggle, and both parents will only end up feeling discouraged, angry, and defeated. Rather than insisting on one's own way, and repetitively arguing one's point, parents should try to understand what their spouse is feeling. His or her feelings may seem illogical or ridiculous, but these feelings are very real and very valid to him or her. It is important to respect those feelings, fears, or anxieties. Empathy with one's spouse is more important than control.

No matter how much you are convinced that your way is right, it might be important to give in and do it your spouse's way and see how it works. Another alternative is to switch off who is in charge, and help your child understand that there are different ways of doing things.

You and your spouse may have divided the child-rearing roles, so that you always handle certain situations, such as getting your child dressed in the morning, or helping your child with homework. But if this is not working well, you might consider switching and having your spouse take over this role. Several surprising things might happen: your spouse might have a novel approach that will work because she is not as emotionally caught up in the matter as you had become; or she might finally understand why it has been so difficult for you, and stop telling you how to run things from the sidelines; or she might come to you for help and between the two of you a creative solution might emerge.

CASE STUDY: THE SEARCH FOR BALANCE

Sheila and Stan, whose differences over punishment and authority were discussed in Chapter 3, were married for six months when their lives were radically changed: they were granted custody of Sheila's two children who had been living with their father. Sheila had expected that her children would live with her at some point, but due to a very problematic and complicated divorce and custody fight several years before, her children had been living with their father in another state. However, an emergency neglect situation changed all of that. Sheila and Stan were thrust into being custodial co-parents much sooner than they had planned, in the honeymoon stage of their young marriage. (These circumstances may be extreme, but they highlight many of the issues with which ADHD families struggle.)

Sheila's older child, 13-year-old Fred, had multiple problems. Diagnosed with ADHD, bipolar disorder, and learning disabilities, Fred was loud, threatening, and defiant. He intimidated other children with his aggressive behavior and sexually inappropriate remarks. He and his 11-year-old sister, Felicity, were very close, but Sheila and Stan were concerned that Fred's aggressive play was inappropriate for his sister. Although his sister laughed at his antics, she also felt intruded upon and frightened by much of Fred's behavior.

The disruption of the sudden move sent Fred into an impulsive frenzy of testing behaviors, and setting limits was a constant struggle for Sheila and Stan. They were often up all through the night battling with Fred and calling the police. Since nothing seemed to be working, their focus on struggling with Fred shifted to struggling with each other. Neither of them felt effective, but each of them was convinced that the other was wrong. (If you cannot figure out what is right, at least you can identify something that is wrong and blame that for your failures.)

Stan firmly believed that children should not disrespect their parents, no matter what their problems might be, and he found it very difficult to tolerate both children's disrespect of Sheila and him. Stan was also very scared of what might happen if they did not get control of Sheila's children. Fred's behavior frightened him.

Sheila was just as exasperated as Stan was. However, she felt that Stan was too severe in his authority. He was too quick to punish Fred, which, Sheila felt, fueled Fred's resentment and incited his oppositional behaviors. Sheila countered Stan by telling him that these were her children, that she understood them better than he did, and that she should have the ultimate authority, although she was at as much of a loss about what to do as Stan was. Furthermore, the fact that Stan had never had children gave her some sense of security that she must know more about what she was doing than he did.

As more of a wedge got driven between the two of them, Sheila and Stan's effectiveness as a team deteriorated. Much of the resentment the two of them felt toward Sheila's ex-husband became transferred onto their relationship.

Complicating their efforts at limit setting were underlying feelings and motivations about which Sheila and Stan were unaware, or which were put on the back shelf because of the crisis nature of their feelings. Sheila had felt enormous guilt about not retaining primary custody of her children due to her financial inability to either fight the legal battle or to support them. Despite her intention to regain primary custody when she was financially more secure, her children had been seriously neglected during the time she did not have them. She felt like a failure for having left her children unprotected. The no-

nonsense, unsentimental authority that Stan exercised, even though carried out in a way that was not demeaning or abusive to the children, triggered in Sheila feelings related to her ex-husband's punitiveness. Her children's outcries at having any limits set on them elicited her desire to protect them from harm, which was complicated by her feelings of failure at not having done this in the past.

Stan thought Sheila was ineffectual with her children. He and Sheila were just learning to be a team with each other, and they suddenly had to learn how to be both a parenting team and a crisis intervention team. He felt that his marriage was threatened.

Stan had a clear sense of the firmness and consistency necessary for disciplining children, as well as a sense of the importance of the parents being benign authority figures at the top of the family system hierarchy. However, Stan had difficulty understanding the ambiguities and contradictions inherent in children's behavior. For example, he had a hard time understanding why Felicity came to Fred's defense when Fred was punished when in fact she often was driven to tears by his teasing. He had difficulty comprehending that a strong mutual dependency and survivors' bond had developed between Felicity and Fred, and that, despite their conflictual interaction, they experienced themselves as two halves of the same whole. Stan also had difficulty understanding why Felicity was so rejecting of him when her own father had been so neglectful. Fortunately, he was open to learning that Felicity's testing and rejecting behaviors were expressions of her fears and her insecurities, and that her ambivalent feelings about Fred were expressions of different but equally powerful needs. He also came to more fully appreciate that Sheila wanted to be an authority over her children, but she was dealing with a great deal of guilt, confusion over their respective roles with the children, and a lack of knowledge about how to handle this very difficult and stressful situation.

While Stan seemed to boil down the situation to its most simplified form, Sheila tended to act upon the complexities and ambiguities. While Stan's position overlooked these complexities in favor of consistency, Sheila's position often seemed to be held hostage to them. While she responded to the various psychological and emotional forces at play, she often was paralyzed in following through on things consistently.

Sheila complained that Stan did not understand the children, which was partially true, but in reality she was saying that Stan did not understand her. Stan's tendency to see things in concrete terms became exaggerated in response to Sheila's criticism of him. The more Sheila was not aligned with Stan, the more threatened he felt by the children's behavior and the more at risk he felt their marriage to be.

Stan felt that Sheila negotiated with the children too much, which undermined her authority. The more she and Stan became polarized, the more Sheila took on the roles of the nurturing and understanding parent on the one hand, and the authoritative parent on the other, flip-flopping between these stances and shutting out Stan. Sheila was making up for lost time with her children, trying to show them the love and understanding that they had missed, and that they so badly needed. She often erred on the side of understanding, and neglected the fact that this was not a normal family situation, with her son's severe behavior problems, her recent marriage, the history of neglect, and the sudden, radical changes in circumstances.

Sheila and Stan decided to seek professional help. Sessions initially took the form of both of them presenting their case as to why they were right and the other person was wrong. Although I could try to apply the tried and true behavior management principles with which I was familiar, and which were available in many of the parenting books that Sheila and Stan were furiously reading in their spare time, I could predict that none of them would work in the present circumstances. Sheila and Stan first needed to be able to listen to each other and understand the needs, fears, and motivations that were underlying their actions, their positions on discipline, and their feelings toward each other. They also needed to see me engage their children as a benign but firm authority figure, setting clear limits and expectations on their behavior, while attempting to build a relationship with them through humor and respect, and at the same time tolerating and engaging their oppositional tendencies and rejection of me with kindness and humanity as well as with an insistence on their respect.

We initially focused on what was right about each of their positions on discipline without implying that the other would therefore be wrong. I tried to help each partner articulate his or her needs and fears, suspending the discussion of their behavior and focusing on their emotions instead. Fortunately, Sheila and Stan had a very strong commitment to each other and loved each other very much. As difficult as this situation was for them, they sat and listened to each other and to me over many hours, often going back to the same issues repeatedly.

Meanwhile, in family meetings, Stan was incredulous at the children's rejection of me. This ranged from simply disregarding what I had to say and pretending that I was not even in the room to direct verbal expressions of hatred and name-calling. I was able to engage Felicity in her hostility by exaggerating the qualities about me that she did not like through self-deprecating humor to the point of absurdity. In front of her mother and stepfather, her oppositional stance and rejection of male authority, which she liberally expressed at home toward her stepfather, became points of engagement with me. At the same time, I was respectful of her decision to dislike me and whatever it was that she thought I stood for. I did not reject her for her needs. I demonstrated to Stan that I could insist on his stepdaughter's respect without trying to control whether she liked me, and this allowed us to have a more peaceful coexistence.

Fred did not respond to humor as well as Felicity did. He often did not understand it. He had difficulty picking up the subtleties and the nonverbal cues in my humor, and he rarely made eye contact. I therefore did not engage his hostility toward me except to set limits on clearly inappropriate behavior or language. Rather, I appreciated and pointed out to Stan and Sheila behaviors that expressed the positive side of his ambivalence toward me and his attempts to establish a relationship with me. For example, in his first meeting in my office, Fred noticed a Koosh Ball on my toy shelf. He showed off to me a trick he had learned of tossing the ball up toward the metal support rods of my suspended ceiling, which caught the fibers of the ball and left the ball dangling from the ceiling. Each time Fred came to my office he did his trick. Sometimes I had totally forgotten that the ball was up there, and it was still dangling from the same spot the next time that the family came for a session. I admired Fred's ability to do the trick and told him that I looked forward to it on each visit. I also let him know that no one else had shown me that trick, and that sometimes I discovered the ball hanging from my ceiling during the week, which made me think of him and gave me a chuckle.

Another important aspect of Stan's attempt to exert control over the situation, and his anxiety when he was unable to, was his very understandable desire to protect Sheila. Sheila had experienced a great deal of heartbreak during her life. Stan saw his role as her protector, which suddenly became very complicated and difficult.

Stan and Sheila demonstrated many of the elements of male–female relationships that influence and complicate raising an ADHD child. As we can see, Stan took a very logical, goal-directed, linear, no-nonsense approach to discipline, which emphasized the hierarchy in the family and minimized the complexities of emotional understanding. Sheila was more caught up in the emotional complexities of her relationships with her children, and was less able to detach herself and adopt an instrumental approach. Her efforts were more subject to the vicissitudes of her own guilt, needs, and efforts to nurture her children. Her relationships with her children were marked not only by a need to establish her authority over them, but also by her efforts to be aligned with them. It was not enough for Sheila to keep her eye on the end result—appropriate behavior. She could not operate so instrumentally, even when she was certain that her disciplinary behavior was appropriate and fair. She could not help but feel the pain and distress that her children felt, and she needed to try to experience this fully. To do this, she needed to place herself on more of an equal footing with her children, which made it more difficult for her to maintain a consistently superior stance hierarchically.

Although Stan had a good handle on behavior management, his efforts were ineffectual without an empathic understanding of Sheila, and without Sheila's having an empathic understanding of him as well. Too often, parents get into a hierarchical power struggle with each other over who is right and who is wrong, but the important power relationship in the family is that between the parental and the child subsystems. Engaging in an "I'm right, you're wrong" struggle with one's spouse creates a conflict in the parental subsytem that impedes the ability of the parents to work together and to function as authoritatively as a team of equals.

Stan and Sheila were coached to cease their accusatory messages and their directives to each other about what the other should or should not do. Sheila was encouraged to talk to Stan about her feelings of guilt and failure and her fearful need to protect her children. Stan was encouraged to verbalize his feelings of confusion, his fear of rejection by the children, and his fear of losing Sheila. Once they understood the other's needs better, and felt more understood themselves, they were able to decrease their emphasis on controlling each other's behavior.

Sheila worked on her need to micro-manage Stan's relationship with her children. She allowed him to discipline them and to make mistakes without intervening. Stan was able to react to the children's rejection and provocation of him with greater calm, now that he could turn to Sheila to bolster his self-esteem. Sheila also became firmer in her limit-setting and was less tolerant of her children's verbal disrespect.

When Felicity escalated her acting out with declining grades at school and more defiant behavior at home, Stan and Sheila were able to focus their attention on how to respond to Felicity together instead of focusing on what the other was doing wrong.

When Felicity and Fred began to express wishes to contact their biological father's family, Stan's initial reaction was one of extreme anxiety and fear. Instead of rushing to control the situation, Stan waited for a therapy session to discuss this with Sheila. Rather than just focusing on what to do, Stan and Sheila were able to discuss their feelings and fears and listen to the feelings of the children before making a mutual decision about how to handle the situation.

It is very important for the parents to work at symmetricality in their relationship. This is true even if two adults have worked out a power arrangement that has a hierarchical structure to it. The path to symmetricality runs through empathy—the attempt to experience the emotions and meaning that events and relationships have for the other.

MATERNAL DEPRESSION

Mothers of ADHD children tend to suffer from depression at a higher rate than mothers of non-ADHD children. Campbell (1994) found that mothers of hard-to-manage boys who were identified in preschool were rated as having more symptoms of depression and parenting stress at a two-year follow-up. Mash and Johnston (1990) found that for mothers, having an ADHD child leads to lower self-esteem, seeing oneself as less competent and knowledgeable in regard to parenting, feeling less valuable as a parent, and deriving less comfort from parenting. This results in a greater degree of maternal depression.

Moreover, mothers of children who have emotional and behavioral problems tend to blame themselves for their children's problems. The fathers of these children, however, do not tend to blame themselves, but instead blame the mother (Penfold 1985). Both parents, therefore, tend to collude in a belief system that places blame on the mother.

Mothers of ADHD children also come to see their children's problems as being more serious than others might see them. While mothers of non-ADHD children tend to see their children as advanced, mothers of hyperactive children see their children as being delayed in the social, cognitive, self-care, and communicative spheres even when their children's IQs are no different from those of non-ADHD children (Sonuga-Barke and Goldfoot 1995). Mothers of ADHD children have the added stress of perceiving their children as delayed relative to their peers and do not have the comfort that other parents take in the illusion that their child is advanced.

It is important for fathers to understand these feelings, why they might be so, and what they can do to improve the situation. There may be several reasons for the higher incidence of maternal depression.

Children with ADHD are more demanding than non-ADHD children. The number of commands a parent has to give in order to effect compliance, the children's resistance to authority, the need to physically keep up with an active child, and the longer duration and louder volume of tantrums and other emotional displays, are all draining of energy and taxing of one's skills.

Children with ADHD often do not fit the picture of the desired child that the parents had fantasized about. Usually the fantasies of a parent's relationship with his child are influenced by the shortcomings in the parent's relationship with his own parents; the relationship with his child will be better. Having a child is usually fertile ground more for one's hopes, wishes, and dreams than one's fears. Although one might expect parenting to be difficult and challenging, most parents do not start out expecting a negative relationship with their child. However, this is frequently how the relationship with the ADHD child comes to be experienced by mothers.

A negative relationship with one's child is very damaging to one's own self-esteem. Not only does the mother wonder "What's wrong with my child?" but she also wonders "What's wrong with me?" She wonders why she cannot connect with or discipline her child, why she cannot enjoy being with her child, why she values time away from her child more than she values time with her child, and why she has such intense anger at her child. She wonders what is wrong with her maternal instinct that she feels such hatred and revulsion sometimes. Her feelings of anger and disappointment are matched by her feelings of inadequacy. She questions whether she is fit to be a parent. How could she have been so wrong about her own needs and abilities?

What makes matters worse is that her husband seems to get the children to listen better than she does. She feels ineffective, inadequate, and ashamed. She sees herself as a poor parent and an inadequate spouse. And when her husband contributes good, sound ideas about child management and discipline, she is unable to carry them out effectively or consistently. But fathers have the luxury of giving input and, since they tend to be absent most of the day, relying on the mothers to carry out these suggestions. Since both parents collude in the assumption that running the household and raising the children are primarily the domain and responsibility of the mother, it is the mother's self-esteem that suffers when the child cannot be disciplined.

Even when fathers are inadequate in enforcing discipline with their ADHD children, they have more permission to opt out of child-rearing responsibilities. In this culture they are encouraged to focus on the external world of work rather than on the children. As Paterson (1976) has pointed out, fathers are less vulnerable to the feelings of depression, anxiety, anger, confusion, and isolation that caregivers in distressed families experience because they do not see family management as a significant part of their identity and role description. Their identity is based on positive experiences outside the home, such as at work, which enables them to keep more of a healthy balance of positive and negative experiences in their lives.

It is not only the differences between the ADHD child and other children that create a feeling of isolation, and, subsequently, depression in the mother, but also the differences between mothers and fathers. The differences in styles, communication, and problem solving between mothers and fathers are useful and helpful to parents and children if they can be integrated into a larger whole, where each is valued and contributes to the child's development and the parents' parenting in ways that make each parent more adaptable, flexible, and effective. When the differences are experienced by the parents as being right or wrong or effective or ineffective, the mother will feel more isolated.

When both parents are able to recognize that the experiences and beliefs of men and women are different and legitimate, that each is necessary and valuable, and that the integration rather than the opposition of the two is what is important in raising a healthy and successful child, both parents will feel less isolated and the mother will probably feel less depressed.

Arnold (1995) has researched the risks inherent in dissimilar views on child rearing. He found that the more the views of a couple were dissimilar, the more the father's reactions to the child's misbehavior tended to be marked, on the one hand, by the father's displays of anger, irritation, and frustration, which Arnold termed *overreactivity*, or on the other hand, by a failure to enforce rules, a tendency to give in to the child's misbehavior, and coaxing or begging the child to behave, which Arnold characterized as *laxness*. The tendency for the father to be overreactive increased with the greater number of ADHD symptoms that the father himself had. Arnold described overreactivity and laxness as two dysfunctional disciplinary styles.

As Herzog (1966) points out, the child internalizes an experience of self based not only on his identification with his mother and his father, but also on his experience of his mother and father's relationship. What this implies is that it is not enough for each parent to have loving, calm, and understanding relationships with the child for the child to develop a healthy sense of self, but it is also necessary to take into account the relationship of the couple to the child. The child will internalize his sense of stability, his identity as a giving, loving, calming, provoking, conforming, or anti-authority self, based on how his parents relate to each other. For the ADHD child, it may be more difficult than the normal child to integrate all of these diverse sources for the development of the self, and it may be more important to have relative consistency in the experiences with individual parents and with the parents as a couple.

Brad, a 7-year-old child with ADHD, was much loved and valued by his parents, Norman and Debbie. Brad did special activities with both of his parents. In general, Norman and Debbie shared common values in teaching Brad rules of behavior and courtesy, and the importance of education, responsibility, and initiative.

Norman, however, had a tendency to ridicule Debbie in front of their children. Norman had an irreverent, but rather juvenile, sense of humor, which at times was charming and amusing, but which he found difficult to turn off when others wished to be serious with him. He had grown up with a very depressed and neglectful mother, whom he had to entertain in order to get attention, but at whom he felt a great deal of anger and disappointment. When Norman and Debbie's three children behaved rebelliously toward Debbie, Norman joined in "in good fun," and could not understand why his wife did not appreciate the joke.

For example, Brad frequently got into control struggles at dinner, in which he refused to eat and criticized Debbie's cooking. Norman, who had his own dissatisfaction with Debbie's cooking, joined in, which led to escalating control struggles between Debbie and her children at dinner. This escalated Brad's noncompliance, as well as eating and elimination problems, which became part of his control struggle with both parents.

This ADHD child was forced to integrate different but loving relationships with both of his parents, and there was a strongly conflictual, control-struggle–oriented, highly critical, dominant-submissive relationship between his parents, in which he was a participant. He developed into a boy who had severe peer problems, who could not accurately read social cues, and who got into control struggles with peers and with teachers.

Not all of Brad's difficulties were directly caused by his parents' relationship, but integrating his individual relationship with both parents and his relationship with them as a couple was confusing to him, given his parents' conflict. The nature of his parents' conflict was then reflected in some of the difficulties he had functioning in the world.

It is in both the father's and the child's interests to have a mother who is not depressed. Mothers tend to be less depressed when they feel a sense of partnership and collaboration with their husbands.

Lewis and colleagues (1981), reviewing the literature on father–infant interaction, concluded that the father's degree of interest in his infant is likely to increase the mother's level of interest. Research supported the conclusion that mothers tend to explore and smile with their infants more often when they are with their husbands than when they are alone with the infant. In families with male children, there is an interrelationship between the extent to which the father played with the infant, the mother's mood, the father's esteem for the mother in her role of mother, marital tension, the mother's competence in feeding the infant, and the infant's alertness, motor maturity, and irritability.

There are several important implications in these findings. One is that the father's esteem for the mother's skills as a mother influences the mother's competence in the vitally important area of feeding the infant. Another is that the father's esteem for the mother is related to a decrease in marital tension. While this might seem to be intuitively obvious, many couples' interactions around disciplining an ADHD child are based on mutual criticism and misunderstanding.

Similar to the kind of attention the ADHD child gets, the mother often gets negative criticism from the father (punishment and aversive control) for her perceived shortcomings and failures, and a lack of positive feedback for her successes. A decrease in marital tension is obviously in the self-interest of the father.

It is interesting to note that the more fathers were involved in playing with their children, the more the mother's mood improved and the higher the father held the mother in his esteem for her parenting skills. A father's involvement with his child enables the father to experience the child first-hand, and to empathize with the mother's experience of caring for the child.

Family therapists sometimes instruct the couple to switch roles in their management of their ADHD child's misbehavior.

In one such family, the mother, Barbara, was having difficulty getting her 6-year-old son Alex to go to school. Getting Alex dressed and out the door in the morning was a major struggle. Alex's father, Victor, was out of the house by 5:00 A.M. to go to work, so he was always spared the trials of getting Alex ready in the morning.

Barbara's control struggles with Alex escalated to the point where she was afraid of hurting him. Victor was sympathetic to Barbara's stress and anxiety, but he did not understand why it was so hard to get Alex ready to leave in the morning. Although the couple agreed on a behavior management system of points, rewards, and punishments, the point system was not working. In coordinating with the school, Barbara continued to be overwhelmed, and Victor continued to give advice in the form of: "Why don't you just . . . ?"

I instructed Victor to stay home for a week and get Alex ready for school. After some resistance to disrupting his work schedule, he agreed, and he came in the next week looking overwhelmed and confused. He had resorted to yelling, commanding, coaxing, and threatening, and could not find a consistent way that worked. Barbara, on the other hand, took on the role of giving clear commands and feedback as to what Victor should do to be more effective. Victor became more confused as to what was right, and more emotionally involved, and Barbara became more instrumental in her thinking.

Fortunately, we were then able to formulate a plan to which both Barbara and Victor could agree (because now they had each had a chance to be the caregiver and the advice giver), that was clearer and more consistent than Barbara's original approach, that was carried out with more authority, that had both parents willing to try new approaches, that let Barbara act with a greater sense of authority, and that allowed Victor to return to work.

It is not just the participation in discipline and in play time that is important in the development of respect by the father for the mother. The literature shows that fathers often play more with their children than do mothers, which forms the basis for an exciting, stimulating relationship. It is also important for the father to engage in interactions with his children that simultaneously develop a strong bond and relationship with the children *and* develop greater empathy for his wife.

These experiences are available in day-to-day caregiving. Many fathers feel like good fathers when they use their free time to play with or run errands with their children, and they are indeed being good fathers. However, a different sort of bond is developed with the child and with the mother when the father is involved in changing diapers, toilet training, feeding, dressing, and bathing his children.

Young children interact with the world mostly through their bodily needs. It is how these bodily needs are met that gives the child a sense of safety, security, freedom from pain, soothing, and mastery over the environment. Erikson (1963) calls it the development of a sense of basic trust in the world and in others. It is in the active care of the child's physical needs that the parent becomes the representative, the personification to the young child of a good, giving, need-meeting world. This bond is different from the play bond. This involvement with the child's bodily processes and physical needs is difficult in a different way than are playing, disciplining, running errands, or making a living. The more this caregiving is considered the province of mothers, the greater the empathy gap between mothers and fathers. The less fathers participate in caregiving, the poorer the bond between father and child.

GUILT

One issue with which mothers often struggle in disciplining their ADHD child, and which frustrates fathers, is guilt. This can be especially poignant if there is one ADHD child in the home and one or more non-ADHD children. The mother finds herself reacting to and treating the ADHD child differently than she does the other children. She expresses more anger at the ADHD child, disciplines and deprives the child more, and is the target of the child's anger and frustration to a greater degree. This might lead her to compensate for her own animosity and punitive behavior by being overly affectionate at times, and by holding back discipline when it is warranted. She might find herself vacillating between being overly harsh and overly lenient.

So much of raising an ADHD child is counterintuitive. We like to see ourselves as nurturing parents, as giving our children opportunities to develop their talents and to experience the world. The ADHD child needs firm and consistent limits, despite his protests to the contrary and expressions of distress and anger. When it might be all right to compromise with a non-ADHD child, it might not be the best thing for an ADHD child. Parents have to retrain themselves in how they discipline. When there are also non-ADHD children in the home, it can feel like one is operating two systems of child-rearing simultaneously. This can be very confusing, as it becomes necessary to think through each move rather than respond naturally. It becomes more apparent that one is not being as nurturing as one would like when the non-ADHD siblings are treated in a more natural way and are easier to nurture. The underlying hostility that builds up in the mother is another source of distressing guilt for her, which can paralyze her in her efforts to be firm and consistent.

Roberta is the mother of Luke, a 9-year-old, very intelligent, likable third grader with ADHD and extremely poor frustration tolerance. Whenever Luke was the least bit frustrated, he experienced it as if a switch were thrown, sending electricity throughout his entire body. He would go on rampages, throwing things, destroying objects, and, if his mother was in his way, kicking, hitting, and biting her. These tantrums could continue for two hours. Roberta, who was home with Luke and his three younger, non-ADHD siblings, frequently had to restrain him. Luke's father also had to discipline him sternly, but since he worked full time, he was spared the majority of Luke's outbursts.

Roberta became the target of Luke's frustration and anger, and she felt this very personally. Luke learned how to manipulate his mother. With his threats of outbursts, he succeeded in stopping his mother from doing things that he was not in the mood for, such as running errands. She had given in to Luke's tantrums and threats of aggression. This served to reinforce his use of and threat of aggression. Roberta's behavior made it more likely that Luke would throw a tantrum or use aggression in the future.

Roberta and Luke had *aversively conditioned* each other's behavior. Roberta's behavior of giving in to Luke's demands had been reinforced and conditioned by the prospect of an aversive stimulus, namely his tantrums and aggression terminating. Luke's tantrums and aggressing toward his mother had also been reinforced and conditioned by the termination of an aversive stimulus, namely his mother commanding him to do something that he did not want to do.

Roberta and Luke's interaction, which was normally very loving, became for Roberta unbearably antagonistic during Luke's outbursts. She understood the need to be firm and consistent, even if it meant ignoring or timing out a tantrum for two hours. However, Luke outlasted her in endurance. Exploring why Roberta found it hard to stand firm with Luke, she became tearful and acknowledged the great deal of guilt that she felt at becoming so angry at him and punishing him so sternly when she was able to shower more love and affection on her other children. As she talked about her guilt and how paralyzing it was at times, her husband understood her better and was able to adopt a more active role with Luke and to be more understanding and forgiving of Roberta's very human inconsistencies. In addition, by discussing her guilt and receiving validation rather than condemnation from the therapist and her husband, Roberta was better able to tolerate disciplining Luke more consistently when the situation called for it.

Nancy, a very competent, loving, and intelligent mother of an ADHD college student, broke down in sobs in my office, fearing that she had failed to adequately prepare her son to survive in life. Although he was highly intelligent, talented in languages and literature, and oriented toward a professional career, he periodically did things that were impulsive and lacked judgment. He would stay up most of the night talking to friends before having to drive home a long distance. During the drive, he would fight falling asleep at the wheel, and he had narrowly avoided several accidents and arrests. He also had a tendency to be too open with people. He would think nothing of driving or walking into a high-crime area of the city to ask directions, or of striking up conversations with strangers indiscriminately.

Nancy had responded to her son's high activity level and defiance through the years by being very controlling. This was a consequence of her natural tendency to be in charge of things (she was a corporate executive) and of her husband's laid-back style. Sitting in my office, she wondered aloud if she had been too controlling and intrusive, and too anxious about her child's ability to cope, if she had not given him adequate opportunity to try things on his own and learn from his mistakes. He was now a young man whom she considered too naive to effectively confront the realities of life.

Her fear for her son led her to analyze her own behavior over the years now that he was out of the house and she had time to think, and the feelings of failure came crashing down on her. Even with a sophisticated understanding of ADHD, she still wondered if she could have done a better job in preparing her son for life.

A parent's reactions to his ADHD child are influenced by what the parent believes to be sound child management, what he has found works with his child, his own personality, and his own upbringing. Now that Nancy was no longer involved in the day-to-day cauldron of child rearing, where much of the activity is action and reaction, and now that she was able to see what in some respects was her "finished product," she could step back and see how things might have been better.

Most thinking parents believe that they could have done better. When the child has a disability, the need to make his life better can take on the quality of desperation. There is guilt for even producing a child with a disability, even if the disability was out of the parents' control. There is the feeling that the parent should have protected the child and failed.

Nancy's grief could not be comforted with reassurances. Nor did she take comfort in hearing that the ADHD was out of her control. It is a parent's job to have control and to teach the child to cope with any adversity. She criticized her own controlling nature, even as she defended it as having been the best way to deal with her son in the context of the family.

Nancy needed to talk. She needed to be listened to. She needed to understand who she was and how her feelings and actions made sense, despite their imperfections. She did not need reassurance, explanations, or solutions.

Providing the kind of listening that Nancy needed is difficult for most men to do, even men who pride themselves on being sensitive. There seems to be a natural inclination to give answers, to solve the problem, to make messy feelings go away, and to analyze. It is difficult for men to leave things unfinished and messy. Fathers of ADHD children need to learn how to listen to their wives and help them with their guilt, not through rationality, but through actively being available to listen and enabling them to work things out for themselves.

CALMING DOWN

The moods and behaviors of ADHD children often infect the entire family, so that everyone starts to feel and act the way they do.

Ten-year-old Bradley was so controlling and aggressive that he often sparked a family-wide free-for-all of yelling and screaming that lasted for hours. The tantrum took on a life of its own, an inertia that Bradley's parents felt unable to stop and were compelled to carry out until everyone was too exhausted to go on.

Bradley's parents, both highly educated professionals and generally soft-spoken people, tried to be a tag team, only to find the interaction continuing at the same or more intense level when the other spouse took over. Further tag-team switching occurred, a cycle that repeated itself until both parents were in Bradley's room arguing and physically struggling with him.

This scenario happened rarely, but when it did both parents felt out of control, helpless, and defeated. Given the circumstances of fatigue, and Bradley's desire to do something that was not permitted, Bradley could be set off suddenly and violently, yelling at his parents, crying, and throwing things. His parents tried talking to him, using time-outs, ignoring him, and restraining him. None of these methods worked. Over time, the parents came to anticipate these interactions with dread, and they became conditioned to quickly lose their patience and respond out of fear and frustration. Since the parents' frustration became more easily triggered over time, this became a factor in their interaction with Bradley, leading to a quicker escalation of the tension. Both parents would become quickly drawn in to trying to control Bradley, thereby losing control of themselves.

Just as we try to teach ADHD children to recognize the signs of anger and frustration in themselves as it is building, in order to prevent it from hitting them suddenly in full force and thereby overwhelming their coping abilities, it is important for parents to recognize and heed the warning signs in themselves and to intervene when they are noticed. Once we become enraged at our child it is often hard to act objectively and follow through with our plan for managing the child's behavior. If we act out of anger, we have ceded the struggle to our child.

As the child sees the parent becoming more angry and frustrated, he will often either withdraw and become less responsive, or he will become stimulated by the parents' mood and become more agitated or anxious, and therefore more difficult to control.

Recognizing the warning signs of building anger and frustration should not be too difficult after a while. Most arguments between family members follow a certain pattern. Therefore, most of the arguments with a child are predictable.

You can usually tell from the circumstances and your child's mood the course that the argument will take and the outcome. Knowing this, it then becomes possible to end the interaction before it escalates. If you find yourself getting angry and involved in an interaction that will escalate and be nonproductive, it would probably be a good idea to leave the room. The child might be disappointed in the termination of the interaction and try to get you to stay. He might feel upset at his loss of control over the interaction, or he might feel sad at the prospect of being alone. In the latter case, your child might be able to calm down just for the reward of having you stay. Leaving the room allows you to stay out of the interaction until you are calm enough to maintain control. It is also important to develop signals for family members to calm each other down or derail the interaction. I helped one boy and his parents develop a signal to give to each other when any one of them felt that an interaction was getting out of control. They bought several pairs of Groucho Marx disguise glasses with the eyebrows and nose attached. Whenever anyone noticed an interaction escalating, he or she would grab one of the disguises, put it on, and continue to talk to the other person in disguise. It was impossible for any of them to take themselves seriously at that point.

Spouses should develop signals to communicate to each other the need to calm down and not take themselves so seriously. Some spouses say "Cool it" or "Easy." Others prefer to make up words that only make sense to the two of them, which sometimes have some humor to them. They can either sound silly or have a humorous, private meaning. The partners can agree that when one of them says this word or phrase, the other will take it as a signal to calm down or back off. It can also communicate a willingness for the calmer spouse to take over at the moment. For this to work most effectively, you not only have to be willing to give your spouse the signal, but you also have to be willing to accept the signal rather than seeing it as interfering or controlling. You have to be able to accept your need to control your emotional reactions better, rather than insisting on being caught up in them and having them control your interaction with your child.

COMMUNICATION

Since there is plenty that goes wrong in raising an ADHD child, there are plenty of opportunities for blaming your spouse for messing things up. Everyone who raises an ADHD child messes things up quite a bit. After developing a behavior management plan, parents are ashamed to report that they have been inconsistent in following it, that they failed to keep up the charts, or that they gave in to yelling at their child. They see themselves as bad parents because of these failures. Most parents of challenging ADHD children already doubt themselves enough as parents; they do not need to add to their feelings of guilt or inadequacy. Just the fact that they have set up a plan or sought professional help means they have already admitted that things are not perfect and that they do not have the answers.

Problems with maintaining behavior management plans become opportunities to learn why certain things work and others do not, opportunities to learn more about the personal styles and preferences of the parents, opportunities to learn more about the particular challenges posed by this child, and opportunities to learn about the likes, dislikes, and needs of the child.

Parents of ADHD children say that they do not know what to do to help their child and manage his behavior. However, some are so frustrated, not only with the child but with themselves and each other, that they engage in destructive blaming of the other. Some couples can carry on endlessly with examples of things that the other has done wrong. Rather than focus on the present and on what can be done better from now on, they persist in bringing up the past, unable or unwilling to move on to more productive pursuits. In therapy sessions their tone is often accusatory, and they talk incessantly about their spouses rather than about themselves, and about things that the other person always or never does. The accused then counters with a denial, or with examples of things that the accuser did wrong, in order to balance the argument. As the argument heats up, the partners then make statements as to how the other person is feeling, or the other person's state of mind, such as "You don't consider anyone else's feelings," or "You hate it when I . . . ," or "You always get angry when . . . ," or "You're so mean whenever . . . "

Aside from venting frustration, there is no use to this line of discussion. People argue about the facts, giving different accounts of what transpired. We are on much firmer ground when we discuss our own feelings, not what we assume to be the feelings and experiences of the other person. We stir up much less conflict if we say, for example, "I feel hurt when you talk to me that way," rather than "You are so mean when you use that tone of voice." The second statement shifts the argument to whether or not your spouse is really being mean, which is an argument without end, but the first statement is not debatable. Beginning your statements with the word *I* rather than *You* keeps the focus on feelings and experiences rather than on accusations.

SUMMARY

- Learn empathy and emotional understanding from your spouse.

- Believe your spouse when she says things are bad. You should respond to your spouse's feelings, not to your different perceptions of your child's behavior.

- Show your spouse you can be consistent and follow through. This will help her follow through consistently.

- Manage your anger. Be aware of how your anger gets in the way of being effective in managing your child's behavior and in working as a team with your spouse. Become aware of the early warning signs that your anger is building.

- Develop cues to help both of you to calm down and provide relief for each other.

- Communicate daily.

- Attend school meetings, counseling sessions, doctors' appointments.
  - Ask questions—prepare a list of what you want to discuss and questions you have. Being organized will help the professionals respond to your needs and know what they have to do to please you. It also sends a message that the professionals have to respect you, that you will be asking things of them. There is no such thing as a stupid question. If something is bothering you, it is important. It is the professionals' job to understand your needs and respond to them.
  - Act interested, make eye contact, question what you do not understand.

- Do not end a child's time-out that your spouse started. Do not intervene in a punishment you did not originate without consulting with your spouse.

- Take time with your spouse; go out together.

- Write down behaviors and consequences and stick to them so as not to react emotionally.

- Help your spouse practice emotional distancing.

- Discuss feelings in communicating with your spouse. Use "I" statements.

- Turn off the TV and spend time interacting with your children.

- Have your wife tell you about her day with your child or children and just listen without commenting or giving advice.

- Give your wife some respite from child care responsibilities. Take your child out to breakfast, drive your child to school, take your child out for the day to a museum or on a hike.

- Understand your spouse's guilt by actively listening and not jumping in with the answers.

❖ C H A P T E R   8 ❖

Co-Parenting after Separation or Divorce

LOSS ISSUES FOR CHILD AND FATHER

Children of divorce have adjustments to make in their lives that can foster flexibility and adaptability in the child, but can also breed their own unique set of problems. The ways in which divorce affects children with ADHD require special consideration, because the adjustments they and their parents have to make are intensified.

Loss of the noncustodial parent, which is often, although not always, the father, typically brings with it feelings of sadness and grief in the child. Even if the child does not directly express sadness, even if he denies feeling sad, his behavior is often an indication that he is having difficulty handling this great upheaval in his life. Parents often report an increase in problem behaviors at school, a greater number of conflicts with peers, an escalation in the seriousness of conflicts with others, and the reemergence of behavior problems that had previously been brought under control.

For non-ADHD children, being apart from their father might elicit feelings of longing; they might wonder what the father is doing, anticipate what they will do together during the next visit, or wish that the father was present so that they could show him things they

216 FATHERING THE ADHD CHILD

did or made. When they finally see their father, they act on these longings and needs by telling him what they have done, showing him what they have made, or doing an activity with him that they had been thinking about all week.

But those things that make being with the father reinforcing might be difficult to keep in mind for the ADHD child, especially for the younger child. When transitioning to being with the father for visitations, the ADHD child might not have kept in mind what he was anticipating doing with or telling his father, or the different rules and expectations in his father's home. Even if the ADHD child has made the transition from his mother's home to his father's home before, he might act like he is experiencing these things for the first time.

Perhaps the biggest problem that many separated or divorced fathers face is the loneliness they feel for their children on a daily basis. This is true even for fathers who were out of the home much of the time because of work demands. These fathers feel more cut off from the day-to-day knowledge and emotional involvement with their children.

Many mothers complain, often legitimately, that their husbands were not very involved on a daily basis with their children anyway, did not spend much time with them, did not participate in caregiving chores, and did not take the time to learn about their child's ADHD. Because of the mothers' anger and bitterness about this, it is often difficult for them to understand how much their ex-husbands miss their children. There are few sources of empathy for the feelings of separated or divorced fathers for the pain they feel at being separated from their children, especially for fathers who have been found wanting by their wives or ex-wives. Out of frustration, many of these men bond with other divorced men, and channel their frustration into legal action, exacerbating the already adversarial nature of the divorce, visitation, and custody processes.

Men have legitimate rights, needs, and complaints that lead them to seek legal redress. However, if these fathers' longing for contact with their children was understood and responded to by their ex-wives, in spite of their anger, the adversarial nature of the legal process could be greatly reduced.

THE NEED FOR FATHERS' CONTINUING INVOLVEMENT

Many divorced fathers feel that because they were minimally involved in child care, their children were more attached to their mothers, and the mothers have been the primary parent, and because the fathers are intensely angry and bitter, their children will do just fine without their active and frequent presence and involvement in their lives. This is far from the truth. In fact, the absence of fathers has been found to have potentially serious effects on the emotional well-being of children. With the greater vulnerability to aggressive behavior for ADHD children with hyperactivity, it should concern fathers that delinquent adolescent boys were found to differ from nondelinquent boys by the absence of a father (Anderson 1968). Differences between delinquents and nondelinquents were found in children as young as 4. These findings imply that father absence can seriously affect the internal controls that boys develop over their behavior and therefore their ability to behave in a socially appropriate manner. Hoffman (1971) similarly found that boys in the seventh grade whose fathers were absent were more aggressive than boys whose fathers were present. He also found that these boys accepted less blame for their problems, conformed to rules less, and had a lower level of moral judgment.

The loss of a father through divorce has also been found to negatively impact the self-esteem of boys and girls (Parish and Taylor 1979). For girls, not having a father has been related to disturbances in their relationships with males, including more attention-seeking, increased attempts to be physically close to males, and communicating greater openness and responsiveness (Hetherington 1972).

Although having an *involved* divorced father has positive implications for the child, there still are problems associated with the divorce that the fathers must be aware of. Being involved with their children does not absolve them from dealing with problems. Frequent contact with the father has been associated with more behavior problems as reported by the mother (Healy et al. 1991). So, although you and your child might be gaining a great deal from your contact with each other, this benefit might not translate into better behavior when he is at home. Although it might be difficult to see how a child who has two involved parents, despite a divorce, can possibly exhibit worse behavior at home, it is important to take the mother's report seriously if this occurs. In fact, for older children, regular and frequent contact with their divorced father actually intensified loyalty conflicts, guilt, or anxiety.

UNDERSTANDING THE EX-WIFE'S POINT OF VIEW

Many fathers bring on the wrath of their wives by minimizing their wives' concerns about the behavior of their ADHD children. Because children commonly pose much less of a behavior problem for the father than for the mother, many men blame the mother's poor parenting for her difficulty with the child. This discrepancy becomes more pronounced when the parents live in different homes. The child sees his father less frequently and in a different setting, thereby introducing more novelty to the experience of seeing the father, which in many cases is more conducive to good behavior. In addition, the child and father are more removed from the routines and rhythms of daily life and are free to have fun. This, too, makes their interaction unusual, adding further novelty and decreasing the expectations of conforming to a structure.

It is therefore very important for the noncustodial father to understand that the mother's experience of the child's behavior is very different from his own, and that this might not have anything to do with the adequacy of either one's parenting abilities. The more the father is able to empathize with the mother's experience of parenting, the more likely it is that the mother will be able to work with the father without resentment and hostility.

This understanding must often go beyond just acknowledging the mother's difficulties and not blaming her for them. The father might be called upon to give direct and concrete support in the parenting arrangements he makes during his time with the child. For example, it might be important for the father to follow a younger child's nap schedule, to maintain the point or token system that the mother has implemented, and to continue whatever restrictions the mother has imposed on the child, such as not using the car or attending parties. Although it is important to respect the separation of the father's and mother's households after divorce, it is even more important for the two households to coordinate their efforts with a child who has ADHD. This puts a continuing strain on a relationship already fraught with tension and conflict. However, consistency and follow-through are vitally important for ADHD children. But one thing that must come before consistency in the parents' management of the child's behavior is mutual empathy on the part of the parents.

It is important for the mother to understand that just as perfect consistency was never possible given two different parents with different personalities and styles, and different relationships with their children, consistency between two different households will be even more imperfect. When the children visit their father, it *will* be mostly fun, and the schedule will not resemble any real-life schedule that the children normally follow. Naps, bedtime, and behavioral expectations might be different.

Neal and Linda, a divorced couple in their early thirties, repeatedly got into these types of struggles. They had three active boys, ages 5, 6, and 11; the younger two were hyperactive. The couple had been divorced for almost four years, and the children stayed at Neal's house every other weekend. Although there was animosity between the parents, they cooperated very well in sharing custody. Both gave highest priority to their children having good relationships with both parents. Neal was present at every doctor's appointment and school meeting, and Linda consulted Neal on every issue concerning the children's health or education.

Neal and Linda experienced the split in perceptions that is very common with parents of ADHD children. Linda often was overwhelmed by the aggressive, overly active, and impulsive behavior of the two younger boys. Neal agreed that the boys were rather active, but felt that they just had a lot of energy that needed to be channeled. During the boys' weekend visitations with him, they were on the go all the time, going places and doing things that the boys enjoyed. They had a rich experience when they were with Neal. However, when Neal returned them to their home on Sunday nights they were wound up, and Linda had to settle them down for bedtime. She felt that the children were more wired than they would have been if Neal had given them naps early in the afternoon, rather than allowing them to fall asleep in the car on their way back to her house. This made them less tired in the evening, when they should have been more tired. She insisted that, for the sake of consistency, Neal follow the same exact schedule that she did during her time with the children.

Neal was able and willing to accommodate Linda's request to some extent. He tried to give the younger children a nap early in the afternoon if they were home, and he tried to prevent them from napping in the car on the ride back to Linda's. However, Linda persisted in her anger at Neal for not agreeing to the same exact schedule that she adhered to, citing the need for consistency with hyperactive children. The parents' ability to mutually empathize with each other broke down over this issue, as it had in the marriage over other conflicts. Both parents became increasingly angry at each other and inflexible in their positions. Neal returned to blaming Linda for not being effective in controlling the children's behavior. Linda was confronted with her need to control Neal, and with her difficulty accepting the fact that they were divorced and that she could not make decisions for him. She was eventually able to be more flexible and accept that they would not have total consistency in their management of the children's behavior, and Neal was better able to make compromises in his own schedule with the boys.

HELPING THE CHILD KEEP A MENTAL IMAGE OF FATHER

While the divorced father might spend a good deal of time between visits thinking about his child, the child with ADHD might not spend a lot of time thinking about his father, as his father is not immediately present. Furthermore, anticipating the long-range future is not a strength of children with ADHD. Therefore, when the ADHD child is reunited with his father, it may be a more jarring transition than it is for the non-ADHD child. A non-ADHD child might grow accustomed to repeated transitions of this nature, and learn what to expect and how to contain his feelings. An ADHD child, however, is more likely to experience a sense of disruption when the scene changes, even if he has experienced similar changes in the past.

It is important for the ADHD child to have some aids that will help him to keep his father in mind when they are separated. This idea was introduced earlier in helping the child cope with a father who is often away from home. One simple way to do this is to give the child a picture of his father or of him and his father together during a happy moment. The child can keep this picture in his room. The child can also have a calendar (making the calendar with the father would be an excellent project), indicating when he will see his father and helping him to count the number of days until that occurs. The calendar should be colorful and stimulating so that the ADHD child will notice it. It can be illustrated with photographs or drawings of father and child, and of the activities that they plan to engage in.

It is important to provide these external supports for a child's internal representations. This is similar to the support we provide for children for their adherence to rules. Although the child with ADHD might know and might be able to state the rules of behavior of the household or of school, it takes repeated, consistent external reinforcement of these rules (in the form of visual and auditory cues or reminders, and rewards and punishments) over a long period of time, for the child to internalize them, that is, to make them his own and to be able to generate behavior in accordance with these rules in the absence of external support.

In the absence of the consistent physical presence of consequences in the environment, it is difficult for the ADHD child to guide his behavior internally. The same holds true for keeping in mind someone who is not actively and physically present. Early in life, children become capable of developing internal representations of external objects and people who are important to them. Through repeated experiences of seeing, touching, and otherwise sensing and interacting with people and things in the environment, children come to hold images of these objects and people in their minds. Therefore, when a child encounters familiar people or objects at another time, he knows them and what to expect from them. He has ways of interacting with them. If the objects have changed slightly, he will still be able to recognize them.

The attention of the ADHD child is so controlled by what is immediately present in the environment that his internal representations of objects and people seem to have less of an effect on his behavior than they do on the normal child's developmental experience. His more immediate needs, feelings, and moods rule his interactions with the world around him, causing his behavior to be more impulsive than that of his peers. His behavior is less likely to be ruled by what he knows to be stable and long-standing properties of the people and objects in his world, especially if he does not have daily contact with them. Therefore, it is necessary to provide external support, through reminders and through the repetition of rules and information, that will reinforce the internal representations that are there.

DIFFERENT RULES AND LIMITS

As mentioned above, the ADHD child has more difficulty coping with transitions and with changes in rules and expectations than does the non-ADHD child. When parents are separated or divorced, there are even more of these changes and transitions with which to cope on a frequent basis.

Many divorced mothers of ADHD children complain that they get their children back from a weekend with their father all "revved up" and difficult to settle down. Many divorced fathers complain that their ex-spouses expect them to have the exact same rules and expectations that exist in the mother's house, without recognizing that the situations are so different as to make that impossible. Many fathers believe that the mother's rules and expectations are too strict and unfair. Many mothers believe that the father's expectations are too lax and that limits are too permissive.

When the parents disagree so fundamentally, consistency is impossible, and the transitions from one home to the other are much more difficult for the child. The child is continuously stepping out of one set of rules and into another. Furthermore, each set of rules is invalidated by the other parent. Children know when their parents disagree with each other. When one parent does not believe that the other's rules are legitimate, it undermines the authority of that parent in the eyes of the child.

Helping the ADHD child with the transitions between his parents' homes involves (1) both parents having an understanding of ADHD; (2) both parents being willing to adjust their rules and expectations to the reality of their child's ADHD symptoms; (3) both parents having an understanding of the rules, expectations, and limits in the other's home; (4) both parents communicating about the child's activities, behaviors, and emotional state; and (5) both parents preparing the child for each transition in a consistent manner.

Both parents understanding the nature of ADHD and the needs of the child with ADHD is crucial to the success of managing the child's behavior and to the child's emotional well-being. When a child has ADHD, dismissing or discounting its effects on his functioning subjects the child to inconsistent feedback, which can be quite harmful. For the child to get the message that limits or rules are unimportant in one setting and centrally important in another is confusing and harmful to his success in learning to manage his own behavior. The child will be subjected to a lack of control in one setting, which might promote even stronger efforts to control him in the other setting. Therefore, he might experience confusing vacillations between undercontrol and overcontrol by the environment, which will promote poor internal regulation of his own behavior as he matures.

Even if one parent does not totally agree with the rules and limits in the other parent's home, it is important for him or her to understand them and the rationale behind them. This will help the child cope with transitioning from one environment to another.

It is important to prepare the child in a similar way each time for the transition from one parent's home to the other's. The preparation should be a ritual to make the transition as predictable as possible. In this way, the child can come to rely on this ritual, which will make the process of transition easier to remember and internalize. It should not be assumed that the child knows that he is stepping into a situation with different rules and expectations, or that he can adjust his behavior accordingly just because this has been previously done or discussed.

It also helps the child to know what the plans will be during his visit. Being able to predict what will happen and what will be expected of him provides the child with structure and predictability. Unexpected changes can be quite disruptive.

PREPARING FOR TRANSITION

Preparing your child for his return to his mother's house, or for visitation with his mother if you are the custodial parent, should become part of the regular routine. It is best to find a time to sit down with your child shortly before he is to return to his mother's house, to say good-bye and review the behavioral expectations for him. For example, you might say, "I am going to bring you back to your mother's house. We will leave at 4 o'clock. Remember, when you get home, walk in the door calmly, put your things down, say hello to your mother, sit down, and listen to what she tells you to do. I want you to remember to listen and cooperate. Now, repeat to me what you are going to do when you get back home." Make sure your child makes eye contact with you and repeats the sequence of behaviors that you have just reviewed with him. If he makes an error, gently correct him. When he has finished, give him a lot of praise for his attention and cooperation. If your child has a special behavior problem on which you are working, such as hitting his sibling when he gets home, or watching TV instead of listening to his mother, include this behavior in your instructions to him: "Remember, the rule is to keep your hands and feet to yourself," or "Remember, stop first and listen to your mother; do not go into the TV room." It is of course a prerequisite that you have familiarized yourself with the routines and rules that your child has at his mother's house.

If transitions pose a particular problem for your child, you can make a chart that will list specific behaviors that are expected of him during the transition, such as "Cooperate," or "Keep hands and feet to yourself," or "Talk, don't hit," and have him earn stickers or points for compliant behavior. The chart should be posted in a prominent place in the home into which the child is transitioning.

Just as your child might need this kind of structure for dealing with his transitions from your home to his mother's, he might also need assistance transitioning from his mother's home to yours. To help him with this, you can have a similar conversation with your child as he enters your home: "Remember the rules here: Have fun in a safe way, do what I tell you to do, and use words if you are upset—no hitting." Again, have your child repeat this to you while maintaining eye contact. It is important to make this part of the expected, predictable ritual for your child. Keep a chart in your home too to help provide immediate feedback to the child who has difficulty with transitions.

PUTTING THE CHILD IN
THE MIDDLE OF PARENTAL CONFLICTS

Divorce usually brings with it many unresolved feelings about one's ex-spouse and about oneself. Divorces happen for unhappy reasons. Even when a divorce is agreed upon by both parties in an amicable fashion, there is still the disappointment of something promising that was supposed to be lifelong not working out.

Although consistency is an important ingredient in child rearing, that quality is strained when the parents are divorced and living separately; at the same time, the ADHD child's need for it has increased. If you are the noncustodial parent, it is easy to resent the intrusions in your life with your child by the demands that your ex-wife makes for consistency with her methods of child rearing. It is also easy to resent having to report to your child's mother on your activities during your visitations. Furthermore, if you do not live with your child on a daily basis, and your emphasis when with him is on having fun, it might be difficult to see the need for strict schedules and behavior management.

The resentment you might feel toward your ex-wife can easily get communicated to your child, directly or indirectly. This might take the form of complaining out loud about the rules, restrictions, or expectations of your ex-wife, or through acting out by returning your child late, or bringing him back tired or unwashed, or through other means such as withholding child support payments or harassing your ex-wife through the legal system. If you have ADHD yourself, it might be even more difficult to check your impulses to say or do these things, or to understand the effects of what you are doing.

All of these behaviors put your child in the middle of your conflict with your ex-spouse. They discharge your tension by involving a third party in your conflict with her. When this third party is your child, it puts the child into a loyalty bind and is destructive to the child's self-esteem, feeling of well-being, ability to trust in the world, and sense of mastery over the environment around him.

Whatever your belief in the legitimacy of your complaints about your ex-spouse, it is destructive to involve your child in your feelings. It is important to examine whether your reactions toward your ex-spouse are irrational. The stronger your rage is, the more likely it is that there is an element of irrationality to your feelings. You might be justifying an irrational amount of rage because you have some legitimate gripe against your ex-spouse that to you justifies anger without bounds. It is often a good idea to discuss this with a professional, as intense rage can control your life and that of your child, even when some of the anger is justified. Even if you believe that you have been careful about protecting your child from your own feelings about his mother, if your feelings are strong your child will probably pick up on them.

Whether your feelings toward your ex-spouse are rational or not, it is important for the sake of your child to examine whether you are doing things that put your child in the middle of your conflict with her. If you are not following through on the arrangements that you made for visitation, then you might be acting in a way that creates more conflict and confusion for your child.

It is important to stick to the visitation schedule that you have worked out. This includes picking up your child on the day and at the time that you have agreed upon. You should keep your child for the period of time that was stipulated and deliver him back to his mother on time. Planned telephone calls should be made as scheduled. Anger at your ex-spouse for the breakup of your marriage, for your financial problems, or for her lifestyle should be kept to yourself and not discussed or commented on in front of your child. If there are living arrangements that compromise the child's safety or well-being, this should be discussed with the proper authorities. Arguments with your ex-spouse should not be aired when you are picking up your child or dropping him off.

SUMMARY

- It is more difficult for the ADHD child to keep in mind the differences in rules about behavior in two different homes.

- Fathers often feel enormous pain at their separation from their children, even if these fathers did not spend a great deal of time at home.

- It is crucial for fathers to remain involved after the divorce; the absence of fathers from the home has been linked to problems with antisocial behavior and self-esteem in children.

- Frequent contact with the father after divorce might increase problem behaviors in the mother's home, and can intensify loyalty conflicts in the child, so continued cooperation between the parents is essential.

- When the mother is the custodial parent, it is important for the father to respect the rules and schedules of her household, and make accommodations for the child's normal schedule.

- Custodial mothers have to come to terms with the fact that when the child is with the father, their time will be more fun and carefree, and the father will not have to cope with the same behavior problems.

- It is important to help the child maintain a mental image of the father in his absence, through the use of photographs and calendars.

- The differences in the rules between the two households can be particularly confusing and frustrating for the ADHD child.
  - The child should be prepared for each transition by reminding him of the rules in the other house, the sequence of behavior that he is expected to follow when he enters the other parent's house should be reviewed, and there should be a ritual established for this preparation to make it as predictable as possible.
  - The child should be informed ahead of time of the plans for his visit to the non custodial parent.

- The disagreements and resentments that divorced parents might feel should not be discussed in front of the child. The visitation arrangements or child support payments should not be used to express resentment. This puts the child in the middle, which is destructive to his self-esteem, feelings of security, and ability to trust others.

When You and
Your Spouse Disagree

The emphasis on consistency and teamwork in child rearing has pro-
moted the myth that parents always have to agree or at least pre-
tend that they do. This is not true, although one would hope that
two people who married each other would have enough in common
to at least see things in similar ways.

Disagreements between spouses are commonplace, and not all
disagreements can be resolved. Recall the case of Cora and William
James, who could not agree on rules for dinnertime with their hyperactive son. Unfortunately, when couples are at an impasse, one parent either passively gives in but harbors hidden resentments, or one
or both try to force the other to see things their way. It is difficult for
two people to agree to disagree.

With an ADHD child, especially one who is hyperactive, aggressive, or moody, parents often feel that nothing goes right. Very few
parents raising such a child have a firm sense of their own adequacy.
No matter what the parent tries, it never works for long. To protect
their self-esteem, their sense that they are good and adequate, many
people blame their spouses when things go wrong. And, with an
ADHD child, one always has plenty of proof at hand, even for the
most competent of parents.

It is easy to blame your spouse for what does not work, rather than see that it is probably the way you are working together. Parents often treat each other in the nonproductive way that they treat their ADHD child. Parents say to each other, "You always give in!" You're never consistent!" "You're too lenient!" "You don't try to understand her!" When parents get to the point of utter frustration and helplessness, they often tune in to the negatives in their spouse's behavior, ignore the positives, and overly generalize the negatives with words like *always* and *never*. They also start to attribute motives and feelings to their spouses: "You don't care!" "You think you're always right!" They communicate almost exclusively in "You" statements rather than "I" statements.

John and Brenda both had a loving, nurturing relationship with their 7-year-old son, Paul. They had worked hard to arrange their work schedules to be with him whenever he was home from school. Their interaction with him was warm and playful. He readily ran to them, sat on their laps, and smiled in their presence. In spite of their abilities as parents, they could not agree on anything having to do with child rearing. Brenda was very structured and insisted on a consistent schedule of medication and activities. John, who had ADHD himself, was much less structured, and he rebelled against Brenda's emphasis on structure.

Brenda felt anxious that John would forget to give Paul a medication dose, or neglect to take Paul to some activity, or fail to fill out school forms. John would accept responsibility for things, but Brenda would be constantly reminding him of what to do. John felt controlled by Brenda; he knew that he would get things done, but they might not be according to the tight schedule that Brenda had established. He did not feel that it was a big deal if a medication dose was administered late, for example.

John and Brenda became involved in a vicious cycle of blaming each other when things went wrong. Brenda blamed John for being careless and irresponsible, and John blamed Brenda for being controlling and infantilizing. They called each other names, and exaggerated the frequency and impact of what each of them did.

They decided to seek professional help. Their initial sessions quickly and consistently degenerated into petty arguments over how often John had forgotten to do things, or what words Brenda had used in correcting John's behavior, and whether or not her words were hostile and controlling.

It took a lot of work to get John and Brenda to stop arguing about the facts and to start talking about their feelings. They were eventually able to see that it was not important to count how many times Brenda had put John down, or what her tone of voice was the last time she reminded him to do something, but rather that John felt controlled and humiliated no matter what Brenda's intent was. It also was not so important how often John had forgotten things, or whether he had adequately communicated what he was going to do, but rather that Brenda felt anxious and alone in her efforts to take care of Paul. Then the discussion could focus on how Brenda could help John to feel respected, and how John could help Brenda feel secure and reassured. Both were able to realize that they had an investment in their spouse's feeling good about him- or herself and about the other, that it was undesirable to Brenda for John to feel controlled and humiliated, and that it was undesirable to John for Brenda to feel anxious and insecure. Each was able to begin taking responsibility for responding to the other's feelings.

It is this respect for one another's feelings that is more important than the facts of the case. It is more important to listen to and understand one another than to do things the same way. Try to imagine how your spouse feels when you speak to her the way that you do when you are most upset. Imagine someone whose goodwill you depend on speaking to you like that. Pay attention to how you feel in that situation.

When the two of you disagree, understanding each other's feelings might move one or both of you to soften your positions. Either you might see your spouse's point of view more clearly through her eyes, or you might see your own point of view more clearly in terms of the emotional meaning it evokes, and then your stance might lose some of its urgency for you. Understanding your emotional investment in your beliefs might not change your mind as to the right thing to do, but it might diminish your struggle with your spouse over who is right and in control of the situation. One of you can then decide to be flexible and try things the way the other prefers, realizing that the stakes of continuing a control struggle and stalemate are much higher than trying a course of action that might not work perfectly.

If the two of you simply cannot agree, no matter how much understanding and empathy you attempt, it might be workable for each of you to try your own approach with your child, and switch off each day, week, or month. The situation in which you try this has to be chosen with care, however, because of the risk of confusing your child and yourselves! Or you can agree to try one person's method for a limited period of time and assess whether it has worked. Try to define beforehand the criteria on which you will judge success or failure. Identify a specific behavior of the child's that you want to change, such as staying seated at the dinner table or waiting to speak without interrupting others.

One of you might favor a point system in which the child earns points or stickers for each good behavior, to be traded in for privileges. The other might believe that taking things away will be the only method that will have an impact. You can agree to try the point system for two weeks, and that this approach will be deemed successful if, by the final five days, your child has earned the majority of stickers for four of those days. If the method does not work well, you can then try the other way. This should be done in a spirit of scientific discovery, not in the spirit of proving yourself right and your spouse wrong. The two of you should adopt the attitude that you are trying to come up with the best way to objectively manage your child's behavior and help your child. You are willing to try different things and take some risks, evaluate the effects of what you do, and change what you do in accordance with your goals.

Another way to deal with disagreement is through the thoughtful division of labor. You and your spouse can designate certain areas of family life for which each of you will have authority to set rules, standards, and limits.

Sue and Ralph had very different styles with their children. Sue tended to be firm and give no second chances, while Ralph negotiated more and bent the rules. Sue was firmer with the children but also encountered stronger resistance from them because of her inflexibility. Under Ralph's authority, the children tended to take longer to get things done; their resistance was milder in intensity, but more prolonged. Both Sue and Ralph were adequately authoritative, but Sue became impatient watching Ralph direct the children, and Ralph got upset seeing how little fun Sue and the children had when Sue was trying to get things done. Sue and Ralph did not have any serious disagreements about their goals for their children's behavior, or about the severity of their 5-year-old's ADHD and what he needed.

To make their home environment more harmonious and leave themselves more relaxed, they agreed that Sue would handle the organization of the family around dinnertime, and Ralph would orchestrate the evening routine from bath to bedtime. They agreed not to interfere with each other, except to give gentle advice or if the other person asked for help. This system worked fine because of their trust in each other and their belief in each other's parenting skills.

SUMMARY

- Despite the emphasis on consistency, it is not possible for two people always to agree.

- Strong disagreements often mask emotional needs, fears, and anxieties that must be understood before people can adjust their behavior. Understanding and communicating these feelings can allow people to be more flexible.

- There are times when both parents will not be able to agree on a way of dealing with the child's behavior.
  - In some situations, it might be workable to alternate methods of coping.
  - You can agree to try one method for a limited period of time, and agree on a way to objectively evaluate the results.
  - You can try a division of labor where the father is responsible for rules and expectations in some areas of family life, and the mother is responsible for other areas.

Coming to Terms
with Your Own Fathering

The parenting that we received influences the way we ourselves parent and how we feel about ourselves as parents. The influence that our parents have had on us is usually subtle and not readily obvious. We might feel that we have escaped repeating some of the more hurtful or objectionable aspects of our parents' parenting only to find ourselves unintentionally doing the same things with our own children.

Often we feel that we parent adequately enough, despite any disappointments we might have in our own parents, until an unexpected challenge taxes our coping abilities. Raising a child who has ADHD is one such challenge. The demands made on a parent's patience, time, and parenting skills can be so overwhelming that one might find oneself reverting to the unproductive way one's own parents coped with frustration. But it may be possible to draw some sense of what it means to be a good parent and to parent in better ways than one's own parents did. However, when raising an ADHD child, even what may be intuitively obvious as good parenting is not always effective. For example, empathy and understanding might work with a non-ADHD child, but with an ADHD child might result in an escalation of the behavior problem and the child's frustration and emotionality. Knowing when to be empathic and when to set limits is a different process with children with ADHD than with non-ADHD children.

In confronting our feelings of inadequacy as fathers, the fathering that we received as children inevitably comes under scrutiny, and an ADHD child certainly creates pangs of inadequacy in fathers. As men, we like to be in control and to be authorities. We are taught to be in control of ourselves and of our families. A child running the show does not fit with this image, and it is not good for the child or the family. When the family is in chaos because of the demands of an ADHD child and the parents' inability to control him, the father feels helpless about protecting his family from this threat from within. Out of his helplessness, the father might respond by becoming overly controlling or by becoming passive and distant, removing himself from the situation. If he grew up with an angry, explosive father, he might become angry and overly controlling in dealing with the family situation. If he grew up with a passive father, he might react by spending more time at work, leaving the disciplining to his wife.

With the challenges that the ADHD child poses, the inadequacies of one's own father can limit the resources on which one can draw to find alternative ways to approach problems. Therefore, one's own fathering might leave one feeling that one does not have adequate parenting skills. The more flexible, involved, loving, and authoritative one's own father was, the more productive alternatives in fathering behavior one was exposed to as a child.

If one's disappointments in one's own father are pervasive, and there is little good feeling to draw on, one might tend to fear one's own inadequacies and feel trapped in them. If a father feels that he has been harmed by his own father, he might be fearful about becoming more involved as a father himself and therefore harming his child (Bell et al. 1961).

Many fathers of ADHD children whose own fathers were alcoholic grew up in homes where there was much unpredictability, emotional volatility, and emotional distance on the part of the father. Their fathers were often irrationally punitive, and, in some cases, violent when they were drunk and emotionally distant when they were not.

In other cases, the father was a quiet drunk who did not disturb the household, but who was semiconscious when he was there.

These fathers do not want to raise their children the way their fathers raised them, and they have a sense of what appropriate parenting is. But the conflicts and frustrations caused by their ADHD children often stir up some of the anxieties they experienced as children themselves, such as their sense of helplessness, rage, and despair. Some men opt out of parenting and require a great deal of firmness mixed with patience on the part of their wives to reinvolve them in dealing with their children's behavior. Many of these men are successful at managing work and managing other people at work. Avoiding dealing with their children's behavior problems enables them to avoid the feeling of failure. Avoidance of the demands of others is also a common tactic of individuals with ADHD, something that many of these fathers discover or suspect they have.

Some fathers remember their own fathers as disciplinarians who were absent from the home due to work responsibilities. Thus, their own difficulties in disciplining their ADHD children drive them to spend more time at work. They want to be different from their own fathers, but they have only seen their fathers exhibit competence in the realms of discipline and work, and discipline was administered harshly and angrily. These fathers are aware of the destructive effects of harsh physical punishment, although they may at times feel tempted to use it.

When these fathers feel that they have failed as disciplinarians and in bringing peace and order to their households, in controlling their own children, and in providing their wives with happiness, they have nothing else to fall back on. Their concept of masculinity often does not include being nurturant and asking for help from their spouses. Even if they theoretically know that it is okay for a man to be nurturant and emotionally vulnerable, they are not sure how to go about doing this.

To make matters worse, these fathers often withdraw from direct involvement in discipline. Their interactions with their children become increasingly argumentative. Each time they try to intervene to set limits, they get roped into a control struggle that they usually lose. When they do win, they rarely feel good about it.

Because work is the arena in which they feel competent, valued, listened to, and masculine, and because the financial rewards make a positive contribution to their families, they spend more time at work. They are willing to leave child management to their wives, not necessarily out of a wish to pass the buck or to be unfair, but out of a gut feeling that the children are in more competent hands with their mother in charge. These men have no idea that their wives feel as much of a failure as they do.

Their wives feel their absence acutely and profoundly. They feel abandoned, and they are deeply resentful of their husbands. They feel that they are left on their own to fail, to cope with an overwhelming situation, while their husbands enjoy adult company, the satisfaction of working, and an escape from the realities of home. The interaction between wife and husband comes to parallel that between mother and child. The father comes home and the mother demands that the father take over and be involved. The father, feeling incompetent, either avoids taking responsibility, makes feeble attempts to interact with his children, or comes on too strongly and overdoes it. The mother becomes more frustrated and takes over, communicating her feeling that the husband is a failure.

It is in times of crisis like this that lacking a nurturing, fatherly role model, a father who was cooperative, admitted his faults, and dealt with adversity in a firm but loving manner, leaves one at a loss for how to cope productively. These men have to talk about their own disappointments in their fathers and at times do some grieving before they can develop a cooperative way of working with their wives to manage their children.

The concept of the destructive power of fathers, while mothers are long-suffering saints who keep the family together, can reinforce the feeling that one's father was the bad parent and one's mother the good parent. But usually the situation is more complex. Whatever your father's flaws, your mother married him and, in many cases, stayed married to him. Even if you attribute this marriage to your mother's youth and innocence, financial realities, religious beliefs, or cultural mores, it is still true that they established a relationship in which they accommodated to each other. In many families, the mother was loving but failed to protect the children from their father's excesses. In other instances, the mother became so emotionally dependent on the children that the children became her defenders, which alienated the father even more from his children and prevented any small possibility of some positive relationship developing.

Some men are so convinced of the good parent–bad parent dichotomy that they are unable to see any good in their fathers. Not having any good feelings or memories of their fathers puts them at a disadvantage in seeing themselves as whole and complete as fathers themselves. Of course, it is possible to be a good father despite lacking good fathering oneself. Awareness of the negative influences of one's father can certainly teach one a lot about what not to do. However, a man not getting what he needs from his father has a profound effect on his self-esteem. There is always a sense of something missing, which in turn creates a sense that there is something lacking in what one has to give as a father and some deep uncertainty about whether one is doing it right or is adequate enough.

Many fathers of children with ADHD had impaired fathers themselves. There is a higher than average incidence of psychological problems in the parents and family members of ADHD children. Given the biological nature of ADHD, this is not surprising. Many men whose children are evaluated for ADHD realize that they themselves have been coping with ADHD their entire lives. It then stands to reason that the fathers of these men may have been prone to ADHD or other psychological problems.

There is also a higher incidence of substance abuse in parents of ADHD children. It is possible that many of the alcoholic grandfathers of ADHD children had undiagnosed ADHD themselves and were medicating themselves because it was hard to cope with the demands of the world for reasons that nobody could explain to them. This only left one person to blame, and the feeling of failure could have been overwhelming.

In the normal process of parenting, when one is confronted with a challenge or a developmental milestone, it is common for a parent to ask himself, "I wonder how my father or mother would have handled this?" If a man's father was abusive or physically or emotionally unavailable, it is impossible to answer this question in a way that would offer productive guidance. It is then more difficult to feel good about oneself as a father in the face of questions that one cannot answer or problems that defy solutions. One does not have the family history, which is part of one's identity, to draw on as a resource. Having healthy parents as part of one's experience is more powerful and valuable than reading about the right thing to do in a parenting book. So there can be a profound loss for the father confronting this lack in his own past, along with strong feelings of disappointment and betrayal. The sadness and anger that these revelations create can preoccupy one's thoughts and prevent a man from taking productive, creative action. To be the kind of father that your ADHD child needs, it is important that you come to terms with your feelings about your own father.

There is a sense among many men that to think or feel anything critical about their fathers is a sign of disloyalty. Many stories of emotional neglect and even abuse end with these words: "But I really can't blame him. He did the best he could. He didn't have the greatest childhood himself." It is great that a man can be compassionate about his father's shortcomings and try to understand the larger picture, but not at the expense of the man's own right to have feelings of anger and disappointment. Men often have difficulty allowing themselves to be angry at their fathers, for fear of being disloyal and therefore being a bad son, which is another form of failure.

Many men are in touch with their anger, but they are so angry that they cannot allow themselves to say anything good about their fathers. This extreme is equally dangerous. It is as if to see any redeeming qualities in one's father would nullify one's strongly felt anger and disappointment. It is as if these two things, strong anger and an acknowledgment of some good, cannot coexist. This is another form of rigid thinking that limits one's perceptions and one's options and prevents one from appreciating people's true complexity. People, impaired or not, are a mixture of good and bad qualities. Being unable to appreciate this in one's own parents can very well make one less tolerant of one's own mistakes. It can force one to be perfectionistic beyond reason, and unforgiving of oneself and others.

It is therefore important to try to see one's father and mother as three-dimensional human beings, with both good and bad qualities. It helps you to see yourself as a three-dimensional human being and to forgive yourself for your shortcomings, many of which will be painfully apparent to you as you cope with raising a child with ADHD. Your father and mother developed a relationship that was mutually created and mutually sustained. For whatever reason, they chose each other and, perhaps, stayed together, and decided to have a child or children together. They both are responsible for creating their relationship, and whatever bad qualities existed in their union is in some way shared by both of them. This may be hard to accept if the visible signs of "badness" were only obvious in one parent, and the other seemed to be a saint. However, intimate relationships are complicated, and an impaired parent functions in the context of a marriage and a family system.

We must appreciate the complexity of family life. Understanding that your father's behavior existed in a context, and may have been unintentionally supported by the behavior of your mother or others, does not negate the pain, anger, and disappointment that you might feel about your father. In coming to terms with the limitations of your own father, it is important to have not just your anger and disappointment, but also some larger way of understanding your father. This does not mean that you have to let him off the hook for his errors, but if possible you should try to enrich your understanding of him.

Gregory grew up with a father who worked long hours and always complained about the demands on him, how hard it was to make a living, and how unfair everyone was to him. Gregory had the constant sense that his father was "under siege," always being short-changed by his superiors and treated unfairly by the world around him. His father never seemed to get a break. When Gregory's father was at home, he was usually irritable and critical. Whenever he got a phone call, after hanging up he would utter some angry invective about the person, indicating that the person was taking advantage of him or being irresponsible. Gregory's childhood was difficult. Although he was intelligent and had many friends, his performance at school was erratic, he had difficulty with athletics, and he was highly anxious. As an adult looking back on his childhood, Gregory could see evidence of ADHD in himself and his struggles in and out of school.

Gregory's father's attempts at helping him with his homework always ended with his father losing patience with him and becoming very angry and critical. When Gregory did not understand the way his father was explaining something, his father did not attempt to explain it in another way, but persisted in repeating himself as if he was trying to cram it into Gregory's skull in exactly the way he understood it. His father, who played sports in high school, frequently promised to spend more time with Gregory and practice basketball. However, the time never came.

Gregory always yearned for a closer relationship with his father, which never materialized. He remembered when he was in college making conscious attempts to engage his father in conversation and solicit his advice on matters about which his father might be knowledgeable. Unfortunately, these conversations usually were unsatisfying for Gregory, as his father failed to tune in to the issues that were important to Gregory and went off on tangents that were only of interest to him. This reminded Gregory of the feelings that he often had as a child doing homework with his father.

Gregory remembered his mother as being very involved and caring. She knew everything that was going on with him in school and in his social world. She was outwardly expressive and affectionate.

Gregory's memories of his childhood therefore focused on a critical, distant, self-centered father, and a warm and loving mother. He always thought that his problems stemmed from his inadequate father. It took him a long time to realize that his mother also played a role in his relationship with his father. He remembered that his mother would often make offhand comments about how difficult her life was with Gregory's father. He also remembered many painful comments that his father made to him, likening him to his mother in unflattering ways, as if Gregory and his mother were allied against him. He remembered how rejected and unmasculine he felt when his father made those comments.

In putting this together, he understood how much his mother needed him for emotional support to cope with the dissatisfactions in her own life, and how she formed an emotional alliance with him that froze out his father. This fueled Gregory's father's alienation from him, and turned his father to look toward Gregory's siblings for his feelings of adequacy, and away from Gregory.

In spite of Gregory's strongly negative feelings toward his father, he realized that his siblings did not share his anger. The father they saw was flawed in the same ways that Gregory experienced him, but there were also softer feelings they had that mitigated their anger and made their disappointment less pervasive. They had gotten something emotional from their father that Gregory did not feel.

As Gregory reflected on these impressions of his siblings, he realized that they saw the same man that he did, that their impressions did not contradict his, but that there was a dimension to his father that they also saw that made him more complicated. Gregory was able to remember instances when his father expressed pride in him indirectly and from a distance. Perhaps his father's feelings toward him were not as uniformly critical as Gregory had assumed.

This small change in Gregory's perception of his father helped him to begin to see some positive qualities in his father, such as his ability to work hard and his dedication to providing for his family. He was also able to develop some compassion for his father, realizing that his father had to be emotionally limited not to be able to express pride or love directly to his son, and that his father was trapped by his inability to bridge the distance from Gregory and break through the alliance between Gregory and his mother.

Seeing his mother as being partly responsible for his relationship with his father helped Gregory to see his mother as less ideal and more human. Gregory came to realize that he had gotten some valuable things from both of his parents. He still felt angry and disappointed in his father, but now he had something in addition to his anger and disappointment.

Seeing both his parents as more human enabled Gregory to see himself as more human as well. When he was involved in the emotional rollercoaster of raising his own hyperactive child, he often found himself automatically reacting like his father did, with impatience and controlling anger. These similarities with his father might have devas-

244 FATHERING THE ADHD CHILD

tated him previously, but Gregory was now able to see them as parts of himself to be aware of and to work on. His increased awareness and acceptance of these traits in himself, and his understanding of his father's influence on him, enabled him to consider alternative ways to react, which was more productive than defensively denying these traits out of his fear of them and his fear of becoming like his father.

Gregory's impatience and irritability—signs of his own ADHD and of learned behavior from his father as a model—were also an area of difficulty for Gregory and his wife. His wife was often surprised at how quickly he would react in a negative fashion and how often she felt that the anger was directed at her. They used to go around in circles, arguing about why Gregory was so angry and why she was so sensitive to his expressiveness. As Gregory shared his thoughts about his father with his wife, they were able to approach his emotionality more often with a sense of humor. As Gregory was named after his father, his father was often called Big Gregory. Whenever Gregory reacted in a way that his wife found objectionable and irrational, and if she happened to have the presence of mind to do so, she would comment: "There goes Big Gregory." It was not long before Gregory started to employ this phrase, and both he and his wife would then enjoy exaggerating Gregory's argumentative behaviors in a way that was reminiscent of his father.

By using humor in this way, Gregory and his wife were able to accept Gregory's identification with his father, to distance himself from automatically acting like his father, and to find alternative ways to relate to each other.

SUMMARY

Coping with your disappointment in your father involves several steps:

- Recognize your own rigid thinking about your father, especially if you tend to see him as all bad and your mother as all good.

- Accept your own anger and disappointment in your father as legitimate; you do not have to give them up.

- Try to see your father's behavior in the context of his marriage to your mother and his own life experiences. This is not to let your father off the hook for his failings, but rather to see him as a human being.

- Accept that you may share some of your father's undesirable traits and that this does not make you a bad person or a bad father.

- Catch yourself responding like your father when you are disciplining your children or disagreeing with your wife. Your more unpleasant traits are more likely to come out when you are under stress.

- Develop a sense of humor about your father's negative traits and your similarities to him. Some things are not funny, but in retrospect some awful memories and experiences can be treated with humor. The humor does not make the situations any less serious, but it enables you to have some distance from them and to see yourself as human.

- Understand that despite your father's negative traits, he might have had some commendable ones as well. Try to think of people with whom your father had positive relationships and what they saw in him that they valued. Try to think of the reasons that your mother might have been drawn to him in the first place. This does not excuse his negative characteristics, but it enables you to see him as more of a human being, which might have a beneficial effect on your perception of yourself.

- Accept that you might have some similarities to your father and that some of these traits might be ones that you do not admire. If you can accept your father as more human, you might be able to accept yourself as human, too.

❖ CHAPTER 11 ❖

Discovering that You Have ADHD

NARCISSISTIC INJURY

Receiving a diagnosis of a disabling condition in one's child can be a frightening and worrisome event. It is difficult to come to terms with changed expectations and to manage the disability. There is fear and concern about the child's well-being and health. Will my child achieve all that he is capable of? Will he have a hard time through life? Will he make it? Will he be accepted by others? Will he find a partner and be loved?

One important component of the grief and confusion that accompanies any diagnosis that affects one's expectations of life is the blow to one's self-esteem and one's image of oneself—one's identity. There is an unshakable aspect of ourselves that persists over time, that is constant no matter how many changes occur in our lives. Internally, most of us have an enduring sense that we are the same person from childhood through adulthood, that there is a continuity of self over time. Aspects of our selves might change, such as certain personality traits, preferences, likes and dislikes, skills, and fears, but our basic self remains. We and others can identify the same essential person throughout the course of time.

Our identity is based on some core, unquestionable assumptions about ourselves. These vary with individuals, but they may involve such things as values and beliefs, physical appearance and physical capabilities, gender, and intelligence. When we experience something that challenges the truth of these core assumptions, such as when someone does something that is totally at odds with his belief system (such as criminal activity, marital infidelity), or we experience something that disturbs our most basic sense of competence or safety (such as traumatic victimization), we are shaken to our foundation. Our sense of our own ability to deal with the world, to make it safe for ourselves, and to be able to survive, is profoundly disturbed.

Not only do these experiences disrupt our self-esteem, our identity, and our basic feelings of competence, effectiveness, and goodness, they also constitute what is known as a *narcissistic injury*. Our narcissism is the basic feeling of self-love and well-being that we have, that is based on experiences beginning in early infancy. It is our basic sense of wholeness and integrity, that there is a basic goodness and worthwhileness about us, and that there is a consistency in the person that we are over the course of time.

For most of us, a core part of our identity is the ability to function independently and to be physically intact. Men are acculturated with the importance of physical integrity. Men are conditioned to compare themselves with peers along the dimensions of physical strength, of being able to meet physical challenges, and of being able to "conquer the world." Physical weakness is not only an unfortunate problem to be dealt with, it takes on the form of a moral shortcoming in men. Men are also conditioned to be competent in earning a living and supporting others financially. They see any impairment in competence as indicating moral weakness. This stems somewhat from the role men are conditioned to take in the world. It also stems somewhat from the physically oriented competition that boys engage in and from men's orientation to seeing relationships in terms of hierarchical arrangements. Being weak or having a lack or loss of capacity makes one lower than others, not as good, not as valuable. This is a failure for men.

This experience of failure at having a disability, the feeling of being defective, is also true for men when it pertains to their children. Fathers identify with their children. Hearing the news that one's child has ADHD—a lifelong disability—is, for many men, a blow to their feelings of competence and wholeness. Our children are extensions of our own sense of power, control, and competence in the world. Since children are our creations (biologically and/or emotionally), they represent us to the world. How they feel affects how we feel. How they are seen by others affects how we are seen. For fathers this is especially true with sons. Men identify with their sons and often want their sons to be just like them. Learning that their sons might have serious problems in coping with the world leaves many men feeling wounded.

This wound is compounded for the fathers who realize, during the course of their child's evaluation, that they have had similar problems. This is often pointed out to the men by their wives. However, fathers often harbor unstated suspicions that what they are seeing in their children was true about themselves when they were children. These fathers often recognize the impulsivity, the violation of rules and authority, and the failing grades. They recall with regret and sadness how they never finished school, or how they never achieved their potential. They recall their frustrations with work and family, their sense of failure and incompleteness in their lives. Some have even forgotten that they once thought they were intelligent and capable of achieving. They have put this in the back of their minds so they can cope with everyday realities with less pain and regret.

After a recent evaluation on a 5-year-old child, the mother, Paula, turned to me and asked: "Now, what can we do about getting my husband evaluated?" Lee, the father, looked at me sheepishly and, with Paula's prodding, admitted that he is forgetful, that he fails to follow through with things, and that he is impulsive. In fact, he had a long history of underachievement.

As Paula recounted, with humor, Lee's list of household projects that he never managed to complete, Lee alternately agreed with her or complained that she was exaggerating. Lee insisted that he finished the work on their son's room and the deck, albeit after dragging these projects out for the better part of a year. He laughed as he told stories of his wild times in high school, the fights he got into during his years in the service, and his years of alcohol abuse until the day came when he could not remember how he got back home one night and decided to quit. He discussed his constant feelings of restlessness, which had diminished somewhat over the years.

Lee also talked about his own father's alcoholism, his chaotic moods, and his disruption of the household. Lee held onto some feeling of dignity and responsibility, as he insisted that his wife was exaggerating.

Lee had to concede the veracity of Paula's points when she reminded him of the comments of his sister, which supported her observations. With ADHD, it is usually more reliable to depend on the observations of others than on the reports of the individual involved. Although individuals may be aware of their inattentiveness, irritability, and inconsistencies, they are often not aware of how much they deviate from the norm, or of how much they disrupt the lives of those around them, and confuse those with whom they are close.

People have an interest in maintaining their self-esteem and their image of being a good person. Men are very sensitive to any indication of imperfection, especially when it affects their adequacy, their prowess, their ability to make a living, and their ability to take care of their families, whether that involves financial, material, or emotional needs. Coming to terms with one's own ADHD means confronting one's imperfections, as well as one's own painful history of underachievement, failure, goals not reached, and dreams not realized.

ADHD FATHERS WITH ADHD CHILDREN

Being a father with ADHD raising an ADHD child is like standing in a hall of mirrors. Everywhere you look you see your reflection, and you cannot get away from it. Interacting with your child when he is impulsive and hyperactive stirs up your impatience and irritability and you respond impulsively. Confronting you child's poor control over his emotions stirs up your anger, which you act on impulsively. Reason can go out the window when the two of you are interacting.

You can help your child with his ADHD only if you come to terms with your own. Otherwise, you will respond to your child in ways that are not helpful and that make the situation worse. If you do not acknowledge the role that ADHD plays and has played in your own life, you will unknowingly escalate your child's symptoms. The greater number of symptoms you as a father have, the more you will tend to react to your child's misbehavior with anger and frustration (Arnold 1995). This is the opposite of what ADHD children need when they are being disciplined.

ADHD children with poor control over their emotions require a firm, consistent, predictable, and calm environment in order to help them gain and maintain control over their emotions and behaviors. Nothing elicits chaos like chaos. If a child is out of control, an out-of-control parent will make things worse. This is true both in the short run, in dealing with the immediate situation, as well as in the long run, in what the child learns about self-control and appropriate behavior over time.

In working with parents of an ADHD child, I always ask what disciplinary methods they use. I ask this in a nonjudgmental, fact-finding way. I am not interested in condemning their child-rearing practices. By showing up in my office they are already admitting to having difficulty. I am genuinely interested in what works for them and what does not work. If I find out that a disciplinary practice works for them that I would not feel comfortable using myself, I have to wonder why it does work, why other methods do not, and if there are other methods that the parents are not using or are using ineffectively that could provide the same benefit, and with which I would feel more comfortable.

Most parents include yelling on their list of disciplinary methods. When I ask parents to tell me which of their methods work and which do not, yelling usually makes the list of methods that do not work. I then have to ask myself and the parents why people would continue to engage in behaviors that do not work. One reason that we do this is our own impulsivity. We are continually struggling with the conflict between our impulses and the need to control them. There is nothing like raising children to challenge our impulse control when it comes to managing our anger. We are expected to withstand assaults on our sense of control and authority without becoming angry, punitive, or explosive ourselves. Children with impulse control problems, such as those with ADHD, challenge our self-control even more.

If a parent is already vulnerable to a loss of self-control, ignoring this vulnerability will not improve his relationship with his child or his spouse. Picture an ADHD child entering his classroom in school. Imagine the children are walking around the room without direction. Each child is doing something different and everyone is talking at once. The teacher has not planned any clear structure for the day. She is going to do things spontaneously. She is harried, yelling, and complaining. No one is listening to her. She becomes more agitated, anxious, and angry, and alternately yells, pleads, and quietly encourages her charges to take their seats and do their work, in which none of the students have been instructed in advance. Obviously, this exaggerated scenario illustrates the effects of a disorganized, impulsive teacher on the entire classroom. This is similar to the effects that a disorganized, impulsive parent has on the atmosphere at home.

Compounding the challenge for an ADHD father is the increased stimulation and unpredictability that an ADHD child provides. Having ADHD, the father benefits from structure and predictability, just as his child does. Too much external stimulation makes it harder to settle down and focus. Having an ADHD child in the house, with a high-activity level, constantly shifting from one task to another and failing to follow rules or actively disobeying them, can make the home environment overstimulating for the ADHD father. The father then becomes more disorganized and impulsive, yells more, is more punitive and erratic, and engages in inconsistent, emotion-driven attempts to control the child, rather than working with preplanned, long-term behavior management strategies.

The ADHD father has the dual task of organizing his child and organizing himself; he cannot help his child until he first helps himself. Consider the ADHD father coming home from work in the evening, and facing dinner with the family (although he is probably a little late since he misjudged the time it would take him to get out of the office), getting the children ready for bed, doing paperwork, making telephone calls, and preparing for work the next day. He walks in and his children noisily greet him or run past him chasing each other. Coming from the quiet and privacy of his car, where he was in total control, he is now bombarded with stimulation that he had no part in creating and to which he now has to react. He is flooded with stimulation not only from without, but also within, as he is anticipating everything he has to do that evening and wondering how he is going to get it done. Furthermore, he is feeling tired, stressed, and emotionally spent. He has little to give and he is too drained to know how to ask for what he needs. At first he tries to be patient and loving. He tries to get his children to slow down and give him a kiss or tell him about their day. But they are too stimulated to shift gears and give their father what he wants and needs. Then he tries to talk to his wife, who is simultaneously listening to him, attending to the children, and informing him about the bills, the plumber, the children's new shoes, and the company coming this weekend.

The father's head is buzzing. He is thinking about how he will get his work and preparation done tonight. He is barely listening to his wife. He starts shutting down. When his children make demands on him, or when their evening bedtime routine does not go as planned, he gets angry and irritable. He tries to force his children to do what he wants them to do, so he can get it over with and get on with the evening. What he had always thought would be an enjoyable part of the day has turned into a grim chore.

Some of this scenario is common for fathers in general. However, the problems are compounded when raising an ADHD child, and then complicated further when the father has ADHD. The ADHD father will tend to be more disorganized, have more unfinished work and tasks piled up, and be more angry and irritable at the disruptions at home. If he does not recognize his own ADHD, he will be prone to wondering why the children will not behave rather than facing the question "How can I be more organized and rational in my approach to my children?"

The father's anxiety about and preoccupation with all the work that he has to do that evening is compounded by the disorganization that prevented him from getting more of the work done during the day. This same disorganization prevents him from being able to plan for tomorrow so he can reassure himself that he will have time to complete his work then. Because he has not planned and organized, everything comes crashing down on him when he comes home, and there he does not have the work environment to structure his time.

ORGANIZING TIME

Failure to organize one's time leaves one vulnerable to being overwhelmed by everything at once. If the father described above could agree to set aside the early evening to see his wife and children, and go through the evening routine with his children without doing any work, and then schedule a time later to make his telephone calls and do his work, he will at least be segmenting his time for the different tasks he has to do.

This father can also review his use of time at work to see how much he wastes in nonproductive activities. He might carry around an index card and record everything he does and the amount of time it takes. He might be surprised at how much time he spends talking to other people about non–work-related subjects, listening to other people complain or tell stories irrelevant to work, waiting for people, drinking coffee, and being on hold on the telephone. Once he has this information, he can decide where and when to set limits. He might not want to eliminate all non–work-related chatter and socializing. After all, the friendly contact and personal relationships that we form make it worth going into the office and provide stimulation, enjoyment, meaning, and self-esteem for us. But being aware of the amount of time spent on each activity allows one to make choices and strike a balance. Not having this information leaves one at the mercy of one's impulses.

The person with ADHD might consider this monitoring and organizing too restrictive and might look at it as taking all the fun and spontaneity out of life. It would be just like this person to see this in all-or-nothing terms, as taking away *all* of his fun and spontaneity, instead of *some* of it. Monitoring one's time and putting oneself on a schedule does rob one of some spontaneity and fun. Life would certainly be a lot more fun if we could do what we wanted whenever we wanted. Add to this the ADHD person's tendency to resist structure and defy authority, and his need to act on impulse, and there are serious impediments to imposing more self-control.

There is a price to be paid for monitoring, scheduling, and organizing yourself, and for setting limits on what you want to do at the moment. However, there is always a price to be paid for everything. Not monitoring and scheduling yourself leaves you at the mercy of having too many things piling up at once, not enjoying your time with your family because your mind is buzzing with all that you have to do, and feeling pressured and overwhelmed. As soon as you recognize that both scheduling and not scheduling exact a toll, you are then in a position to make choices about what price you want to pay, and then exerting some control over those choices.

Scheduling time and planning ways to use it productively frees up time for what you want to do. However, making use of that newly freed-up time can also be a problem. One ADHD father occasionally found himself with unscheduled time at the office. Initially he relished the idea of finally getting some things done that he had been putting off, such as paperwork and phone calls. However, he would sit down at his desk, ready to be productive, and his mind would be flooded with everything that he had to do. He became paralyzed trying to decide what to do first. As soon as he started doing one thing, he began to do two other things simultaneously. For example, he would begin reviewing notes from a meeting and decide to return a phone call at the same time. As he talked on the phone and read meeting notes he tried to file things. He ended up hearing half of what was said to him on the phone, unsure if he had communicated everything that he had wanted to communicate, and having fragments of disconnected thoughts on his notepad (he had also tried to take notes on his phone conversation as he was reviewing notes from the meeting!).

It can be hard for an adult with ADHD to do only one thing at a time. Doing three things at once, although often a product of the person's restlessness, disorganization, and impulsivity, is often justified as being more efficient. However, the product of these efforts is often sloppy and disorganized. In many cases, it would be far more efficient to do one thing at a time and to structure your time so the important things get done and the unimportant things take up much less time. Then, you might have more time for the really important things, like enjoying the time you spend with your children.

To make an index card monitoring system easier to use, you can use a separate card for each day, and mark off the time, using each line for a 15-minute interval. It can look something like this:

MONDAY, AUGUST 4	
9:00	1:00
9:15	1:15
9:30	1:30
9:45	1:45
10:00	2:00
10:15	2:15
10:30	2:30
10:45	2:45
11:00	3:00
11:15	3:15
11:30	3:30
11:45	3:45
12:00	4:00
12:15	4:15
12:30	4:30
12:45	4:45

Keep these cards in your pocket and jot down everything you do throughout the day. At the end of the week, add up the time you spend in nonwork, nonproductive activities. Determine what percentage of your time this amounts to. Decide what percentage of your time you want these things to take up. Decide which behaviors to decrease or eliminate. Write down what your goal is in terms of using that time, that is, what you plan to do instead. Estimate how much more you will get done of things that are important to you in one week, one month, six months, and one year. Estimate how much personal time this will free up for these time periods. Estimate the value in the amount of stress and worry this will save you and how much more you will enjoy your personal time now that you will not have to be preoccupied with everything that you have not finished.

Also use your cards to account for time that you might not have much control over, but which you could put to better use. For example, you might have to make telephone calls, which might mean being kept on hold often during each month. Write down all of the things you could do while on hold. If you can do paperwork, make sure to keep the work near the phone so it will be available.

Adults with ADHD consistently complain about their poor sense of time. This is affirmed by their spouses. They usually have an unrealistic sense of how long it will take to do things or how long it will take to get from one place to another. They often underestimate the time required, so they are frequently late, rushed, harried, and overloaded. They end up disappointing family members. Part of the reason for this is that they do not take into account all the details they will have to attend to in order to get out of the office at the end of the day, or to run an errand. They also do not anticipate that they are sure to be distracted by things that derail their pursuit of their goal. In addition, ADHD adults frequently find it hard to say no to others and to set limits. So, if someone asks to talk to them, they stop and talk.

It takes practice to say no to other people. You can use your time chart to highlight those things that you wish you could say no to, and then begin saying no when those things occur again.

SELF-SOOTHING

Irritability and alcohol use commonly accompany ADHD in adults. Alcohol use can be a way of self-medicating uncomfortable feelings, such as anxiety, depression, and restlessness. Irritability gets triggered easily, as the individual has great difficulty tolerating frustration and needs to be in control. Nothing challenges a person's control like raising children, and no children challenge an adult's control like ADHD children.

You cannot train your child to self-soothe if you cannot soothe yourself. Many ADHD adults know what it was like to grow up in chaotic families. ADHD children more commonly have parents with some problems in psychological functioning. Many ADHD adults can look back at their own childhood and recognize that when they needed soothing and comforting, they got more stimulation, emotion, and anger instead. Rather than respond in ways that helped the child calm down when in distress, many parents responded to their child's volatile emotions and behavior with volatility of their own. The real needs of the child were not attended to. In fact, the child got the exact opposite of what he needed.

Many ADHD fathers re-create this atmosphere in the families they establish. The stresses of living with and being responsible for a child with ADHD trigger some deep-seated response, perhaps fear, that in turn triggers a volatile response. The child's actions trigger the adult's fear of losing control. In return, the adult reacts strongly in order to regain control, but the manner in which he reacts leads to a loss of control over his own emotions and subsequently over the situation.

Before the ADHD father teaches his child to self-soothe, he must practice it on himself. The first thing to do is to recognize the anger building up inside before it hits full force. Try to recognize the early warning signs of anger. Some people experience muscular tightness in certain areas of the body, such as the neck, head, shoulders, or abdomen. Others feel their faces getting warm. Sometimes there is a change in one's breathing pattern to shorter, more shallow breaths. Some people just know that they will explode if provoked for one more minute.

The buildup of anger often goes unrecognized because it is such a subtle thing. Many people explode without seeing it coming. This is especially true for people with ADHD, who tend to react more impulsively and suddenly, with the full force of emotions bearing down at once.

If one learns to pay attention to what goes on inside oneself, one can come to recognize the more subtle signs of anger building and can learn to head off a loss of control. Trying to tell a person who is active and impulsive to slow down and meditate on what is going on inside of him might be met with skepticism and scorn. However, if you have gotten this far in the book, you are clearly open to changing. So try this exercise: Sit comfortably in a chair. Close your eyes. Breathe in slowly, steadily, and deeply, taking long, slow breaths, filling your lungs completely, then exhaling completely. Let your mind scan your body, wandering up and down. You will notice that some parts of your body feel relatively cool and others feel warmer. Some parts of your body feel pressure from the chair or from clothing you are wearing, while other parts feel free and unencumbered. You will also notice that some parts of your body feel tense and other parts feel relaxed. You might notice variations in relative relaxation and tension. These differences in temperature, pressure, and tension exist all the time, but we usually screen them out.

After you have done this exercise, make a list of the possible sensations that precede your explosions of temper. Copy this list on an index card to carry around with you during the day. Every time that you become aware of one of these sensations, take out the index card and place a checkmark next to that feeling. Also, take your index card out of your pocket every hour or so and take an inventory, checking off any of the sensations that you were aware of experiencing since you last checked the list. Since you might be recognizing these internal sensations for the first time, you will probably notice feelings that you did not think of including in your original list. Add these to your list and continue to monitor them.

Once you are better able to recognize the early warning signs of anger, you can stop an interaction when you experience these sensations. It is best to remove yourself from an interaction that is destined to escalate. You can simply walk out of the room, stating that you are too angry to deal with it productively at the moment, and come back when you have regained control of yourself.

Another thing that you can try when you experience these feelings coming on is to close your eyes and breathe deeply, as in the exercise above, and focus on your breath and your internal sensations. If you think that this looks funny and out of character, imagine the effect it could have on interrupting an interaction that is headed for disaster!

CHANGING PATTERNS OF ARGUMENTS

It is also worthwhile to identify those situations that predictably lead to arguments and control struggles. We fall into the same traps, the same control struggles, and the same arguments time after time. Most of us can predict when we will have an argument with our spouse or children by just knowing the topic, our mood, and the other person's mood.

If you write down the last five arguments you had with your child or with your spouse, you can probably recognize enough of a pattern that you can predict the next five arguments. Here is where knowledge can be power. Instead of passively and helplessly following along this path to doom, you can consider restructuring these situations. Doing something unexpected can have the effect of interrupting the pattern so new behaviors emerge.

A colleague of mine told a story that illustrated his attempts to separate emotionally from his mother and be seen by her as a separate, adult human being. When he was in his twenties, he would often visit his mother during vacations from graduate school and occasional long weekends. Every time he was about to leave, his mother would pull out some shirts or other articles of clothing that she had bought for him and give them to him. My colleague felt infantilized by his mother's actions. His mother still picking out his clothes at his age embarrassed him and made him feel childish. He and his mother then engaged in their routine separation dance of her insisting he take the clothes and his insisting that he did not want them. This routine both delayed his departure and also left them both feeling angry, hurt, and confused. It prevented them from separating emotionally, since it enabled them to maintain a strong emotional tie to each other in which they were actively in each other's thoughts and hearts, albeit through guilt and confusion.

One weekend, after a typical visit, my colleague's mother offered her usual stack of shirts as he was leaving. Instead of arguing and resisting, he looked at his mother and enthusiastically said, "Thanks Mom, that's great. But did you get me any shirts with blue stripes? You know I love blue stripes!" His mother was speechless. He took the shirts and put them in his suitcase, smiled, and kissed his mother good-bye. He responded in a similar manner on the next visit. Following that, his mother's gift-giving became much less frequent, and when she gave him clothes she was less excessive about it. She did not give him gifts every time he visited, and there was less of a forced quality to her giving to him. He had some regrets, as now he had to buy more of his own shirts on a graduate student's meager income!

To restructure a repetitive situation, it might be helpful to visualize it first, although sometimes it just happens spontaneously. First, choose a conflict that happens fairly often and fairly predictably with your child. Next, close your eyes and imagine, step by step, behavior by behavior, everything leading up to the conflict. Think of the outcome you would want instead of what typically happens. Examine your responses each step of the way, and ask yourself how you could respond differently so that a different outcome, preferably the one you desire, could occur.

Select a place in the sequence of interactions in which to substitute a new response for the old one, and imagine the same scenario, step by step, with your new response inserted. Then imagine the outcome following the new response.

Mark and his 5-year-old daughter Alexa got into struggles almost every night at bedtime. Alexa would get lost in each step of her evening routine, sometimes staring into the mirror as she brushed her hair repeatedly, or taking an inordinately long time to pick out her pajamas, frequently changing her mind. She often would not respond when her father cued her to begin the next step of her routine. Mark often repeated himself ten or more times, as he stood in the bathroom waiting for Alexa to brush her teeth, while she was nowhere to be seen. By the time they settled down to read, Mark was irritated and exhausted. Alexa would often be silly and noncompliant, prolonging the evening while getting off the track. When Mark tried to set limits at that point, his nerves were already frayed, and he felt controlled by his daughter. Alexa quickly became defensive, and accused her father of yelling at her and hurting her feelings. As Alexa would not take responsibility for her behavior, Mark became angrier, and Alexa would tantrum more. There usually came a time in their argument that Alexa told her father that she was going to push him out of her room, or physically overpower him in some way. He usually dealt with these comments as defiance and tried to put Alexa in her place, or he tried to ignore the comments.

Mark thought that this last interaction might be a good place to intervene and change his response. He imagined the argument escalating as it typically did, but this time, when Alexa threatened to push him out of her room, he imagined inviting her to do this. With a smile on his face, and a twinkle in his eye, he imagined himself saying to Alexa, "Let's see you do it, big shot!" The next night, when Alexa was so angry that she threatened to throw him out of her room, he responded in the new way, and she started giggling and pushing and jumping on him. They became very playful, and apologized for hurting each other's feelings. Although this did not stop the problem of tension building in the first place, Alexa and Mark now had a tool by which to stop the interaction from escalating too much once it got started.

VERBAL MEDIATION

Adults with ADHD get bored very easily. Earlier, I suggested that fathers of ADHD children sit and observe their children at play without intervening to change the play. Just observing, or doing anything that involves prolonged concentration in a way that does not generate a lot of activity or sensory stimulation can be very taxing for an individual with ADHD. The father with ADHD may be unable to sit still long enough to attend to his child.

Using verbal mediation helps to focus attention and screen out distracting stimuli and thoughts. It can also enhance memory. If you are observing your child play and trying to inhibit your impulse to interject or control the play, you can consciously describe to yourself what you are seeing to keep yourself focused. This also provides you with an activity to do while you sit still, so you are less likely to express you fidgetiness by interrupting your child or getting up from where you are.

Describe to yourself everything your child does in sequence, as if you were talking to someone who could not see what was happening. You might find yourself noticing things that you had not noticed before, such as details and subtleties of your child's behavior, personality, preferences, and emotional reactions to things. There might be a fuller appreciation of who your child is as a separate, unique person. Your child will also see that you, as his father, are paying attention to him, closely, perhaps for the first time. This type of active, involved interest from an adult is not lost on children.

THE FATHER'S FATHER

Earlier, the experience of being a father with ADHD raising a child with ADHD was likened to a hall of mirrors, seeing oneself and one's child continually reflected in each other, trapped in a closed system of ADHD-type actions and reactions. This hall of mirrors becomes even more complex and controlling when the ADHD father comes to terms with his own father's ADHD or shortcomings. In a previous chapter, we explored the father's dealing with disappointments in the fathering he received as a child. It is possible that some of the shortcomings of one's own father were due to ADHD or some other condition, such as depression or alcoholism.

The anger at one's father for not doing things differently might not go away, but recognizing that one's father might have had limitations that were not totally under his control can add understanding to that anger and perhaps soften the effect of the disappointment. If you grew up in chaos and disorganization, it is natural to vow that you will be different when you get to be a parent yourself. This is a laudable goal, but it is important to recognize that your early "training" or "programming" might have conditioned you to react in the same way as your father. Add to this your own ADHD and related problems, and you can understand that just intending to do things differently probably is not enough. You have to retrain yourself by developing organizational strategies such as the ones outlined here.

COMMUNICATION WITH YOUR SPOUSE

It is important to recognize the impact that your ADHD has had on your relationship with your spouse. Many men have the best intentions of being good partners and empathic, supportive listeners. However, their wives experience them as quite different and feel their husbands' attention as fleeting and shallow (Weinstein 1994). The husband needs to understand and appreciate that even if he intends to listen, and is indeed concerned and caring, this does not get him very far if his spouse does not feel understood and listened to.

Often, the spouse makes the mistake of accusing the husband of not caring and not listening. She might say to him, "You never listen to me! You don't care about me! All you care about is your work! If you cared you would pay attention!" In the case of the ADHD husband, she might be confusing inattention with lack of caring. He might be unaware of the effects of his behavior; he might indeed care, and he might feel that he is listening. In fact, he might be listening as well as he can.

The spouse would be on firmer ground if she presented her complaints in terms of her feelings. This would avoid an argument over what the two of them believed were the facts, which neither of them could win. Thus, the spouse could say, "When you look all around the room, or when you will not sit still, I don't feel listened to," or "I don't feel cared for when you do not sit still, look at me, and pay attention. I need to feel that you are listening to me."

Arguing over your intentions is nonproductive. It is important to take responsibility for your behavior, even if your intentions are the best. Being accused of having bad intentions (such as not caring or being mean) might not be fair, but neither is excusing your behavior just because your intentions were good. Many men use the excuse that they did not mean to hurt their wives, or be late, or neglect to do something that they were being counted on to do, as a way to get off the hook. The wife of one such man said to him, "I am not questioning your intentions. If I believed you were the type of man who meant to hurt my feelings, I would not have married you. I need you to understand that when you don't act responsibly in these ways you hurt my feelings and I need you to behave differently."

You need your spouse to tell you not just to pay attention, but specifically what behaviors she needs to see that signal to her that you are paying attention (that make her feel attended to). Maybe she wants you to make eye contact, or perhaps she wants you to stop looking at the newspaper, or to sit down instead of pacing. Have her specify these behaviors and remind you of them each time she wants to talk to you.

When your spouse tells you what she needs you to do to demonstrate that you are paying attention to her, use verbal mediation to remind yourself of this when you are attending to her. You can remind yourself, in your thoughts, to look at your wife and not pick up the newspaper or the mail. It would also help for your spouse to cue you that she wants to talk to you and wants your attention instead of just launching into a discussion unannounced. She can say, "I'd like you to listen to this," or "I'd like to tell you something important." One important component of attention is an orienting response in which we cue ourselves that there is something in the environment that demands or merits attending to. Individuals with ADHD might need some reinforcement to activate this orienting response.

If your spouse wants you to listen, and it is not a good time for you to tune in, such as when you are tired after a very trying day at work, communicate this to your spouse. Tell her what frame of mind you are in. Let her know that you want to listen but that you cannot now because you are too tired. Tell her when you will be more available to listen. This is far better than forcing yourself to do what you are not capable of, doing it poorly, resenting your spouse for it, and having her resent you for not paying attention.

COMMUNICATING YOUR LIMITS

It is also important for you to take responsibility for other limitations you might have. Fathers with ADHD often feel that they have to do everything for everyone and accept whatever demands people make on them. They have difficulty saying no, and difficulty gauging how much time they are actually committing themselves to when they take on another project. It rarely occurs to them to say, "I can only do one thing at a time well. Let me finish this and then we can talk about this other thing." Fathers with ADHD often get frustrated when they are in the middle of doing one thing, and their spouse or child asks them to do something else. Although the spouse or child might not expect him to respond to the request until he is finished with what he is doing, the ADHD father might feel burdened and irritated at the request. He might feel that he is being expected to do two or three things at once. The second request might derail him from completing the first. However, he might not be very good at communicating this to his spouse or child. He might feel that it is his job to do all of these things and might feel ashamed if he cannot meet these seemingly simple demands. It is important for the ADHD father to communicate his limits, and explain to his spouse the best way for her to communicate her expectations of him.

MEMORY PROBLEMS

It is also important for the ADHD father to take responsibility for his memory problems. Many disappointments and misunderstandings are caused by the simple fact that he does not remember what he was told. Many fathers with ADHD have missed too many important events in their children's lives, such as soccer matches, parent–teacher conferences, and therapy appointments because they did not remember where they were supposed to be and when they were supposed to be there.

Like your ADHD child, if you are an ADHD father you probably "listen" to others while you are busy doing something else or thinking of something else. Your wife and children are probably used to hearing you say, "Uh-huh," but are no less frustrated by it. They can cue you to look at them and stop what you are doing while they talk to you, and they can ask you to acknowledge that you have heard what they just told you. They cannot remember things for you, however. You need to develop a system to aid your memory.

Strategies for memory enhancement for ADHD adults have been written about elsewhere (Weinstein 1994). Notebooks, index cards, and other written organizational systems are helpful. The key is to record things immediately. If you delay recording something important, you are almost certain to get distracted by something else and forget it. It is important to have available at all times some tool that you will use to record important information. A pen and an index card are small and portable. Another useful tool is the pocket voice recorder that operates on a computer chip and requires no tapes and no complicated operation. Get into the habit of recording what you need to remember.

Develop a system of organizing your notes every day. Choose categories that are meaningful to you, such as personal phone calls, business calls, financial matters, and children's activities. Use a calendar so you know when you have to do things. Set a goal for the date when you plan to complete each task. Record warning signs for important deadlines so you know in advance when something important is coming up. A personal digital organizer can be helpful. But memory systems are only as good as the people who use them. Yours must be user friendly, convenient, and enjoyable to use. The sense of empowerment it gives you may be reinforcing enough to keep you using it. But it is not enough to record things. There has to be a time of day set aside for reviewing your notes to yourself, checking your voice recorder, and organizing the information so it is useful. For example, you can set aside a few minutes after dinner to review what you have recorded, transcribe it into categories, put it on a calendar, set goals or deadlines, and cross off what you have already done.

> Larry, an ADHD father, was very good at writing down things that he had to do. Ideas for projects, telephone calls, and paperwork he had to complete all found their way onto pocket-sized scraps of paper that he carried around in his breast pocket. Every day when he came home from work, he would take the stack of papers out of his pocket and put them aside, only to put them back in his pocket when he left for work the next day. The stack of papers got larger over time, with a variety of colors and sizes. Some started getting worn and frayed, adding interesting textures to the collection. Occasionally during the day, he would take out the stack and thumb through it, discarding some and replacing the rest in his pocket. One day, Larry panicked when he could not find his important stack of notes. He felt that he could not function without his notes because he might forget to do something important, although he usually neglected to check them anyway. Later that week, he went to pick up his dry cleaning and, as he was about to exit the shop, the owner called to him and asked him if he had left something in one of his jacket pockets as he handed him an envelope with his multicolored, multitextured stack of notepaper in it.

Checking one's notes daily might seem like a lot of effort to someone who feels he has no time to spare and who lives from moment to moment. However, the time that such a simple system can save you each day will more than make up for the extra organizational effort.

HELPING YOUR CHILD, HELPING YOURSELF

If being an ADHD father with an ADHD child is truly a hall of mirrors, then helping yourself will help your child, and helping your child will help you. Working with your child on his organization, social skills, self-soothing, and anger management will have a beneficial effect on your own skill development in these areas. Practicing these strategies with your child, teaching your child to become better at self-monitoring and at generating alternative strategies, will result in new learning for you, if you are open to it.

SUMMARY

- Learn self-soothing; you cannot calm your child if you cannot calm yourself.

- Organize yourself; you cannot organize your child if you cannot organize yourself.
  - Organize your physical effects.
  - Manage your time; you will not have time to help your child unless you learn time-management strategies for yourself.
  - Plan your long-term projects and responsibilities.
  - Take responsibility for your memory problems.

- Anticipate times and topics of conflict, and plan strategies to deal with them.

- Deal with your alcohol or drug problems.

- Communicate your limits to others.

- Learn anger management; recognize early warning signs of anger.

- Learn alternative behavior management strategies to yelling.

- Be open to learning new ways to teach your child.

- Plan time with your spouse.

Summary and Future Directions

When we consider the needs of ADHD children, we can appreciate how multiple and complex they are. To a parent they can seem overwhelming. ADHD children need the adults responsible for them to have an understanding of their disorder and of how their unique personalities combine with their ADHD to make them the people that they are. They need help with organizing their time and physical surroundings, focusing their attention, getting work done productively, fitting in socially and in school, controlling their impulses and their activity level, setting goals, delaying gratification, developing social skills, doing homework, believing in themselves and liking themselves, and asserting their needs.

ADHD children need parents who are patient, knowledgeable, understanding, dedicated, involved, and relatively sane, who can tolerate frustration, control their own anger and impulsivity, be flexible and consistent at the same time, discipline rationally when they are feeling irrational, work with others as a team, and communicate their own and their child's needs to others in the face of misunderstanding, ignorance, and prejudice.

The needs of the parents of ADHD children are equally serious. They need patience when faced with massive frustration with their children's behavior, and with the frustration and lack of understanding of their families, friends, and their children's school. They need fresh ideas and solutions when they have run out of tricks. They need knowledge and understanding when their time and training are limited. They need to cooperate when they are at odds with their spouses or ex-spouses. They need to advocate for the needs of their child whom they might experience as frustrating and ungratifying. They need to give more of themselves when they are getting less in return.

ADHD children also need their fathers. The physical or emotional absence of fathers in the lives of ADHD children is very painful to the children, can have detrimental effects on their emotional well-being, and on their ability to successfully cope with the demands of the world.

Fathers need to feel effective in parenting, and the struggles of parenting an ADHD child can lead a father to make himself more removed and distant from the daily responsibilities and pleasures of parenting. ADHD children need the active presence of their fathers.

The differences between mothering and fathering make it vitally important that both parents be involved in parenting the ADHD child. These differences also make conflict more common, but the advantages of having conflict and working it out are immeasurable.

Fathers often cede control of the ADHD child to the child's mother, feeling that the mother understands the child's needs better, or spends more time with the child, or is better able to interact with professionals involved in the child's care. They often clash with their spouses over how serious the child's problem is, or whether the child even has a problem, and how to set limits, communicate with the child, and help the child with school. In this process, fathers often take themselves out of the picture. The child unfortunately loses the special and unique things that the father has to offer, as does the mother.

Fathers often are able to look at the problem of ADHD and define clear goals for their child in terms of behavior and performance. They often are very good at planning and at keeping on track with limits and consequences. They can be scientific in their approach, recognizing what does and does not work.

The questioning and the doubt that many fathers bring to the professionals evaluating and treating their children can be a healthy thing. It forces the professionals to carefully consider the reasons for the diagnosis and treatment. It also forces the professionals to understand the father's point of view, which can be the first step to developing a strong working relationship with him.

Fathers are often good at recognizing when their spouses allow their emotions to interfere with effective and consistent limit setting. However, fathers often allow their own anger to get in the way of their efforts. Anger is often so much a part of a father's personality, and often seems justifiable by what the child does, that the father fails to notice it as a problem. Anger is often a problem when fathers take an authoritarian approach to parenting. These fathers assert their authority with no allowance for questions or explanation. Children learn obedience but little understanding, and do not develop important skills in negotiating with authority figures.

Fathers are often good at directing their children in what to do, in exciting and stimulating them, and in challenging them to adapt to someone else. They are often less adept at providing empathy for their child, in seeing the world through their child's perspective. In this area they often can learn a great deal from the child's mother.

Fathers and mothers tend to see things differently. While this creates ample opportunities for conflicts, it also creates fertile ground for collaboration in a way that gives the child the benefit of two ways of seeing things and of problem solving. For the child to benefit from the different perspectives of his mother and father, it is necessary for the parents to understand, accept, and value their differences.

Raising an ADHD child requires constant parental involvement. It is essential for both parents to learn as much as possible about the disorder, to work with their child to help him compensate for his deficits, and to serve as their child's advocate in negotiating with the world around him. It is essential for fathers to know the teachers, therapists, coaches, and physicians who are involved with their children. One father commented that he made it his business to know each of his son's teachers through the years so that when a problem arose, they would see him as part of the solution rather than part of the problem.

Fathers often have a lot to cope with themselves in raising an ADHD child. It is very likely that the father himself will have ADHD and will therefore tend to respond impulsively to his child's behavior. Fathers have their own problems with adequacy and self-esteem, especially if they suffered profound disappointment in their relationships with their own fathers.

It is therefore important for fathers of ADHD children to come to terms with their own fathering and, if applicable, their own ADHD. Getting oneself evaluated, if there is a suspicion of ADHD, is very important. A trained therapist can help you deal with your child's problems in ways that are helpful. Your disappointment with your own father might be influencing your self-image as a father and your own feelings of adequacy. A professional can help you to sort these things out.

Therapists tend to have a more difficult time reaching fathers than they do mothers. Research that examines in greater detail the different ways in which mothers and fathers respond to therapists emotionally and behaviorally would be helpful: What are the differences in how each parent feels validated or discounted, satisfied or angry? To what extent does each put into practice the advice of the therapist? Are there different types of input to which each responds better? Understanding that there are important differences between mothers and fathers, how can this knowledge be used to teach or train mothers and fathers to respond more productively to each other when it comes to raising an ADHD child? There are several parent training programs that are useful for parents of ADHD children to develop better parenting skills, but they might be more effective if they took into account the differences between mothers and fathers in how they see their children and relate to them, and how they problem-solve around their children's deficits.

It is my hope that this book will be useful in helping the fathers of ADHD children become more active and effective in their fathering, so they will feel more valuable as parents, so they will derive greater satisfaction from parenting, and so their children will thrive in the world. It is also my hope that the needs of fathers, their perspective on ADHD, and their strengths and weaknesses will be better understood by them, their spouses and ex-spouses, and the professionals who work with them.

I am interested in hearing from fathers, mothers, and professionals concerning the observations you have about what works and what does not work in fathering children with ADHD. I can be reached at my office at 12 Parmenter Road, Londonderry, NH 03053.

References

American Psychiatric Association. (1987). *Diagnostic and Statistical Manual of Mental Disorders, Third Edition Revised.* Washington, DC: American Psychiatric Association.

—— (1994). *Diagnostic and Statistical Manual of Mental Disorders, Fourth Edition.* Washington, DC: American Psychiatric Association.

Anastopoulos, A. D., Spisto, M. A., and Maher, M. C. (1994). The WISC-III Freedom from Distractibility Factor: its utility in identifying children with Attention Deficit Hyperactivity Disorder. *Psychological Assessment* 6: 368–371.

Anderson, R. E. (1968). Where's dad? Paternal deprivation and delinquency. *Archives of General Psychiatry* 18: 641–649.

Arco, C. M. (1983). Pacing of play stimulation to young infants: similarities and differences in maternal and paternal communication. *Infant Behavior and Development* 6: 223–228.

Arnold, E. H. (1995). *Father involvement and children with ADHD.* Paper presented at the Association for the Advancement of Behavior Therapy, Washington, DC, November.

Baker, D. B. (1994). Parenting stress and ADHD: a comparison of mothers and fathers. *Journal of Emotional and Behavioral Disorders* 2: 46–50.

Barkley, R. A. (1981). *Hyperactive Children: A Handbook for Diagnosis and Treatment*. New York: Guilford.

—— (1987). *Defiant Children: A Clinician's Manual for Parent Training*. New York: Guilford.

—— (1990). *Attention Deficit Hyperactivity Disorder: A Handbook for Diagnosis and Treatment*. New York: Guilford.

—— (1993). A new theory of ADHD. *The ADHD Report*. October, 1: 1–4.

—— (1994). Impaired delayed responding: a unified theory of attention deficit hyperactivity disorder. In *Disruptive Behavior Disorders in Childhood*, ed. D. K. Routh, pp. 11–58. New York: Plenum.

—— (1995a). Is there an attention deficit in ADHD? *The ADHD Report*, August, 3: 1–4.

—— (1995b). *Taking Charge of ADHD*. New York: Guilford.

Baumrind, D., and Black, A. E. (1967). Socialization practices associated with dimensions of competence in preschool boys and girls. *Child Development* 38: 291–327.

Bell, N., Treischman, A., and Vogel, E. (1961). A sociocultural analysis of the resistances of working-class fathers treated in a child psychiatric clinic. *American Journal of Orthopsychiatry* 31: 388–405.

Bellinger, D. C., and Gleason, J. B. (1982). Sex differences in parental directives to young children. *Sex Roles* 8: 1123–1139.

Bhavnagri, N. P., and Parke, R. D. (1991). Parents as direct facilitators of children's peer relationships: effects of age of child and sex of parent. *Special Issue: Family-Peer Relationships, Journal of Social and Personal Relationships* 8: 423–440.

Blanchard, R. W., and Biller, H. B. (1971). Father availability and academic performance among third grade boys. *Developmental Psychology* 4: 301–305.

Brachfeld-Child, S. (1986). Parents as teachers: comparisons of mothers' and fathers' instructional interactions with infants. *Infant Behavior and Development* 9: 127–131.

Brachfeld-Child, S., Simpson, T., and Izenson, N. (1988). Mothers' and fathers' speech to infants in a teaching situation. *Infant Mental Health Journal* 9: 173–180.

Braswell, L., and Bloomquist, M. L. (1991). *Cognitive-Behavioral Therapy with ADHD Children.* New York: Guilford.

Bright, M. C., and Stockdale, D. F. (1984). Mothers', fathers', and preschool children's interactive behaviors in a play setting. *Journal of Genetic Psychology* 144: 219–232.

Bronfenbrenner, U. (1967). The psychological costs of quality and inequality in education. *Child Development* 38: 909–925.

Brooks, G. R., and Gilbert, L. A. (1995). Men in families: old constraints, new possibilities. In *A New Psychology of Men*, ed. R. F. Levant and W. S. Pollack, pp. 252–279. New York: Basic Books.

Buchoff, R. (1990). Attention Deficit Disorder: help for the classroom teacher. *Childhood Education*, Winter, 86–90.

Buri, J. R., Louiselle, P. A., Misukanis, T. M., and Mueller, R. A. (1988). Effects of parental authoritarianism and authoritativeness on self-esteem. *Personality and Social Psychology Bulletin* 14: 271–282.

Campbell, S. B. (1994). Hard-to-manage preschool boys: externalizing behavior, social competence, and family context at two-year follow-up. *Journal of Abnormal Child Psychology* 2: 147–166.

Cunningham, C. E. (1990). A family systems approach to parent training. In *Attention-Deficit Hyperactivity Disorder: A Handbook for Diagnosis and Treatment*, ed. R. A. Barkley, pp. 432–461. New York: Guilford.

Deutsch, M. (1960). Minority group and class status as related to social and personality factors in scholastic achievement. *Monographs of the Society for Applied Anthropology* 2: 1–32.

Deutsch, M., and Brown, B. (1964). Social influences in Negro–white intelligence differences. *Journal of Social Issues* 20: 24–35.

Dodge, K. A. (1986). A social information processing model of social competence in children. In *Cognitive Perspective on Children's Social and Behavioral Development*, ed. M. Perlmutter. Hillsdale, NJ: Lawrence Erlbaum.

Dykman, R. A., and Ackerman, P. T. (1993). Behavioral subtypes of attention deficit disorder. *Exceptional Children* 60: 132–141.

Edwards, G. (1995). Patterns of paternal and maternal conflict with adolescents with ADHD. *The ADHD Report*, October, 3: 10–11.

Erikson, E. H. (1963). *Childhood and Society*, 2nd ed. New York: Norton.

Faigel, H. C., Sznadjderman, S., Tishby, O., et al. (1985). Attention deficit disorder during adolescence: a review. *Journal of Adolescent Health* 16: 174–184.

Fash, D. S., and Madison, C. L. (1981). Parents' language interaction with young children: a comparative study of mothers and fathers. *Child Study Journal* 11: 137–153.

Fish, K. D., and Biller, H. B. (1973). Perceived childhood parental relationships and college females' personal adjustment. *Adolescence* 8: 415–420.

Fisher, S. F. (1973). *The Female Orgasm: Psychology, Physiology, Fantasy*. New York: Basic Books.

Forehand, R. I., and McMahon, R. J. (1981). *Helping the Noncompliant Child: A Clinician's Guide to Parent Training*. New York: Guilford.

Fowler, M. C. (1980). *Maybe You Know My Kid*. Secaucus, NJ: Carol Publishing Group.

Frederick, B. P., and Olmi, D. J. (1994). Children with Attention-Deficit/Hyperactivity Disorder: a review of the literature on social skills deficits. *Psychology in the Schools* 31: 288–296.

Garber, S. W., Garber, M. D., and Spizman, R. F. (1995). *Is Your Child Hyperactive? Inattentive? Impulsive? Distractible?* New York: Villard Books.

Giddan, J. J. (1991). Communication issues in Attention-Deficit Hyperactivity Disorder. *Child Psychiatry and Human Development* 22: 45–51.

Gleason, J. B. (1975). Fathers and other strangers: men's speech to young children. In *Developmental Psycholinguistic Theories and Applications*, ed. D. P. Dato, pp. 289–297. Washington, DC: Georgetown University Press.

Gray, J. (1992). *Men are from Mars, Women are from Venus*. New York: HarperCollins.

Guevremont, D. C., and Dumas, M. C. (1994). Peer relationship problems and disruptive behavior disorders. *Journal of Emotional and Behavior Disorders* 2: 164–172.

Halperin, J. M., and Sharma, V. (1994). Investigation of modality-specific distractibility in children. *International Journal of Neuroscience* 74: 79–85.

Hancock, L. (1996). Mother's little helper. *Newsweek*, March 18, pp. 50–56.

Healy, J. M., Malley, J. E., and Stewart, A. J. (1991). Children and their fathers after parental separation. In *Annual Progress in Child Psychiatry and Child Development*, ed. S. Chess and M. E. Hertzig, pp. 45–61. New York: Brunner/Mazel.

Herzog, J. (1982). On father hunger: the father's role in the modulation of aggressive drive and fantasy. In *Father and Child: Developmental and Clinical Perspectives*, ed. S. H. Cath, A. R. Gurwitt, and J. M. Ross, pp. 163–174. Boston: Little, Brown.

——— (1996). The difference between mother and father: research findings, clinical implications. *Psychotherapy Forum* 2: 5.

Hetherington, E. M. (1972). Effects of father absence on personality development in adolescent daughters. *Developmental Psychology* 7: 313–326.

Hoffman, L. (1981). *Foundations of Family Therapy*. New York: Basic Books.

Hoffman, M. L. (1971). Father absence and conscience development. *Developmental Psychology* 4: 400–406.

Jacobs, E. H. (1991). Self psychology and family therapy. *American Journal of Psychotherapy* 46: 483–498.

——— (1995). Fathering the ADHD child. *New Hampshire Learning Disabilities Association Newsletter*, Spring, pp. 1–4.

Johnston, C., Pelham, W. E., and Murphy, H. (1985). Peer relationships in ADHD and normal children: a developmental analysis of peer and teacher ratings. *Journal of Abnormal Child Psychology* 13: 89–100.

Kohut, H. (1971). *The Analysis of the Self*. New York: International Universities Press.

——— (1977). *The Restoration of the Self*. New York: International Universities Press.

——— (1984). *How Does Analysis Cure?* Chicago: University of Chicago Press.

Koziol, L. F., and Stout, C. E. (1993). Conceptualization of ADHD as an executive function disorder. In *Handbook of Childhood Impulse Disorders and ADHD: Theory and Practice*, ed. L. F. Koziol, C. E. Stout, and D. H. Ruben. Springfield, IL: Charles C Thomas.

Lamb, M. E. (1981). Fathers and child development: an integrative overview. In *The Role of the Father in Child Development*, pp. 1–70. New York: Wiley.

Landy, F., Rosenberg, B. G., and Sutton-Smith, B. (1969). The effect of limited father-absence on cognitive development. *Child Development* 40: 941–944.

Lavoie, R. D. (1995). Life on the waterbed: mainstreaming on the home front. *Attention* 2 (1): 25–29.

LeChanu, M., and Marcos, H. (1994). Father–child and mother–child speech: a perspective on parental roles. *European Journal of Psychology of Education* 9: 3–13.

Lefkowitz, M. M., Huesmann, L. R., and Eron, L. D. (1978). Parental punishment: a longitudinal analysis of effects. *Archives of General Psychiatry* 35: 186–191.

Lessing, E. E., Zagorin, S. W., and Nelson, D. (1970). WISC subtest and IQ score correlates of father absence. *Journal of Genetic Psychology* 67: 181–195.

Lewis, M., Feiring, C., and Weinraub, M. (1981). The father as a member of the child's social network. In *The Role of the Father in Child Development*, ed. M. E. Lamb, pp. 259–294. New York: Wiley.

Lozoff, M. M. (1974). Fathers and autonomy in women. In *Women and Success*, ed. R. B. Kundsin. New York: Morrow.

Maag, J. W., and Reid, R. (1994). Attention-Deficit Hyperactivity Disorder: a functional approach to assessment and treatment. *Behavioral Disorders* 20: 5–23.

MacDonald, K., and Parke, R. D. (1986). Parent–child physical play: the effects of sex and age of children and parents. *Sex Roles* 15: 367–378.

Malone, M. J., and Guy, R. F. (1982). A comparison of mothers' and fathers' speech to their 3-year-old sons. *Journal of Psycholinguistic Research* 11: 599–608.

Mash, E. J., and Johnston, C. (1990). Determinant of parenting stress: illustrations from families of hyperactive children and families of physically abused children. *Journal of Clinical Child Psychology* 19: 313–328.

Maslow, A. H. (1968). *Toward a Psychology of Being*, 2nd ed. Princeton, NJ: Van Nostrand.

Maxwell, A. E. (1961). Discrepancies between the pattern of abilities for normal and neurotic children. *Journal of Mental Science* 107: 3–307.

McLaughlin, B. (1983). Child compliance to paternal control techniques. *Developmental Psychology* 19: 667–673.

McLaughlin, B., White, D., McDevitt, T., and Raskin, R. (1983). Mothers' and fathers' speech to their young children: similar or different? *Journal of Child Language* 10: 245–252.

Mills, R. S. L., and Rubin, K. H. (1990). Parental beliefs about problematic social behaviors in early childhood. *Child Development* 61: 138–151.

Osherson, S. (1995). *The Passions of Fatherhood.* New York: Fawcett Columbine.

Parish, T. S., and Taylor, J. C. (1979). The impact of divorce and subsequent father absence on children's and adolescents' self-concepts. *Journal of Youth and Adolescence* 8: 427–432.

Paterson, G. R. (1976). The aggressive child: victim and architect of a coercive system. In *Behavior Modification in Families*, ed. E. J. Mash, L. A. Hamerlynck, and L. C. Handy, pp. 267–316. New York: Brunner/ Mazel.

Penfold, P. S. (1985). Parents' perceived responsibility for children's problems. *Canadian Journal of Psychiatry* 30: 255–258.

Phares, V. (1992). Where's poppa? The relative lack of attention to the role of fathers in child and adolescent psychopathology. *American Psychologist* 47: 656–664.

Pope, A. W., Bierman, K. L., and Mumma, G. H. (1989). Relations between hyperactive and aggressive behavior and peer relations at three elementary grade levels. *Journal of Abnormal Child Psychology* 17:253–267.

Power, T. G. (1985). Mother– and father–infant play: a developmental analysis. *Child Development* 56: 1514–1524.

Power, T. G., and Parke, R. D. (1983). Patterns of mother and father play with their 8-month-old infant: a multiple analysis approach. *Infant Behavior and Development* 6: 453–459.

Radin, N. (1981). The role of the father in cognitive, academic, and intellectual development. In *The Role of the Father in Child Development*, ed. M. E. Lamb, pp. 379–428. New York: Wiley.

Reader, M. J., Harris, E. L., Schuerholz, L. J., and Dencklo, M. B. (1994). Attention deficit hyperactivity disorder and executive dysfunction. *Developmental Neuropsychology* 10: 493–512.

Reardon, S. M., and Naglieri, J. A. (1992). PASS cognitive processing characteristics of normal and ADHD males. *Journal of School Psychology* 30: 151–163.

Robins, P. M. (1992). A comparison of behavioral and attentional functioning in children diagnosed as hyperactive or learning disabled. *Journal of Abnormal Child Psychology* 20: 65–82.

Santrock, J. W. (1972). Relation of type and onset of father-absence to cognitive development. *Child Development* 43: 455–469.

Schachar, R. J., and Tannock, R. (1993). Inhibitory control, impulsiveness, and Attention Deficit Hyperactivity Disorder. *Clinical Psychology Review* 13: 721–739.

Sciara, F. J. (1975). Effects of father absence on the educational achievement of urban black children. *Child Study Journal* 5: 45–55.

Silver, L. B. (1991). *Attention Deficit Hyperactivity Disorder: A Clinical Guide to Diagnosis and Treatment.* Washington, DC: American Psychiatric Press.

Slomkowski, C., Klein, R. G., and Mannuzza, S. (1995). Is self-esteem an important outcome in hyperactive children? *Journal of Abnormal Child Psychology* 23: 303–315.

Solomon, M. (1980). Self psychology and marital relationships. *International Journal of Family Therapy* 8: 211–226.

———— (1985). Treatment of narcissistic and borderline disorders in marital therapy: suggestions toward an enhanced therapeutic approach. *Clinical Social Work* July: 141–156.

———— (1989). *Narcissism and Intimacy.* New York: Norton.

Sonuga-Barke, E. J. S., and Goldfoot, M. T. (1995). The effect of child hyperactivity on mothers' expectations for development. *Child: Care, Health and Development* 21: 17–29.

Starrels, M. E. (1994). Gender differences in parent–child relations. *Journal of Family Issues* 15: 148–165.

Sutton-Smith, B., Rosenberg, B. G., and Landy, F. (1968). Father-absence effects in families of different sibling compositions. *Child Development* 38: 1213–1221.

Tannen, D. (1990). *You Just Don't Understand: Women and Men in Conversation.* New York: Ballantine.

Umansky, W., and Smalley, B. (1994). *ADD: Helping Your Child to Untie the Knot of Attention Deficit Disorders.* New York: Warner.

Volling, B. L., and Belsky, J. (1992). The contribution of mother–child and father–child relationships to the quality of sibling interaction: a longitudinal study. *Child Development* 63: 1209–1222.

Walker, K., and Armstrong, L. (1995). Do mothers and fathers interact differently with their child or is it the situation which matters? *Child: Care, Health and Development* 21: 161–181.

Wechsler, D. (1991). *Wechsler Intelligence Scale for Children—Third Edition.* San Antonio, TX: The Psychological Corporation, Harcourt Brace Jovanovich.

Weinstein, C. S. (1994). Cognitive remediation strategies: an adjunct to the psychotherapy of adults with Attention-Deficit Hyperactivity Disorder. *Journal of Psychotherapy Practice and Research* 3: 44–57.

Weiss, G., and Hechtman, L. T. (1993). *Hyperactive Children Grown Up: ADHD in Children, Adolescents, and Adults,* 2nd ed. New York: Guilford.

Whalen, C. K., and Henker, B. (1985). The social worlds of hyperactive (ADHD) children. *Clinical Psychology Review* 5: 447–478.

Whalen, C. K., Henker, B., Collins, B. E., et al. (1979). Peer interactions in a structured communication task: comparisons of normal and hyperactive boys and of methylphenidate (Ritalin) and placebo effects. *Child Development* 50: 388–401.

Zentall, S. S., Harper, G. W., and Stormont-Spurgin, M. (1993). Children with hyperactivity and their organizational abilities. *Journal of Educational Research* 87: 112–117.

Index